The Pontoon and Deckboat HANDBOOK

INTERNATIONAL MARINE / MCGRAW-HILL

Camden, Maine ■ *New York* ■ *Chicago*
San Francisco ■ *Lisbon* ■ *London* ■ *Madrid*
Mexico City ■ *Milan* ■ *New Delhi* ■ *San Juan*
Seoul ■ *Singapore* ■ *Sydney* ■ *Toronto*

HOW TO BUY, MAINTAIN, OPERATE, AND
ENJOY THE ULTIMATE FAMILY BOATS

The Pontoon
and Deckboat
H A N D B O O K

DAVID G. BROWN

The McGraw·Hill Companies

1 2 3 4 5 6 7 8 9 10 DOC DOC 0 9 8

Library of Congress Cataloging-in-Publication Data
Brown, David G. (David Geren), 1944–
  Pontoon and deckboat handbook : how to buy, maintain, operate, and enjoy the ultimate family boats
/ David G. Brown.
     p. cm.
  Includes index.
  ISBN 978-0-07-147263-0 (pbk. : alk. paper)
  1. Pontoon boating—United States. I. Title.
  GV836.15B76 2007
  797.1—dc22
                          2007001132

ISBN 978-0-07-147263-0
MHID 0-07-147263-0

Questions regarding the content of this book should be addressed to
International Marine
P.O. Box 220
Camden, ME 04843
www.internationalmarine.com

Questions regarding the ordering of this book should be addressed to
The McGraw-Hill Companies
Customer Service Department
P.O. Box 547
Blacklick, OH 43004
Retail customers: 1-800-262-4729
Bookstores: 1-800-722-4726

Photos by the author unless otherwise noted.

CONTENTS

Contents

10 Maintenance and Customizing 149

Appendix: Legal Matters 172

Index 181

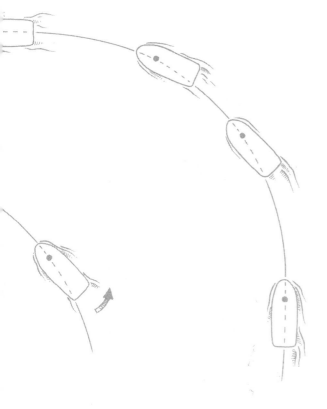

The Fleet: Pontoon and Deckboats

Decisions, decisions. What's right for you? A pontoon boat or a deckboat? If you've narrowed the field to these two choices, you've already admitted a preference for river and lake boating over offshore ocean fishing, sailing, or high-speed powerboat racing. The big decision that remains is choosing between the patio lifestyle of a pontoon boat or the jaunty exuberance of a deckboat. Both are all about having fun on the water. They are the boats of choice for families because of their low-cost versatility. One minute they are flying across the water hauling the kids on an inflatable tube, the next they are in a quiet backwater where the big fish lie in wait. At lunchtime, both types of boat can be beached to let the kids play in the water while the adults break out the picnic basket.

Fun is not limited to just young families, however. Senior skippers are starting to choose pontoon boats for serious angling on lakes and quiet streams. Ol' timers love these boats for the steady casting platform they provide, coupled with their ability to slip easily into shallow water. Deckboats and pontoon boats may not be intended for open-water passages or

Pontoon and deckboats offer similar lifestyles, but they're quite different in construction. A deckboat has a conventional hull (usually fiberglass), while pontoon boats float on long aluminum cylinders. Both offer large amounts of deck space for lounging and entertaining the whole family. (Godfrey Marine [top], Genmar Holdings, Inc.)

hard-core tournament bass fishing, but these versatile boats provide more fun per dollar than anything else afloat—which explains their growing popularity.

Apart from the fun quotient, the construction of pontoon boats and deckboats are as unalike as any two types of watercraft can be. One is a multihull vessel usually built on two long aluminum cylinders; the other is a monohull boat often made of fiberglass. Despite their differences, deckboats and pontoon boats are usually mentioned in the same breath due to the similar lifestyle that each type of boat offers. Both boats are uniquely adapted to the quiet, shallow backwaters of lakes and rivers. This doesn't mean they are slowpokes. Depending upon the power available and the hull design, speeds of 50 miles per hour are possible, even with pontoons. And, while calmer waters provide the most fun, both types of boat are capable of handling larger waters such as protected bays and larger inland waters. Neither boat is intended for the open ocean.

PONTOON BOAT ADVANTAGES
■ Lowest cost per square foot of deck space
■ Backyard patio entertaining afloat
■ Perfect for teaching kids to fish
■ Good swimming and diving platform
■ High initial stability gives sense of security

The similarity between the pontoon-boat lifestyle and life on a backyard patio has not escaped the boatbuilders. Except for the necessary helm station, the interior design of most boats provides couch-style seating around tables for easy entertaining. Optional features include built-in ice chests, sinks with pressurized running water, and stereo systems. Railings and gates keep passengers—particularly toddlers—from going overboard. Overhead, an optional bimini top protects boaters from the hot sun while allowing the lake breeze to cool off the boat.

PONTOON BOATS

Although most pontoon boats are constructed of aluminum, their design draws inspiration from a wooden log raft. In fact, the cylindrical pontoons that support them are still known as logs. Pontoon boats traditionally have two logs, but an increasing number now float on three for greater load capacity and stability. The logs are held together by a grid of beams that create a deck space that's as wide as the boat and nearly the full length of the logs. No other type of watercraft provides more open space than pontoon boats. Boaters use their large decks much like floating backyard patios.

Pontoon Boat Styles

While pontoon boats share a basic rectangular shape, there's a wide range of available deck layouts from different manufacturers, anywhere from open dayboats to enclosed cabin cruisers. Some larger boats have upper decks and waterslides to add to the fun. Pontoon boats are available in sizes ranging from trailerable models all the way up to 40-foot yachts. Unlike conventional monohull boats, no industry-standard names have been established for the differing layouts of pontoon boats. Even so, there are broad general categories based upon size and intended use.

A BRIEF HISTORY OF THE PONTOON BOAT

Log rafts were used by American settlers 150 years ago, but the pontoon concept did not really materialize until the advent of 55-gallon steel oil drums. These could be welded end-to-end into long cylinders. Unfortunately, steel drums have a lot of disadvantages. They are heavy, many contain potentially toxic oil or chemical residues that make welding difficult, and they rust. Plus, the flat end of a drum is extremely inefficient at cutting through the water. The switch to custom-made pontoon logs of welded lightweight aluminum cured these problems. Suddenly, the watercraft that had been the ugly duckling of boating became queen of the lakes.

All-aluminum pontoon boats debuted in the 1950s. One of the first was the creation of S. S. Deputy. His 1958 Sanpan was a hit with the crowd at the Chicago Boat Show. That first boat looked more like a floating back porch than a watercraft, but it had all of the key features of modern pontoon boats. It was almost as if the outboard engine had been created just to power these new craft. In recent years several builders have begun improving the round, barrel-shaped pontoon logs by adding lifting strakes and flat planing surfaces. These give today's pontoon boats speed and agility to match conventional monohull watercraft. (See discussion on planing on page 42.)

TRAILERABLE

Boats in this category are narrow enough to be trailered without special permits on most roads. Trailerable boats can be up to 102 inches (8 feet 6 inches) wide—the maximum for trailering on the Interstate Highway System and most state highways. Some secondary highways and scenic byways still restrict maximum vehicle width to 8 feet. In order to keep the length in reasonable proportion to "street-legal" width, trailerable boats seldom exceed 21 feet in length. The vast majority of pontoon boats measure between 18 and 20 feet in length.

Trailerable pontoon boats are among the most economic craft afloat. Because of their size, they are lightweight and don't require high-horsepower engines for a nice turn of speed. Each manufacturer sets horsepower limits based upon U.S. Coast Guard recommendations. Trailerable pontoon boats are rated from 40 to 100 horsepower.

The tow vehicle must be considered when

Trailering widens your horizons. Highway law restricts boats to a maximum width of 102 inches (8' 6"), which means most trailerable pontoon boats are limited to less than 24 feet in length.

selecting any trailerable boat. Most trailerable pontoon boats weigh between 1,500 and 1,900 pounds. Add to that the weight of the trailer, engine, and any gear carried aboard. The tow vehicle must therefore be capable of safely pulling between 3,000 and 3,500 pounds.

MIDSIZE DAY CRUISERS

This category of pontoon boats range between 21 and 30 feet in length. Because they're longer, the pontoons need to be larger in diameter thus increasing the overall width beyond highway limits. This means most midsize pontoon boats stay in the water all season. Some manufacturers, however, offer both a trailerable and non-trailerable versions of models in the 21- to 25-foot range. The difference is that the trailerable version will be narrower with smaller-diameter pontoons. The wider, non-trailerable version is a more satisfactory boat, so you should only choose the trailerable version if portability is an absolute necessity.

Pontoon Boat Subgroups

Whether trailerable or non-, pontoon boats can be outfitted for a variety of lifestyles. When selecting the right boat, consider these attributes.

FISHING BOATS

Fishing boats are equipped with options such as rod lockers and aerated livewells for keeping

This pontoon boat's stern has been equipped with fishing chairs. (Avalon)

bait alive. Anglers often prefer the 18-foot boats because they are easy to launch on an ordinary ramp. Open space is more valuable to anglers than seating or built-in galleys, so fishing boats have slightly smaller seating areas and a large open foredeck. Fishing chairs on the foredeck or stern allow anglers plenty of room to play fish without swinging their rods into obstructions. (These fishing chairs are only for use only when the boat is at anchor or drifting. They are not intended for use when the boat is in motion.)

FAMILY BOATS

Family boats may have some or all of the fishing equipment, but they're more likely to include amenities such as built-in ice chests and pop-up toilet rooms. These boats usually have a large amount of seating for day-long fun and relaxation.

SINGLE-DECK BOATS

Single-deck boats provide the quintessential waterborne patio lifestyle for which pontoon boats are famous. Look for "living room" seating arrangements, entertainment centers, and sinks with running water.

SUNDECK BOATS

Sundeck boats have a large but lightweight hardtop that covers the steering station and after portion of the deck. This covering is capable of supporting several people for sun bathing or as a launching platform for human cannonballs. This style of boat is extremely popular with families. The area under the upper deck is easily enclosed with canvas for overnight cruises.

LARGE HOUSEBOATS

Houseboats offer all of the amenities of a miniature cruise ship including hot and cold running water, air conditioning, and microwave ovens. Attractive as they are, however, houseboats are

This pontoon boat is perfect for the family. The sides of the boat will help keep your young ones safely corralled. (Genmar Holdings, Inc.)

in a different category altogether from conventional pontoon boats, and are beyond the scope of this book.

Pontoon Boat Construction

The majority of pontoon boats are built of aluminum. Flat aluminum sheets are rolled and welded into cylinders. Due to the limited width of roll-forming machines, the resulting cylinders are not the full length of the finished boat. Instead, several cylinders must be welded into a full-length log. A bulkhead between each cylinder gives the finished pontoon multiple watertight compartments for safety (i.e., if one compartment is punctured, the whole pontoon does not fill with water). An end cap is welded onto the stern and a bow-shaped section is welded onto the front. Finally, two sections of extruded angle stock are welded to the top of the cylinder. These angles increase the rigidity of the log and provide support for the deck. Some manufacturers have upgraded their designs by replacing the simple angle extrusions with custom brackets that provide greater rigidity and better deck mounting.

Single-deck pontoon boats are all about comfort. (Crest Pontoon Boats)

A sundeck gives your boat an extra deck for sun worshippers, yet also provides some shade for those who'd prefer to stay out of the sun. (Crest Pontoon Boats)

Quality construction shows in this "chassis" of a Forest River pontoon boat. The welds are smooth and clean. The metal is not distorted by heat from welding. Beams are attached with bolts that allow replacement of a pontoon should it become damaged.

Welding makes strong, waterproof joints, so aluminum pontoons are impervious to water. Nonetheless, conscientious builders don't assume that all welds are perfect. To check their work, builders pressurize each individual section in a completed log and use gauges to monitor the air pressure over time. If the air pressure decreases there are bad welds or pinholes in the log.

There are different types of aluminum plate a boatbuilder can choose from. Some types are not rated for marine use, but not all so-called marine-grade aluminum is proper for small boats. The grade of aluminum is not as critical if you plan to use your boat only on freshwater rivers and lakes. But insisting upon a true marine-grade metal with corrosion-resisting properties is critical if you plan to venture into salt or brackish waters. Series 5052 and 5086 aluminum are considered best.

PONTOON SHAPE

A cylinder provides natural rigidity at low cost. A cylinder does have disadvantages, however. Buoyancy and speed can both be greatly affected by the shape of a boat's pontoons.

A traditional boat produces an increasing amount of buoyancy as more of the hull is submerged; cylindrical pontoons do the opposite. Most logs float about half submerged. Increasing the passenger load, for instance, submerges more of the log; however, because of its round shape, a pontoon creates less additional buoyancy for each inch of immersion once it's submerged beyond its midpoint. As long as pontoon boats are safely loaded, however, they remain safe and stable.

U-shaped logs, on the other hand, do not

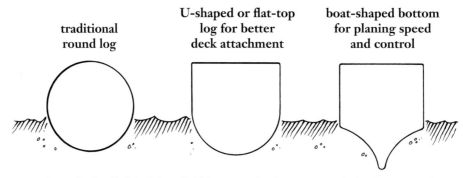

| traditional round log | U-shaped or flat-top log for better deck attachment | boat-shaped bottom for planing speed and control |

Early pontoon boats had cylindrical logs (left) because they're strong and simple to manufacture. Today, however, many builders offer U- or V-shaped logs (center and right) that are designed for better speed and economy on the water. (Christopher Hoyt)

FISHING

Few boats equal the serious angling potential of pontoon and deckboats. Both offer lots of open space to swing a rod, six anglers can work from either type of boat without tangling lines, and both are shallow-draft boats that can get into the coves and backwaters where the big 'uns lurk.

Not everyone is an expert angler. Don't worry. Plenty of good advice is available at any of the big-box outfitter stores as well as at the little bait shop near the launching ramp. Don't be afraid to ask questions, especially about the right tackle for the local waters.

Knowing when to fish is as much an art as it is science: hard-core anglers watch everything from the phase of the moon to the temperature of the water before deciding. Here are some basics tips to get you started:

- Fish tend to bite during the hours prior to the approach of a cold front
- Activity drops off after the front passes
- Fishing in the rain or overcast weather can be productive

(Godfrey Marine)

---

have the inverse buoyancy problem inherent in round logs. As the name suggests, a cross section of a U-shaped log resembles the letter U; it has a round bottom, vertical sides, and a flat top. (Modern U-shaped logs, however, are increasingly less U-shaped. Nowadays, their bottoms are modified to provide planing surfaces. See planing discussion on page 42.)

The flat top of a U-shaped log provides a more rigid and stable platform for deck attachment. Pontoon tops can be made with built-in flanges for attaching the deck beams. These improvements in boat design come at a price. U-shaped logs are more expensive to build.

BRIDGE BEAMS

To make a pontoon boat, two or three logs are placed in their proper relative positions.

Extruded aluminum beams are then attached to span the pontoons. These beams make up the transverse strength of the boat and also support the deck. In the past, most beams were installed 4 feet apart to simplify the installation of 4-by-8-foot plywood sheets for decking. As boats have grown larger, however, many builders have adopted the homebuilder's standard of 16 inches between joists. More joists add transverse support to the pontoons and reduce flexing of the plywood as people move around on the deck.

The common method of attaching beams to the logs is with stainless-steel bolts and nuts. Typically, these are $\frac{3}{8}$ inch in diameter and secured with self-locking nuts. A small number of pontoon-boat builders now weld the deck beams to the pontoons. Each method has its

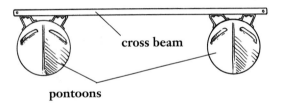

view from bow

cross beam

pontoons

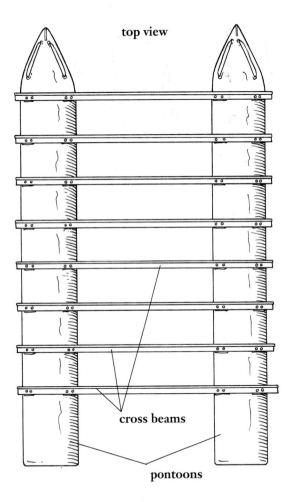

top view

cross beams

pontoons

Brackets welded to the tops of the pontoons provide attachment points for the cross beams supporting the deck of a pontoon boat. The logs give fore-and-aft strength, while the beams provide side-to-side rigidity. (Christopher Hoyt)

advantages. Bolts allow a damaged pontoon to be easily removed for replacement. However, bolts must be checked each year to make sure they remain tight. Welding makes a more rigid framework that requires no such annual maintenance.

DECK CONSTRUCTION

Pressure-treated exterior plywood is the universal material for decks on pontoon boats. "Pressure-treated" refers to the method by which chemicals are infused into the wood to prevent rotting. Treated plywood is easily fitted to the flat deck beams and it muffles sound and vibrations considerably—particularly when compared to an all-metal deck. Wood also stays cooler than metal—a distinct advantage on a hot summer day. Pressure-treated wood is extremely long-lived because its antifungal properties are augmented by the free flow of air over both sides of the deck. The plywood dries thoroughly even after a rough trip.

Indoor/outdoor carpeting covers the plywood decking to provide a comfortable surface

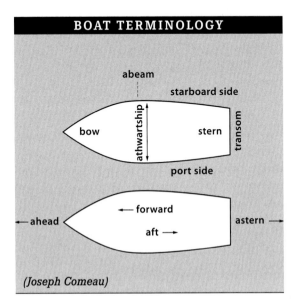

BOAT TERMINOLOGY

abeam

starboard side

bow

athwartship

stern

transom

port side

forward

ahead

aft

astern

(Joseph Comeau)

for bare feet. The edges of the deck are then capped with an aluminum extrusion to give a finished appearance. Deck rails and furniture are then bolted to the deck through the carpeting.

MOTOR MOUNT

Most pontoon boats are powered by a single outboard engine mounted between the logs at the stern. (See Chapter 4 for more information on outboards and other engines.) The motor mount hangs beneath the deck and is bolted or welded to the crossbeams. No part of the boat gets more strain and vibration than the motor mount. The mounts are generally well braced and made of heavier metal than the pontoons. Motor mounts have a hydrodynamic shape that nearly resembles a miniature boat hull under the deck. This allows the mount to move smoothly through the water without creating water turbulence ahead of the propeller. The mount will also have freeing ports to rid itself of water during operation.

The weight and power of an outboard put considerable strain on the motor mount. A good mount is made of properly braced heavy-gauge metal. It should spread the load of the engine over several cross beams. (Mercury Marine)

Inboard/Outboard Power Not all pontoon boats rely on outboard engines. An inboard/outboard (I/O), or sterndrive, engine can be installed in a small "engine room" mounted between the two pontoons. It may also be installed inside the after end of the center pontoon in a tri-toon boat.

DECKBOATS

Deckboats were created by merging the hull style of a runabout with the layout of a pontoon boat. A deckboat's large, almost rectangular deck provides at least some of the patio lifestyle that is characteristic of pontoon boats; however, a deckboat's conventional pointed-bow hull allows it to perform better at high speeds—a boon for waterskiers, wakeboarders, and

tubers. Deckboats can be powered by either outboard engines or inboard/outboard (I/O) drives. Most buyers prefer I/O power for their higher resale value—an important factor if you're thinking about upgrading to a larger boat in a few years. (See Chapter 4 for more information on engines.)

Most deckboats are arranged with a helm station amidships on the starboard side. A

DECKBOAT ADVANTAGES

- Ride and handling of conventional boat
- Easy trailering
- Greater visual appeal
- Higher speed means better waterskiing, tubing, etc.

A BRIEF HISTORY OF DECKBOATS

It is often said that the Gulf of Mexico gets a foot deeper for every mile you go out. That's an exaggeration, of course, but long stretches of protected water along the Gulf Coast from Florida to Texas are extremely shallow. It is not surprising, then, that the first recognizable deckboats were born along the Texas coast in the 1950s. By 1974 the Hurricane Boat Company was producing a deckboat that the company conceded looked like a golden bathtub on a fiberglass barge. Although the appearance of these early deckboats was anything but traditional, boat buyers liked the combination of a real boat hull and pontoon-boat deck. This ungainly craft was as good for fishing as for waterskiing.

Deckboats ride through the water like any conventional boat because they have traditional hulls. The difference is that the decks offer the open space usually associated with pontoon boats. (Genmar Holdings Inc.)

passenger seat flanks the skipper on the port side. Forward there is a large seating and entertainment area. Some boats have limited seating at the stern, while others turn the motor box into a large padded area for sunbathing while anchored or docked. Most deckboats have the added feature of a large open deck at the stern that serves as a platform for swimming.

While all deckboats may have a similar layout, builders vie for the most creative and unique touches. Drawers may be tucked into seats, or an entertainment center may be hidden beneath a hinged countertop. Storage compartments for water skis are common.

The deckboat was originally conceived as a platform for sun and fun on the water. These days, however, some deckboats are also designed and marketed with serious angling in mind. Some deckboats have fishing seats mounted on the foredeck for use when the boat is not under power.

Deckboats can be found in lengths from 18 to 25 feet, with the majority in the middle of this range. In an effort to gain the maximum interior room, most boats are 102 inches wide (8 feet 6 inches), which is the maximum permitted on the Interstate Highway System. While this width should present no problems on most roads, it pays to check local regulations as some rural roads may still be restricted to 96-inch-wide vehicles.

The typical deckboat weighs in at 2,500 to 3,500 pounds. This includes the engine. Adding the trailer and necessary gear means your tow vehicle will haul a total weight of between 3,500 and 5,000 pounds. This trailer weight is within the towing capacity of most midsize SUVs. Deckboat manufacturers typically offer a trailer in a package deal with a new boat purchase. This is usually the most cost-effective way to obtain the right trailer for your new boat.

Deckboat Construction

Deckboats are composed almost entirely of fiberglass. The complex deck shapes of these boats would be far more expensive to create in materials other than fiberglass. That said, some innovative builders of aluminum boats are beginning to reproduce the smooth curves of fiberglass in metal. Look for more aluminum deckboats in the coming years.

COMPOSITE LAMINATE

A fiberglass boat is not made of fiberglass alone. Rather, it is a composite laminate consisting of fiberglass and one of several plastic resins. By itself, fiberglass is limp and no more waterproof than a dishrag. Plastic laminating resins, on the other hand, cure so hard that they are too brittle for boat construction. But combine these two dissimilar materials into a composite laminate, and the result is a wholly new material that is both hard and resilient.

BUILDING PROCESS

The typical fiberglass boat is built in an open mold called a *tool*. The tool is the exact shape and size of the boat. The manufacturer starts by spraying a gelcoat into the mold. The gelcoat is pure resin tinted the color of the finished boat. (In effect, a fiberglass boat is "painted" before it is built.) Once the gelcoat has been applied, the layering of fiberglass and resin begins. This process is called *laminating*. Laminating follows a precise schedule controlling the order of fiberglass layers and the amount of resin. After the resin has cured, the finished part is popped out of the mold.

Most deckboats are composed of at least three different major parts: the hull, the deck, and the interior liner. (For ease of construction, interior liners are often divided into several smaller parts.) The liner is often made with the bases of the seats, galley units, and storage lockers already molded in place. Once the interior is installed in the hull, the deck is lowered over the hull and the parts are fastened. The hull-to-deck joint is an area of critical importance. Most newly built boats use both mechanical fasteners and an adhesive.

RESINS

Three resins are often used in boat construction, but only two are commonly used for mass-produced boats. True epoxy resins are excellent, but expensive. Their use is mostly confined to custom boatbuilding. Polyester resins were the first to be used in high-volume boatbuilding. Vinylester resins have been introduced in recent years to overcome some disadvantages of polyester materials. Both polyester and vinylester resins lend themselves to high-volume production techniques.

- **Polyester**—These styrene-based resins come in two different compositions.

Orthophthalic polyester (ortho) is the most popular for boatbuilding because it produces a strong laminate at low cost. Isophthalic polyester (iso) resins are somewhat stronger and more durable. Iso resins are also resistant to osmotic blistering (cosmetic blemishes in the laminate) and are thus popular for use below the waterline.

- **Vinylester**—Similar to epoxies, these more expensive resins are superior in all respects to polyester. They do not experience osmotic blistering and have excellent bonding characteristics.

Boatbuilders have switched from lower-cost ortho resin to more expensive iso or vinylester resins to reduce osmotic blistering experienced by fiberglass boats kept in the water for the whole boating season over a number of years. However, this blistering does not affect boats that are kept on trailers between weekend outings. There is little advantage to the higher-cost resins unless you plan to wet-dock your boat for extended periods of time.

COLORS

As mentioned above, gelcoats used on boats are made of pure resin that has been tinted to the desired color of the finished hull. The coloring agents that are used to tint gelcoats are similar to those in paint or printing ink. Different colors stand up to the sun better than others. Red pigments fade rapidly under ultraviolet light from the sun. Blues and greens hold up better. Dark colors often become splotchy as they age, while lighter tints last longer. White fades the least of all gel colors.

FIBERGLASS

As stated earlier, resin by itself is too brittle to be used in boat construction. To make a safe boat, builders use fiberglass to reinforce resin. Two different types of glass strands are manufactured—E-Glass and S-Glass.

- **E-Glass** might be considered the "generic" fiberglass fiber. It is the most common type used in boatbuilding

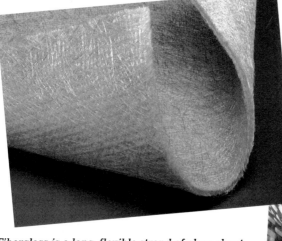

Fiberglass is a long, flexible strand of glass about the thickness of sewing thread. It can be woven into cloth or chopped into mat. These materials are used to reinforce polyester resin in much the same way that steel bars are used to reinforce concrete. (Owens Corning)

because it bonds well with polyester resin and is relatively inexpensive.

- **S-Glass** is a higher-quality product. Developed for use in the aircraft industry, S-Glass is about five times as expensive, but has up to 40 percent greater tensile strength. S-1 Glass is used in the space program, while S-2 finds its way into boats.

No matter whether the fiber is E-Glass or S-Glass, it can be manufactured into a variety of products ranging from fine cloth to chopped mat. Each has a weave or texture intended for a specific application.

- **Cloth** is woven much like cotton and other fabrics used in clothing production. Different fiber counts are available, and the finished cloth can exhibit weave patterns ranging from twill to satin. Boat cloth is a term often applied to a fine weave developed to drape easily around a boat's curves.

- **Mat** is made of chopped strands of glass fibers, usually cut between 2 and 3 inches in length. After a binding agent is applied, mat fiberglass resembles shredded wheat.

- **Roving** is a rough woven fabric made from large bundles of fibers. Woven roving resembles a basket weave. When used in boatbuilding, it builds thickness in a laminate.

- **Directional fabrics** are composed of strands of fiberglass that all lay in the same direction. Fabrics of this type are available in unidirectional, biaxial, and triaxial orientations.

Buying Tips

xcept for discovering true love, few things are as exciting as buying a new boat. This is especially true for a first-time buyer. Unfortunately, many first-timers take home more boat than they can handle. It takes time to develop the skills necessary to dock a big boat or to navigate across open water. Seamanship skills are faster and easier to learn on a modest-sized boat. When the inevitable bumps and scrapes occur, they will be less severe and costly than the same accident in a big, expensive, heavy boat.

Boats increase both in size and expense by the rule of the cube. A 36-foot boat may be twice the length of an 18-footer, but because it's also wider, taller, and more extensively equipped, it's more than three times as much boat. Fuel, insurance, dockage, and storage costs all increase in the same geometric ratio. Starting modestly allows a first-time skipper to learn boat-handling

ALOHA PARADISE 290

With the right accessories a pontoon boat can go on overnight adventures. This Aloha Paradise 290 is equipped with a standup height full enclosure that turns it into a cabin on the lake, any lake.

skills without breaking the bank. A first purchase is not forever. Almost everyone moves up through a progression of boats before finding their ideal boat. Plan from the outset to learn about boating from your first purchase, and trade up to something bigger and better.

If you plan to purchase a trailerable boat, be sure to know the recommended trailer weight limits for your tow vehicle. Consult the owner's manual for your car, or check with a dealer. When you go shopping for a boat, be sure to factor the weight of the boat, motor, and the trailer to determine the total weight you will be pulling. A full discussion on trailering can be found in Chapter 5.

NEW OR USED?

First-time buyers are often tempted to limit their entry cost into boating. The simplest way to cut cost is to purchase a pre-owned boat, but a used boat may not be cost-effective in the long run. Used boats may cost thousands less than new; however, maintenance costs are higher for older boats. So how do you choose the best option?

New Boats

New boats are sold by authorized dealers who have factory support for fixing warranty claims. Whenever you purchase a new boat, you begin a long-term relationship with the dealership. This is where you will go for warranty work and perhaps other repairs.

The price of a new boat includes the manufacturer's warranty; if something goes wrong with a new boat, the manufacturer picks up most or all of the cost of repairs. Used boats, on the other hand, are typically "as is" purchases and the buyer foots any repair bills. Few first-time buyers

PROS OF BUYING A NEW BOAT
■ Manufacturer's warranty
■ Easier financing; possibly lower rate
■ Dealer assistance in learning how to operate boat
■ *You* choose the colors and factory options
■ Trailer included
■ Safety gear included

CONS OF BUYING A NEW BOAT
■ Highest initial cost
■ First-year depreciation
■ Long delivery time if not "on the lot"
■ Cost of adding options

have the expertise to confront the maintenance issues and repairs associated with an older boat. For that reason alone, it's almost always best for newcomers to purchase brand-new boats.

New boats often come bundled with a trailer specially matched to the weight and shape of the hull or pontoons. Plus, most dealers bundle safety gear (life jackets, fire extinguisher, etc.) with each new boat sold. Used boats don't always come with a trailer or all of the required safety gear. This means you'll spend extra time and money purchasing the separate equipment.

For an experienced boater, however, a new boat is not always the right choice. The lower initial cost of a used boat can offset the lack of warranty—if the buyer is familiar with boats and handy with tools. New boats often must be ordered from the factory. Delivery can be weeks or months after the purchase contract is signed. Used boats are always on the lot, so to speak, and can be put in the water the same day the deal is signed.

Depreciation and the cost of options are two often-overlooked factors in boat buying.

PROS OF BUYING A USED BOAT

- Lower cost for equivalent boat
- Immediate availability, aka "buy and float"
- Lowest depreciation
- Many accessories often included

CONS OF BUYING A USED BOAT

- More difficult to finance; higher interest rate
- Limited or no warranty
- Higher maintenance costs
- Repair costs may eventually equal new boat price

Boats depreciate steeply in their first year in the same way cars do. As a boat gets older, however, its value tends to level out or even rise slightly.

Used Boats

While new boats are sold by dealers, used boat sales can be divided into two broad categories: dealer/brokerage boats; and "driveway" boats.

Whether a used boat comes from a dealer or a private individual, there are some advantages to an "experienced" craft. One of the biggest advantages is the low prices on extra equipment. Most owners throw in optional radios, depth sounders, and other amenities with the sale of their boats. The buyer pays a fraction of what these amenities would typically cost if sold separately—used or new.

Depending upon your skill with tools and your available free time, buying an old clunker could be cost-effective. Fiberglass and aluminum both last almost indefinitely. This means it is usually possible to restore an old boat to nearly showroom condition by replacing wooden parts, carpeting, seats, and other furnishings.

Although emotionally rewarding, restoration of an older boat is only a financial success if the initial purchase price is low enough to justify the cost of new materials and your labor. Cost may not be as big a factor if your goal is a highly customized personal boat. (See Chapter 10.)

Lower price and more equipment may seem attractive, but don't overlook some of the disadvantages to used boats. The biggest is wear and tear. No matter how well the prior owner maintained them, the engine, gauges, bilge pump, and so on, have hours of use on them. All equipment has a finite life span, so it is logical that more repairs and maintenance are needed on used equipment than on new. In addition, some lending institutions require higher interest rates when financing a used boat. Financing a used boat often takes a bit more work on the buyer's part.

PRICING A BOAT

New boat prices are set by individual dealers. Although their decisions are based on the man-

REGIONAL POPULARITY

For reasons that are not always obvious, certain brands of boats are more popular in some areas of the country than others. Some brands of equal or better quality may be unknown or even disliked in a particular area. It pays to keep these regional preferences in mind. If you are deciding between a boat that's popular in your area and one that is unknown, go with the popular boat. You will probably get a higher trade-in value when time comes to move up to a new boat.

ufacturer's suggested retail price (MSRP), dealers are free to set their own prices in order to compete with other dealerships.

Used boat prices also vary widely based on year, make, and model. Two identical used boats can have radically different prices depending on their physical condition. Three price books are commonly used to help dealers, brokers, and lenders determine the value of used boats. Each of these books gathers raw data from boat sales around the country to compute a price for each individual model. The three books use different methods for setting prices, so there can be a wide discrepancy in values for a given model. Rather than worry about these differences, use whichever book your lending institution prefers.

The three books are:

- **BUC**—Gives "retail high" and "retail low" prices for each model. It factors in regional preferences and provides a method for factoring in the condition of a particular boat.
- **NADA**—Provides low, average, and high prices for specific models, plus tabular values for engine upgrades.
- **ABOS**—This book is available only to brokers and dealers; it's used to establish trade-in values.

The BUC and NADA books can be purchased, but the high cost of each is seldom justified when making a single boat purchase. Luckily, these books are often available at libraries.

JUDGING QUALITY

New or used, nothing is more important in a boat than the quality of construction. Well-built boats seem to outlast their owners, while those

Boats carrying a National Marine Manufacturers Association sticker are built to a strict set of quality guidelines. To qualify for the sticker program, the builder must use NMMA-approved materials and parts. (NMMA)

of lesser-quality materials and workmanship seldom last a decade. The problem for a first-time buyer is knowing the difference. On the surface, high-quality boats don't look all that different from their bargain-basement cousins. Discerning the difference can't be learned solely through a book. It takes hands-on experience with lots of boats in the real world. There are, however, obvious clues about the quality of the boat that even a novice can observe.

Check for NMMA Certification

The biggest clue is a sticker indicating the boat is certified under National Marine Manufacturers Association (NMMA) standards. NMMA is the only organization to certify pleasure boats and trailers in the United States. To gain certification for a specific model, a builder must submit to a factory inspection. All products and materials used in building that particular boat model must meet applicable U.S. Coast Guard or American Boat & Yacht Council (ABYC) standards. An NMMA-certified boat must contain approved fuel tanks, hose, bilge pumps, ventilation blowers, navigation lights, and other equipment.

NMMA certification should not be confused with stickers the U.S. Coast Guard requires on all new boats under 20 feet long. The Coast Guard sets minimum safety standards,

TAHOE 215

Deckboats have become the most versatile of watercraft. The Tahoe 215 combines the best of a bass boat with the luxury of a runabout. The swivel fishing chairs can be removed if the day's activities include waterskiing instead of angling.

but a NMMA-certified boat, on the other hand, meets not only USCG minimum requirements but also the far more demanding industry standards. It is perfectly legal to build and sell boats that do not carry the NMMA sticker. The NMMA certification process is totally voluntary on the part of the boatbuilder.

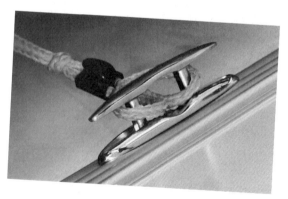

Nothing says more about a builder's overall dedication to quality than deck hardware such as mooring cleats. Good-sized stainless steel cleats attached with through-bolts and backing plates are visible signs of quality construction.

A Once-Over

You can get an overall impression of a boat's quality by simply walking around the hull. On a fiberglass deckboat, put your head close to the transom and peer forward along the full length of the hull. Use the reflections of overhead lights or the sun to help judge the quality of the fiberglass laminate. Reflections that show waves, wrinkles, or dips in the shiny gelcoat might be signs of potential defects in workmanship. Similarly, look along the rub rail where the deck meets the hull. This should be a smooth curve from one end of the boat to the other. Humps and hollows are indicators of construction problems. Be sure to find out what resins were used in the construction of a fiberglass boat. As we discussed in Chapter 1, some resins are better than others. Some deckboats are now being built of aluminum. Give these boats the same reflection test. The internal bracing and framework should not show through the aluminum skin like the ribs of a starving cow.

If you're evaluating a pontoon boat, be sure to closely inspect the logs. Logs must be straight for the vessel to perform correctly. Check the reflection of light along the length of each pontoon. A straight reflection across the welds indicates that the sections were put together with care. If you plan to use the boat in salt water, find out if the logs are made from marine-grade aluminum.

While standing at the transom of either type of boat, take note of the stern cleats. Better-built boats have cast stainless steel or chromed bronze cleats of adequate size. Chrome-plated zinc or other "pot metals" are a lot cheaper, but seldom last. Check one of the cleats to be sure that it is properly through-bolted and reinforced with a backing plate. At a minimum, there should be oversized washers and either self-locking nuts or regular nuts with lock washers. Stern eyes—used for attaching tie-downs when trailering or towing water skiers—should be made of stainless steel U-bolts. If there is a swim platform or a boarding ladder, it must also be attached with through-bolts and backing plates.

Evaluate the Helm Station

Sit in the driver's seat of any boat you are seriously considering. Not all helm stations fit everyone the same. Be sure you have a good view ahead as well as on each side. Make sure the steering wheel is comfortable to hold and that the engine controls come naturally to hand. Helm consoles in dark, matte-finished colors will minimize sun glare. The number of gauges varies depending upon whether the boat has a sterndrive engine or an outboard. (See Chapter 4 for more on engine types.)

For sterndrives, you'll want these gauges:

- Tachometer (indicates engine rpm)
- Oil pressure

- Water temperature (within engine)
- Trim/tilt (indicates angle of the stern-drive's lower unit)
- Ammeter (indicates the electrical draw)

For outboard engines, you'll want these gauges:

- Tachometer
- Water temperature
- Water pressure (indicates flow of engine coolant)
- Voltmeter (indicates if alternator is functioning)
- Trim/tilt

All boats can be fitted with a water speedometer to help judge the actual speed through the water. An hour meter, or Hobbs meter, on the engine is an excellent way of keeping track of routine maintenance. Fuel

Sit down at the helm station of any boat you are considering. Check to make sure the sight lines are good and the controls come easily to hand.

THE STEAK TEST

Surprising as it may sound, you can quickly estimate the quality differences between boats much the same way as you can with steaks—by price per pound. Better meat costs more; the same is generally true with boats. Divide the cost of a boat by its total weight and you'll be able to quickly judge the quality differences between boats. A first-time boater is wise to purchase the best boat for the money, not the biggest or fastest. A better-built boat is cheaper in the long run. It will require less maintenance and will return more of its value when the time comes to trade up or sell.

tanks fitted on sterndrive boats usually have a sending unit for a gauge at the helm station. Outboards with portable gas tanks seldom are rigged with gas gauges on the helm console.

Ask Questions

Once you've narrowed your choices to a particular model, take time to talk to people who bought the same make or model. Learn what they like and don't like about their boats. Take what they say with a grain of salt; owners are not always honest about their dislikes.

UNDERSTANDING DEALERS AND BROKERS

Two groups of people who are helpful in purchasing a boat are dealers and brokers. Even so, they are not really friends of the buyer. Both have primary obligations to other people or companies. Knowledge of how brokers and dealers make their money is useful when it comes time to negotiate the final price of a boat. Just like any other large purchase, the initial asking price and the final "off the lot" price of a boat can be quite different.

WHO'S WHO IN USED BOAT SALES?

- **Dealers.** Dealer boats are boats that were traded in from buyers of new boats. These used boats are now owned by the dealer. Most dealers offer a limited warranty on boats they sell, and they usually help with financing. In some cases, the resale value of the trade-in boat represents the entire profit that the dealer makes "turning" both boats.
- **Brokers.** Brokerage boats are still owned by private individuals who have hired a broker—who is paid a commission—to handle the sale. Some brokers offer limited warranty coverage and may assist with obtaining financing.
- **Private sellers.** So-called driveway boats are offered directly by their owners. (The term comes from the common practice of owners who park their boats in the driveways of their homes.) No broker or dealer is involved. The sale is strictly a "private treaty" between seller and buyer, and the boats are almost always sold "as is" with no warranty. It is up to the buyer to determine the condition of the boat and its value.

BOAT SHOW SAVVY

Shows are an excellent place to see and compare a lot of different boats; however, beware of the "buying frenzy" that dealers create. Sales staffs are at their most aggressive at shows. They have to be. Dealers often do half or more of their annual business during the winter boat shows.

Dealers and the boat manufacturers offer dramatic price cuts at boat shows. It's important to realize, however, that show deals don't necessarily expire on the last day of the show. Discounts can stay alive for a week, a month, or even a whole season—but only if you began negotiating on a new boat at the show.

So, be sure to get the salesperson's card. Talk price at the show, but leave your checkbook on your kitchen table. Attend the show to narrow your choices. Then seek the quiet of your own living room to weigh the remaining options. Make your buying decision independent of last-minute sales pitches and the frenzy.

Boat shows bring a huge selection of pontoon and deckboats together in one place. The price of admission might seem steep, but it's often far less than the cost of driving from dealer to dealer to see the same boats.

New boat dealers have a contractual relationship with the boat manufacturer. One part of that contract is the dealer's obligation to provide buyers with a certain level of service and to handle warranty claims. Not discussed in public are any requirements for the dealer to sell a minimum volume of boats. Special factory sales incentives to dealers are also not always made public either.

A broker is a sales representative engaged by a private owner to market a specific boat. Most of the time, the broker gets paid a commission only after the boat sells. As a result, the broker is more interested in the needs of the seller than in those of the buyer. The line between broker and dealer is not always sharp. New boat dealers usually also sell trade-ins and broker customers' boats. The dealer owns trade-in boats, so is able to negotiate price directly on those boats. Negotiating price on a brokerage boat is a bit more difficult because it requires the agreement of the current owner.

The typical markup on a new boat runs from about 10 to 20 percent of the MSRP. Brokers work on a commission ranging from 10 to 20 percent of the final sales price. These markups and commissions do not leave a lot of margin for negotiating the prices of either new or used boats. Fortunately, there is a way other than price to apply buyer's leverage to the sale.

This is to haggle over optional equipment purchased as a package with the boat. Dealers and brokers take up to a 40 percent markup on options and extras that they install. This larger margin makes bargaining over aftermarket equipment more productive than arguing over the boat price. For instance, dealers will often "throw in" a full set of equipment required by U.S. Coast Guard regulations (life jackets, fire extinguisher, etc.). Or, a broker may arrange to have a major repair done at a considerable discount just to finalize the sale.

(Once you've bought a boat, you'll have to deal with the somewhat unpleasant paperwork that comes with ownership. See the appendix for information that will make the process a little less painful.)

FACTORY OPTIONS FOR BUYERS OF NEW BOATS

Buyers of new construction have the opportunity to customize their boats as they come down the assembly line. Since factory options cannot be fitted after assembly, they make a strong case for buying new rather than used. Here are some factory options that may be available:

- Hull colors and graphics
- Designer upholstery and carpet colors
- Interior layout
- Entertainment systems
- Special fishing gear (e.g., livewells)
- Tubing and wakeboarding towers
- Engine options

Deckboat Exteriors

As mentioned in Chapter 1, deckboat colors are molded into their gelcoats as they are built. The only practical way to get the color you want is to have a tinted gelcoat applied at the factory. Few builders are willing to mix custom gelcoat colors for a single boat, but it's worth asking. When ordering custom colors, keep in mind that sun is the enemy of gelcoat. The high ultraviolet content of sunlight on the water causes colors to fade and the surface to lose its highly polished appearance.

Fiberglass gelcoats can be tinted almost any color. Boatbuilders tend to favor white and other light colors because they fade less in the sunlight. Accent stripes and details printed on self-stick vinyl tape can be easily repaired or replaced by the boatowner. (Genmar Holdings Inc.)

Pontoon boats give open deck space for entertaining or family fun. A wide variety of furniture layouts allow buyers of new boats many options. (Crest Pontoon Boats)

ALOHA

Even though it is within the legal width for trailering, this 29-foot pontoon boat has ample room for entertaining the whole crowd. The double bimini arrangement gives everyone shade from the sun without blocking the breeze.

Pontoon Boat Exteriors

Pontoons are almost always bright-finish aluminum. However, the filler panels of deck fences can be brightly colored. Most builders use pre-painted aluminum for these panels, so the base color is predetermined; however, factory-installed vinyl graphics can add a splash of color.

Interior Colors and Layouts

Most boatbuilders use only one color combination on a specific model for a full production year. A few manufacturers offer two or three choices of interior colors for each model. These choices are intended to color-coordinate vinyl upholstery with the carpet colors into a unified appearance.

Factories offer a variety of interior layouts on each basic hull. Boats geared toward fish-

Factory-original canvas tops always fit well. A local canvas maker can duplicate a factory top or make additional pieces to extend its usefulness.

ing typically have two or more angling seats mounted where there is maximum room to swing a rod. Boats intended for a patio-on-the-water lifestyle feature sinks and built-in ice-boxes. Newer deckboats are sometimes configured for wakeboarding, tubing, and other tow-behind water sports.

Canvas Tops and Covers

Factory canvas is built to the exact specifications of the boat. As a result, factory tops and covers fit perfectly. (Years later, the canvas may be worn out, but those factory-made aluminum or stainless bows that supported it are usually good as new. Having a set of bows as a foundation makes the job of reproducing the old canvas top relatively easy.)

One factory option for pontoon boats that should not be overlooked is a pop-up changing room with canvas sides that offers privacy for changing clothes or a portable toilet.

Safety on the Water

3

Safe boating is fun boating. The image of bold adventurers taking uncertain risks is romantic, but silly. Truth is, dedicated skippers are always concerned with safety. Unfortunately, safety compliance is often viewed as something one does to avoid a ticket.

COMMERCIAL OPERATION

The Coast Guard defines commercial operation as taking passengers on your boat with a reasonable expectation of gain as a result of the trip. Charging money in return for taking someone out is obviously a commercial operation. The term *expectation of gain* can be a little less obvious, however. For instance, a salesman who takes clients boating in expectation of future business is—in effect—running a commercial operation. Exempted from commercial designation are instances like a fishing trip where four or five friends split the associated fuel or docking costs.

To take passengers for hire you must first obtain one of two U.S. Coast Guard licenses.

- **Operator Uninspected Passenger Vessel (OUPV, or 6-pac).** This

license allows you to take up to six people on an uninspected vessel upon waters specified on the license.

- **Master (25, 50, or 100 tons).** This license allows you to take any number of people on inspected vessels within the gross tonnage restrictions on the license.

An uninspected vessel does not receive annual inspections by the U.S. Coast Guard, but is required to have a level of equipment in excess of the ordinary pleasure boat. Uninspected boats are limited to six passengers. Inspected vessels are generally larger, up to 65 feet in length and 100 gross tons. To obtain either license you must meet the minimum required days of sea time and must pass an exhaustive test.

OPERATOR EDUCATION AND LICENSING

After wading through titling and registration requirements (see Appendix) and purchasing all the required equipment, it comes as a surprise to most people that the Coast Guard does not require any sort of operator's license for boats up to 65 feet in length. Things are different on the state level, however, where a variety of mandatory education and operator licensing laws are in effect. Be sure to know the classwork or licensing your boating area requires.

Many states are phasing in adult mandatory education based on birth date. Persons born after a certain date are required to complete an approved course, while those born before the cutoff are not. This "grandfathering" is intended to let people who have been boating their whole lives continue without fear of testing.

An approved course must meet the criteria established by the National Association of State Boating Law Administrators (NASBLA). Courses taught by state watercraft officers qualify. So do courses offered by the U.S. Coast Guard Auxiliary and the United States Power Squadrons. To find the course nearest you, call the BoatU.S. Courseline at 1-800-336-BOAT (2628). Or, go online to www.boatus.com/courseline/default.asp.

REQUIRED SAFETY EQUIPMENT

Federal regulations determine the minimum equipment to be carried by boats of various sizes. Each individual state is free to require additional equipment. For example, most states require that an anchor and line be carried, even though anchors are not among the federal requirements. Most of the specified equipment is the responsibility of the operator to supply. However, two key pieces of fire safety equipment on inboard powerboats—bilge ventilation and a carburetor backfire arrestor—must be supplied by the original builder of the boat. The operator is required to maintain these builder-supplied items in working order.

Personal Flotation Devices

At least one life jacket (personal flotation device, or PFD) must be supplied for every person on board. In addition, vessels over 16 feet in length must have an approved throwable Type IV device. This can be an approved cushion or life ring. All PFDs must be approved by the U.S. Coast Guard, in serviceable condition, and appropriate for the intended use. There are five official types of personal flotation devices.

TYPE I

Type I life jackets provide the most buoyancy. They are effective for all waters, but are especially appropriate for open, rough, or remote waters where rescue may be delayed. It is designed to turn *most* unconscious wearers to a face-up position in the water. These are expensive and seldom used on pleasure boats.

TYPE II

Type II devices are near-shore buoyancy vests intended for calm, inland water, or where there is a good chance of quick rescue. Type II PFDs will turn *some* unconscious wearers to a face-up position in the water.

TYPE III

Type III PFDs are designed to be most comfortable for long-term or continuous wear. They come in many colors and styles including float

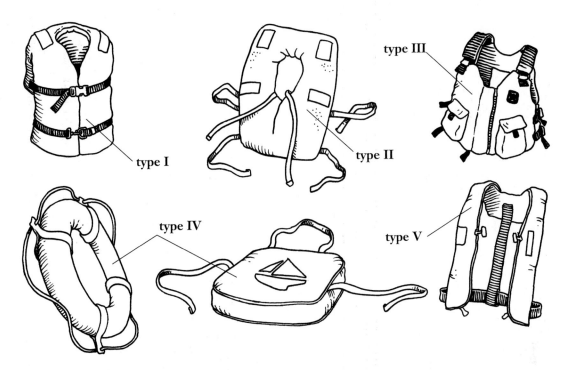

A variety of personal flotation devices (PFDs) are available to fit different needs. They vary from the bulky but secure Type I devices used by commercial vessels to specialized water-ski vests. (Christopher Hoyt)

coats, fishing vests, and vests for other water-sports. Type III PFDs are good for conscious users in calm, inland water or where there is a good chance of quick rescue. They are designed so that wearers can place themselves in a face-up position in the water.

TYPE IV

Type IV devices are throwable (such as life rings and buoyant cushions). A Type IV device is not designed to be worn, but rather to be thrown to someone who has fallen in the water. There are no inflatable Type IV devices.

TYPE V

Type V devices are intended for specific activities. Inflatable devices are included in this category as are some competition ski vests. Type V

devices may be carried instead of another PFD only if used according to the approval conditions listed on its label.

Just carrying the right number of PFDs is not sufficient under most state laws, which require them to be readily accessible. This means they cannot be stored in their original store packaging, in a locked locker, or beneath a pile of gear in the bottom of the boat.

An increasing number of states require that children under a specific age wear a PFD at all times. These rules generally apply to boats under a stated size, or to boats engaged in certain activities. Child PFDs are sized to match the young wearer's weight. It is critical that the PFD fit the child properly. To check for a good fit, pick the child up by the shoulders of the

Children should always wear approved flotation devices when on the water. All PFDs must be sized to the height and weight of the child. PFDs for very young children have flotation collars to support their heads. (Monterey Boats)

PFD. If the fit is correct, the child's chin and ears will not slip through. A child's PFD should be tested in the water immediately after purchase. A PFD will keep a child afloat, but may not keep a struggling child face-up. That is why children should be taught how to put on a PFD and to relax in the water.

Many states require that PFDs be worn when engaging in certain boating or water-related activities. Check with local boating law enforcement agencies to learn which requirements apply in your boating area. Typically, PFDs are required when:

- Waterskiing or engaging in any towed water activity
- While operating a personal watercraft (PWC)
- During whitewater boating activities
- While windsurfing

If you are boating on a lake or waters under the jurisdiction of the Army Corps of Engineers or a local park authority, different rules may apply.

Inflatable PFDs are gaining popularity because they are more comfortable to wear. Unlike conventional fixed flotation devices, however, these new devices provide no support unless properly inflated. This is why inspection of the user-serviceable parts is necessary on a routine basis. The gas cylinder should be intact and not corroded. The indicators on the inflator must be green, or the device is *not* serviceable and does *not* satisfy the requirement to carry PFDs. Coast Guard–approved inflatable devices are authorized for use on recreational boats by persons of at least 16 years of age.

To see this PFD inflated, you'd hardly suspect that it was little more than a harness before it hit the water. Inflatable PFDs do not interfere with activities while you're dry on deck and they provide more buoyancy after inflation than many conventional life vests. (Mustang Survival)

MINIMUM BUOYANCY OF PFDS

Wearable Size	Type	Inherent Buoyancy
Adult	I	22 lbs.
	II and III	15.5 lbs.
	V	15.5 to 22 lbs.
Youth	II and III	11 lbs.
	V	11 to 15.5 lbs.
Child and infant	II	7 lbs.
Throwable cushion	IV	20 lbs.
Ring Buoy	IV	16.5 to 32 lbs.

MINIMUM BUOYANCY OF INFLATABLE DEVICES

Wearable Size	Type	Inflated Buoyancy
Adult	I and II	34 lbs.
	III	22.5 lbs.
	V	22.5 to 34 lbs.

MINIMUM BUOYANCY OF HYBRID PFDS

Wearable Size	Type	Inherent Buoyancy	Inflated Buoyancy
Adult	II and III	10 lbs.	22 lbs.
	V	7.5 lbs.	22 lbs.
Youth	II and III	9 lbs.	15 lbs.
	V	7.5 lbs.	15 lbs.
Child	II	7 lbs.	12 lbs.

Note: The term inherent buoyancy *refers to the buoyant properties inherent in the materials that the PFD is made from.* Inflated buoyancy *refers to that buoyancy that is created by inflating the PFD. A pure inflatable device has no inherent buoyancy, only inflatable buoyancy. A hybrid, on the other hand, has some inherent buoyancy, but it is augmented by the inflated buoyancy.*

Fire Extinguishers

Coast Guard–approved fire extinguishers are required on boats where a fire hazard could be expected from the engines or fuel system. Extinguishers are required when any of these situations exist:

- Inboard engines are installed

- There are closed compartments and compartments under seats where portable fuel tanks are stored
- There are open spaces between the cockpit deck and the bottom of the boat that are not sealed to the hull or not completely filled with flotation materials

COMPARISON OF APPROVED EXTINGUISHERS

Class of Fire	Foam (gals.)	Carbon Dioxide (lbs.)	Dry Chemical (lbs.)	Halon (lbs.)
B-I (Type B, Size I)	1.25	4	2	2.5
B-II (Type B, Size II)	2.5	15	10	10

MINIMUM NUMBER OF HAND-PORTABLE EXTINGUISHERS

Vessel Length	No Fixed System	With Approved Fixed System*
Less than 26 feet	1 B-I	0
26 to less than 40 feet	2 B-I or 1 B-II	1 B-I
40 to 65 feet	3 B-I or 1 B-I and 1 B-II	2 B-I or 1 B-II

*A fixed *firefighting system is built into the engine compartment and triggered automatically if there is a fire. Most small-boat systems use a halon gas deployed from a canister that looks much like an ordinary fire extinguisher. When a fixed system is triggered, the engine is automatically shut down to prevent the fire-suppressing gas from being discharged out the exhaust. An override allows you to restart the engine after the fire is extinguished. Fixed systems are expensive, but provide a real measure of safety for inboard gasoline-powered boats.*

ALOHA 290 SUNDECK

Lightweight aluminum construction makes it possible to add a second deck to larger pontoon boats like this Aloha 290 Sundeck. Optional canvas curtains can turn it into a protected cabin.

- There are closed living spaces
- There are closed stowage compartments in which combustible or flammable materials are stowed
- There are permanently installed fuel tanks

Extinguishers must be labeled as meeting U.S. Coast Guard standards. Less expensive extinguishers intended for home use are generally not acceptable. Look on the label for "Marine Type USCG." To comply with the law, each extinguisher must be stored in a type-approved bracket. Letters are used to indicate the type of fire an extinguisher can put out:

Class A—wood, paper, bedding, etc.
Class B—oil and burning liquids
Class C—electrical

Coast Guard–approved hand-portable extinguishers are all rated for at least Class B fires. They come in three sizes: B-I, B-II, and B-III. Of these, only types B-I and B-II are normally found on pleasure boats. The higher the number, the larger the extinguisher. Extinguisher markings can be confusing because a single unit can be approved for several types of fires. For instance, an extinguisher marked "Type A, Size II, Type B:C, Size I" is considered a B-I extinguisher.

Ventilation

Regulations on bilge ventilation affect mostly deckboats. Manufacturers are required to install ducts to clear explosive gasoline fumes from boats with sterndrive gasoline engines. Boats built after 1980 must also be equipped with one or more power exhaust blowers to remove potentially explosive fumes from the engine compartment. Each exhaust opening or exhaust

Coast Guard regulations require ventilation of engine compartments. Boatbuilders are careful to follow these requirements. It's up to the owner to keep the ventilation system free of obstructions and the blower operating properly.

duct must originate in the lower third of the compartment. Supply and exhaust openings or ducts must each be above the normal accumulation of bilgewater. Powered ventilation is required for every compartment that has a permanently installed gasoline engine with a cranking motor for remote starting.

There are no ventilation requirements for outboard boats where the engine and the fuel tank are located in open air outside the hull of the boat. For this reason, ventilation regulations apply to only a handful of sterndrive-powered pontoon boats. The majority of outboard-powered boats are exempt.

Backfire Flame Arrestor

Carbureted inboard engines are subject to backfires, which could ignite gasoline fumes in the bilge. A Coast Guard–approved arrestor has an approval number stamped into its metal. The device must be suitably attached to the air intake with a flame-tight connection. Automotive air cleaners do not provide adequate flame protection. Beyond not being approved, automotive devices are dangerous afloat. Backfire flame arrestors are not required on outboard motors and therefore seldom apply to pontoon boats.

Bells and Whistles

Federal regulations require an "efficient sound-producing device." Both the federal and state Rules of the Road require certain sound signals that are only possible on a whistle, which is the official term in the Rules of the Road for horn. Look for horns that meet either the ABYC or NMMA standard. Bell signals are required only when at anchor in limited visibil-

ity. Boats over 39 feet 4 inches in length must carry a bell with a 7.8-inch mouth. There are no federal requirements for the size of bells on smaller craft.

Navigation Lights

Navigation lights are displayed by vessels at night to indicate their size, type, and direction of travel. A boat that is operated only in daylight and fair weather does not need lights. However, navigation lights (often called "running lights") must be displayed between the hours of sunset and sunrise, in fog, or in heavy weather when visibility is diminished. New boats should be equipped with light fixtures that meet federal standards. They are identified by "USCG" followed by the certi-

---

FOOD SAFETY

Not every queasy stomach is caused by seasickness. Careless food preparation, handling, and storage can easily result in food poisoning. This is especially true on hot summer days when picnics on the water are most popular. Food safety specialist Dr. Angela M. Fraser of North Carolina's Cooperative Extension Service offers good advice for worry-free summer dining:

- Rapidly chill cooked foods in your home refrigerator before packing them for a trip. Two-thirds of food-borne illnesses are due to improper cooling.
- Hold food at 40°F or colder during transportation. This requires packing your food in a high-quality cooler with plenty of ice. Embed the food into the ice; don't simply set the food on top of the ice.
- Prevent bacteria growth during the

meal by keeping cold foods cold and hot foods hot. Cover all foods to prevent contamination by insects, which can carry bacteria and viruses.
- Throw away leftovers. Uneaten picnic foods that have been sitting in the hot sun for some time are unsafe, particularly if they've been handled by many people.

If you can, bring two ice chests. Dedicate one cooler to perishable foods; the second cooler should be reserved for soft drinks and non-perishable snacks. The perishable-food cooler should be kept closed from the time it leaves your home kitchen until serving time on the boat. Opening and closing the lid causes the ice to melt faster and exposes the food to warm temperatures. Losing cold air is less of a problem with the drinks and snacks in the second cooler, so you can feel free to

---

fied range of visibility in nautical miles (e.g., "USCG 2nm").

Power-driven vessels under 65 feet display a red sidelight to port, a green sidelight to starboard, a white stern light, and a white masthead light. On most pontoon boats and deckboats, the masthead and stern lights are combined into a single all-around white light. There is seldom any problem with the mounting of the colored sidelights and the white stern light. Problems arise with getting the all-around white light high enough that it is not obscured by the boat or its equipment. The rules require that the all-around, or 360-degree, white light be at least 1 meter higher than the sidelights. It is the operator's responsibility to make sure that nothing obscures any of the boat's navigation lights.

Light Type		Arc	On-Diagram
⌒	MASTHEAD	225°	A
◗	SIDE	112.5°	B
⬯	STERN	135°	C
◯	ALL-AROUND	360°	D

Navigation lights warn other boats of your presence. (Joseph Comeau)

open and close that one as much as you need throughout the day. Chipped ice or cubes do not last as long as block ice, but they're easier to pack around food containers.

Thermoelectric coolers have dropped in price over the years to the point that they are competitive with ice chests. Thermoelectric coolers use 12-volt power, so these coolers are ideal for transporting food to and from the boat.

Thermoelectric coolers work fine until the ambient temperature around the box exceeds 88°F. Above that, the internal temperature may not be sufficient for safe refrigeration. For that reason, be sure to transport the cooler inside the car's passenger compartment; summer temperatures inside a car trunk can approach 150°F on a sunny summer afternoon.

Relatively new to the market are portable compressor coolers. These are really true refrigerators that weigh less than 40 pounds. Like thermoelectric devices, they can be powered by the boat's 12-volt system or by 120-volt household current. A thermostat allows for a constant interior temperature, and these portable units can also be used as freezers.

Beware that it takes power to keep coolers running. This is not a problem as long as the car or boat engine is operating. If the engine is off, however, an electric cooler can quickly draw down the battery.

Take precautions with your dinnerware, too. Experienced boaters have learned that inexpensive reusable plastic plates and cups don't blow away like paper plates do. The only drawback with plastic is that bacteria grow quickly in food scraps on used plates. This means dirty dishes must never be reused for a later meal in the same day. Always have extra plates and cups on hand.

TAHOE

The built-in swim platform makes everywhere your favorite swimmin' hole. Aside from being attractive and useful, the platform of this 20.5-foot Tahoe conceals the sterndrive. The engine is hidden beneath the sun pad in the stern.

Anchor and Line

Most states require boats to be equipped with an anchor of sufficient size and a line, or *anchor rode*, long enough for the waters of operation. A considerable length of anchor line is required because the scope (length of rode from the deck of your boat to the anchor) should be 5 to 7 times the depth of water at anchor. A typical 150-foot anchor line provides enough scope for anchoring in water between 20 and 30 feet deep. The size of an anchor depends upon its design and construction. Anchor manufacturers' tables should be consulted. There is no federal requirement for an anchor and line on pleasure boats.

Danforth-style anchors are made of stamped steel with two triangular-shaped flukes attached to a stock. A shank pivots on the stock so the flukes can assume a good digging angle when they reach the bottom. No other type of anchor has the same holding capacity for its weight and cost. Most are made of galvanized steel, although high-tensile steel and even aluminum models are available. Danforth-style anchors are excellent in sand or stiff mud bottoms. Rocky bottoms, however, are tricky with a Danforth anchor. Often the flukes get wedged into the rocks and refuse to come out when you want to retrieve the anchor.

Mushroom anchors are a favorite with river anglers. They range from a big coffee can filled with cement to cast iron specialty anchors coated with plastic to prevent damage to the boat when you haul them in. A mushroom anchor works primarily on weight, so bigger and heavier is best. Smaller anchors will hold for a couple hours of fishing in good conditions, but should not be trusted to keep an unoccupied boat from drifting away.

In use, you can pull the anchor out backwards by motoring slowly over the top of it to reverse the pull on the rode. Use caution not to tangle the rope in your prop.

Visual Distress Signals

These are nonelectronic means of attracting attention or guiding rescuers to your boat in an emergency. Visual signals fall into two categories: day and night. The number of signals depends upon the type selected. A single distress flag satisfies the daytime requirement, but it takes three red flares to meet the legal requirement for night signals.

Visual distress signals must be marked with U.S. Coast Guard approval numbers to meet federal requirements. Flares, for instance, are marked with an expiration due to their limited lifespan; an out-of-date flare does not count as a distress signal. Most states follow federal guidelines regarding distress signals. It's important to note that the Rules of the Road authorize some distress signals which do not meet federal requirements. For instance, continuous sounding of a horn is a recognized signal of distress, but your boat horn does not count toward meeting federal requirements for carriage of distress signals.

Pleasure boats are not allowed to display blue flashing lights. These are reserved to identify law-enforcement vessels when operating in that capacity. Sirens are prohibited on pleasure boats for the same reason. Under most state laws, only police and fire boats may sound a siren.

All boats operating on federal waters and on many state-controlled rivers and lakes must carry distress signals. Signal types range from flags to orange smoke and red aerial flares. (www.mirtoart.com)

SIGNAL TYPES

Day-Only Signals
- Orange distress flag with black ball and square
- Orange smoke signal

Day/Night Signals
- Handheld red flares
- Aerial red flares
- Red parachute flares

Night-Only Signals
- Electric distress light (flashes S-O-S)

ALTERNATIVE DISTRESS SIGNALS
- Waving (a slow-motion jumping jack)
- Firing a gun at 1 minute intervals
- A square over a ball hoisted in the rigging
- Dye markers and smoke signals
- Code flag November over code flag Charlie.
- White strobe (50 to 70 flashes per minute)

VHF Marine Radio

There are no federal or state regulations requiring boats under 65 feet in length to carry a marine radio. Nonetheless, installation of a VHF (very high frequency) radio is *strongly advised* for boats operating on major rivers and larger bodies of water where commercial traffic is commonly encountered. If you choose to carry a marine radio, it must be operated under the regulations established by the Federal Communications Commission (FCC). Operators of recreational boats are not required to be licensed, nor is a station license required for operation solely within the United States. If you plan to cross into Canadian or Mexican waters, however, you will need both a station license for the radio and an operator's license for yourself.

Applications for both licenses come packed with new radios and are available from marine electronics dealers.

VHF Channel 16 is the international hailing and distress frequency. This channel is monitored 24 hours a day by the U.S. Coast Guard and all commercial shipping. To ease congestion on Channel 16, the FCC has established Channel 9 as the calling channel for pleasure boats. All marine radio channels have been designated for different types of messages.

The VHF marine radio is not a citizen's band (CB) radio or a toy. There are strict penalties for violating FCC regulations governing its use. It is unlawful to transmit a false distress alert. Vessels operating in Canadian waters should be aware that Canada has a much more aggressive enforcement policy than the United States.

VHF MARINE RADIO CHANNELS

Channel	Type of Message
06	Intership safety: used for ship-to-ship safety messages and search messages of the Coast Guard.
09	Boater calling: the FCC has established this channel as a supplementary calling channel for recreational craft in order to relieve congestion on VHF Channel 16.
13, 67	Navigational safety: big ship bridge-to-bridge communications. This is also the main working channel at most locks and drawbridges. Channel 67 is for the lower Mississippi River only. Power output of transmitter limited to 1 watt.
16	International distress, safety, and calling: USCG and most coast stations maintain a listening watch on this channel. All commercial ships monitor this channel.
21A, 23A, 83A	U.S. Coast Guard only.
22A	Coast Guard liaison and maritime safety information broadcasts. You may be directed to switch to Channel 22A when talking to the Coast Guard.
24, 25, 26, 27, 28, 84, 85, 86, 87	Public correspondence (marine operator): use these channels to call the marine operator at a public station where services are available. Except for distress calls, public stations usually charge for this service. Note: With the advent of cell phones most commercial operator stations have now ceased operations.
68, 69, 71	Noncommercial ship-to-ship: these channels are for pleasure craft communications.
70	Digital Selective Calling: reserved for DSC signals. No voice traffic.
79, 80	Noncommercial ship-to-ship: available on the Great Lakes only for pleasure craft communications.

USING VHF RADIO

Federal law requires that you initiate radio conversations by calling the other vessel on Channel 16. Recently, in authorized areas boaters can hail each other on the recreational calling frequency of Channel 9. Always call the Coast Guard or other law enforcement agencies on Channel 16. Channel 16 is always used by commercial vessels and distress calling.

Hailing a Vessel

To make a call, first establish contact on either Channel 9 or 16 and then switch to an idle operating channel for your conversation as described below. (Beware of the Channel 16 override feature on many radios. This is meant to automatically return the transmitter to the distress frequency, primarily for emergency situations. If you have the override activated, you can switch the unit to a working frequency but it will automatically return to Channel 16 if you press the transmit button. Also note that the buttons on many microphones are arranged to allow for one-handed operation. Careless handling of a multi-function microphone can result in switching channels inadvertently, making communication impossible.)

Proper radio etiquette is essential. Professional mariners talk in a deliberately polite and formal manner. As a courtesy, address the person at the other end of the signal as captain (or "cap" for short). Keep messages as short as possible and speak slowly with distinct enunciation to prevent misunderstandings. Hold the microphone close to one side of the mouth so you talk past and not directly into it. Speaking into the mike can cause popping sounds.

Before transmitting, monitor the channel for a few moments to make sure it is idle. When hailing another boat for the first time on either Channels 16 or 9, call out that boat's name up to three times, then give your own boat's name. Let's say you're trying to hail the captain of the *Black Pearl* and your boat is is the *Flying Dutchman*.

YOU: *Black Pearl . . . Black Pearl . . . Black Pearl*, this is *Flying Dutchman* calling *Black Pearl*, over.

(The word *over* means that you are turning the conversation over to the other vessel.)

After finishing the hail, listen for a reply. After a minute or so it's proper to hail a second time. But, don't make a career of calling the other boat. Just as you can't wake a dead man by shouting, you can't turn your friend's radio on by repeated calls. A couple of hails is enough, then wait a half hour or so before trying again.

THEM: *Flying Dutchman*, this is *Black Pearl*. What channel do you want to go to, Cap? Over.

YOU: *Black Pearl*, how about Channel Six-Eight? Over.

THEM: Roger, Channel Six-Eight.

(The word *Roger* stands for the letter R, which means the message has been received and understood. Saying "Six-Eight" instead of the more familiar "sixty-eight" helps avoid confusion if there is radio interference. There is no need to over-exaggerate numbers, just speak distinctly. If you want to switch to Channel 8, you would say, "Switch to Channel Zero-Eight." The number zero is never expressed as *oh*.

FCC-issued call signs are not required if you operate only within U.S. waters. If you have a license for your radio, however, you must identify your call sign at least at the beginning and end of each string of transmissions. Otherwise, identify yourself with the name of your boat.

Communicating with Commercial Vessels

If you operate on the Mississippi, the Ohio, or any of the other Western Rivers, you may need to talk to a commercial towboat regarding safety. Sometimes towboat skippers talk on the radio as if they are blowing whistle signals. A towboat will propose to pass on the "one-whistle side," and the other will agree, "Roger. A one-whistle passing." This means exactly the same thing as if the two had exchanged one-blast whistle signals. Both have agreed to steer right and pass port-to-port. As a private boat, it is best to avoid this sort of talk simply because the professionals may think you are just copying something you have heard and do not really understand.

Be sure to use precise radio procedures when you talk to a towboat or other commercial captain. As a rule, they do not want to chat with private boats. One way to make sure the towboat captain understands that you are interested in a safety issue is to say so in your first hail. This bends the rules, but gets the job done.

YOU: Towboat *Sarah Sue*, this is

the pleasure craft *Flying Dutchman* requesting information on how I can pass you safely.

Signing Off

Always identify yourself by boat name and call sign (if you have one) at the beginning and end of each conversation. When you finish talking, you can either stay on the working channel or go back to Channels 16 or 9. If you plan to talk frequently with another boat, the general rule is to stay on the working frequency. In radio talk, you are *standing by*.

YOU: This is *Flying Dutchman*. Out and standing by on Channel Six-Eight.

The word *out* means you have completed your conversation and do not expect any reply from the other station. It is the opposite meaning of *over*, which indicates you are turning the conversation over to the other person for a reply.

If you are *out* on the working frequency, you may indicate that you are returning to one of the calling frequencies.

YOU: This is *Flying Dutchman*. Out and returning to Channel One-Six.

Mayday

Mayday is the spoken equivalent of *S-O-S* in Morse code. It means that you and your crew are in mortal danger and you require immediate assistance. Running out of gas on a sunny day in quiet water is not a mayday situation. Mayday should be used for situations such as a sinking, or a fire. Certain elements must be included in any mayday call.

1. Repeat the word *mayday* at least 3 times
2. Give the name of your vessel
3. Describe your distress as simply as possible
4. Give your location as accurately as you can
5. Give the number of persons on board
6. Repeat the name of your vessel
7. Repeat the word *mayday* at least 3 more times

Be sure to get all the information into your first mayday transmission. You may not get a second chance if the boat sinks or fire burns through the wiring. Wait 15 seconds for an answer and repeat the entire message.

Continue transmitting until somebody responds or your radio sinks beneath the waves.

An emergency that is not life-threatening is introduced with *pan-pan* (pronounced "pawn-pawn"). For example, you would use pan-pan to alert the Coast Guard that your engine has died and you're adrift but not in any immediate danger. You can also use pan-pan to alert the Coast Guard of a life-threatening situation that's occurring on a boat other than your own.

You may also hear commercial vessels use the word *securité* (pronounced "secure-a-tay"). This identifies a message of interest to everyone in the area. For instance, a towboat may use a security call to announce that it's coming around a blind bend in a river.

ALOHA PARADISE 250

The most popular pontoon boat layout has two seating areas. The bow is for conversation and dining. Additional seating is grouped around the driver. This Aloha Paradise 250 also has a refreshment center with sink.

PERSONAL SAFETY

Sun and Fun

Nothing makes a Sunday afternoon on the water more fun than bright sunshine; however, nothing can ruin Monday morning more than too much of it. Harsh ultraviolet light reflects off the water, increasing the effect of sun exposure. The amount of UV light varies with time of day. Tests by the National Weather Service and U.S. Environmental Protection Agency show it can be ten times greater at noon than at 9 in the morning or 6 in the evening. To help people avoid excess UV exposure, the two agencies have developed the "UV Index." This index rates the amount of radiation on a 0 to 10 scale. Listen for it in NOAA Weather radio broadcasts.

SUNSCREEN

Experienced boaters use plenty of sunscreen, even on hazy, overcast days, and also favor wide-brimmed hats that protect ears and the back of the neck.

The *sun protection factor* (SPF) of a sunscreen is intended as a guide to its degree of protection from the sun. The higher the number, the better the protection. SPF 15 is considered the minimum protection on the water. This number is only a guideline. People with sensitive skin usually find they need a higher number than those with darker complexions.

Using a higher-rated product is definitely recommended. Since many people apply less sunscreen than is ideal, dermatologists often recommend an SPF 30 sunscreen. Sweating in the sun, swimming, and other water activities tend to wash the SPF protection from the skin. Reapplication is usually needed throughout the day, even for products claiming to be waterproof.

Older products using PABA as a sun blocker often caused stains on the fiberglass or vinyl upholstery of boats. Most newer products do not contain this ingredient, but it pays to check the label. If you are uncertain, dab a bit on an inconspicuous surface and observe what happens.

SUNGLASSES

Wear sunglasses whenever you are boating in daylight. Polarized lenses work best because they protect against excessive glare. Anglers use this feature to peer into the depths. Polarized or not, sunglasses should block 100 percent of the incoming UV light. Ultraviolet rays cannot be seen, but they still have the power to damage your eyes. Long-term damage from UV exposure may form cataracts in the lens of the eye. The short-term damage is to the photochemical receptors in the retina; overexposure to ultraviolet rays can produce *photokeratitis* (commonly referred to as snow blindness). The symptoms should resolve themselves in about a day. If not, seek medical treatment.

Water Safety

Nothing is more refreshing than a dive into cool water on a hot summer day. Everyone, especially the kids, is going to want to join in. Before things get out of hand, certain safety procedures should be followed. The first is to establish a designated swimming area that can be kept under constant observation by a designated adult. If someone does get into trouble they won't struggle unnoticed. Adults should be encouraged to wear PFDs and they should be mandatory for children.

You can cordon off a swimming area by using buoyant polypropylene rope. The bright yellow color of poly line is easily seen by other boaters. Tie lifejackets or large boat fenders at regular intervals along the line to create a series of "safety islands" for tired swimmers.

The designated swimming observer should have either a coach's whistle or a portable air horn. Everyone swimming should know to immediately come out of the water when the whistle or horn blows. Use this system to get everyone onto the boat from time to time for a rest period and to make sure nobody has disappeared. Also, swimmers should use the buddy system to keep track of each other.

The second big issue is propeller safety. A spinning boat propeller can cause serious injuries or death if it strikes a swimmer. Common sense says that the engine should be shut down whenever swimmers are in the water. Don't just rely on neutral to keep the propeller from spinning. This is particularly true when picking up water-skiers or people who have been tubing.

Another advantage of shutting down the engine is that it stops the production of carbon monoxide in the exhaust. This odorless gas can build up under and around boat swim platforms and it has caused swimmers to become unconscious and drown.

Powering Your Boat

At the heart of every powerboat is the engine. Pontoon boats and deckboats have traditionally gone their separate ways when it came to power. Outboards have been the engines of choice for pontoon boats, even large commercial craft. Deckboats, on the other hand, have been mostly powered by inboard/outboard (I/O), or sterndrive engines.

The reasons for this divergence are the basic differences in the hulls of the two types of watercraft. Pontoons provide a lot of buoyancy, but seldom have enough interior room for a conventional gasoline engine. From the beginning, it was easier to hang a motor bracket between the 'toons and attach an outboard engine. The hull of a deckboat, on the other hand, provides plenty of room for an inboard/outboard engine.

While the pairings of outboard engines on pontoon boats and I/Os on deckboats still

PLANING

At slow speeds, all boat hulls—including pontoons—ride low in the water. This is called operating in *displacement mode*. To get an acceptable turn of speed, however, the boat needs to get out of displacement mode so it can ride higher and *plane* across the top of the water. Once a boat is planing, it is subject to less friction from the water and can go faster.

Deckboat hulls are designed with flat bottom surfaces to help them plane easily.

Unlike deckboats, traditional round pontoon logs do not provide any flat planing surface, but they still rise up as speed increases. Much of the log remains in the water, however, so it takes a lot of horsepower and fuel to gain a fair turn of speed. The solution has been to design pontoon logs with flat planing surfaces instead of round bottoms. Boats with these newer pontoons are capable of speeds over 50 miles an hour.

dominate the market, there are some exceptions. For instance, deckboat manufacturers are starting to take advantage of newer 4-stroke outboards that are now powerful enough to handle larger fiberglass hulls. Newer pontoon boats take advantage of MerCruiser's Vazer sterndrive, which is specifically designed to power trailerable pontoon boats.

OUTBOARD ENGINES

As the name implies, outboard engines are the detachable engines that are mounted on the outside of the boat.

The race between manufacturers to build outboard engines that are both clean-running and powerful has been a face-off between high-tech two-stroke engines and their heavier four-stroke cousins. All of the new outboards represent major improvements over the engines made just a decade ago. The question is which will gain popularity among boaters. At the moment, it appears four-stroke engines will dominate, but not eliminate, two-stroke machines. In the meantime, this competition between technologies has made the boating public the clear victors. We are now seeing wide availability of the best performing, cleanest outboards ever built.

Two-Stroke versus Four-Stroke Technology

Early outboard inventors chose two-stroke technology for maximum output with minimum weight. Two-stroke engines produce a pulse of power every time the piston moves down in the cylinder. A four-stroke engine produces power half as often, on every other downstroke. In theory a two-stroke engine half the size of a four-stroke could produce the same power.

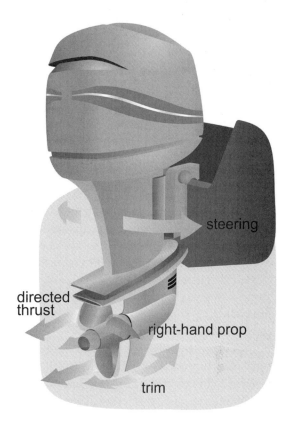

Outboard engine. Boats with outboard engines are steered by pivoting the entire engine on its mount. The directed thrust from the prop will push the stern from side to side thus steering the boat. As we'll discuss later, the engine can also be pivoted up and down to change the boat's trim. Most engines have a right-hand prop, meaning the propeller turns clockwise. (As we'll discuss later, the direction your prop turns will influence the direction of your boat's so-called prop walk.) (Bob Sweet)

ADVANTAGES OF OUTBOARD POWER

- Wide variety of horsepower options
- Easy replacement of old engine
- Excellent power-to-weight ratio
- All but necessary for pontoon boats

Conventional two-stroke engines are light and powerful, but they have a problem with lubrication. The crankcase is part of the air- and fuel-handling system, so two-stroke outboards do not have a pan for lube oil like four-stroke engines. To lubricate the crankshaft it is necessary to mix special lube oil into the fuel. In old-technology two-stroke engines the result was an oil-rich blue exhaust much like that coming from a worn-out jalopy on the highway. Environmental protection laws forced outboard makers to reduce emissions and the simplest solution was to adopt four-stroke engines. Four-stroke technology allows the lube oil to be kept in the crankcase like an automobile engine. Lube oil is not mixed with the fuel, so it does not produce the blue hydrocarbon emission associated with old-technology two-strokes.

Although they're getting a lot of sudden attention these days, four-stroke outboards aren't new. In the late 1950s Homelite/Bearcat pioneered four-stroke outboards by bolting a Crosley automobile engine to a standard outboard lower unit. The results were predictable: a heavy engine that produced no haze of blue exhaust, but was sluggish due to an inefficient gear ratio. This sluggard reputation unfairly plagued four-stroke engines despite the fact Honda brought its first line of high-performance four-stroke engines into the United States in 1973.

At the time, those Honda engines seemed out of place in a world dominated by conventional two-stroke outboard technology. There was no consumer demand for cleaner outboards because exhaust and emission standards were nearly nonexistent.

Updated Two-Stroke Engines

Several manufacturers continue to show faith in two-stroke technology. Newer two-stroke engines now surpass all current emission regulations. Evinrude's E-TEC engines, for example, use a one-way system of lubrication to produce extremely low emissions. Lube oil goes from a tank to the engine where flow is controlled by a transducer sensor. Oil pressure is automatically monitored and adjusted to meet operating conditions. If oil flow fails, the engine is designed to operate at low power output for up to five hours with no oil.

Who Has The Power?

Evinrude says its new two-stroke engines give even the best four-strokes serious competition for speed and power. Two-stroke engines have traditionally held the edge in something called the *hole shot*. That's what bass anglers call the transition from dead stopped to screaming across the water on plane. They want to "get out of the hole," or out of displacement mode quickly.

Four-stroke outboard manufacturers first improved the hole shot by tinkering with lower unit gear ratios and changing propellers. (Conventional two-stroke engines typically use about a 1.8:1 gear ratio, meaning the engine driveshaft rotates a bit less than two times for every rotation of the propeller. This ratio allows conventional

DIRECTED THRUST

Boats with outboard engines or stern-drives use *directed thrust* to steer. When you turn the wheel to port, for instance, the engine's lower unit pivots, and the propeller's thrust kicks the stern to starboard and pushes the boat into a turn to port. Directed-thrust steering allows you to turn the boat even if it's "dead in the water," or not moving.

TUBING AND SKIING

Why the first person volunteered to be towed behind a moving boat may never be known. We do know, however, why the practice became so popular: it's fun. Today, there's no shortage of people who are willing to be towed on water skis, kneeboards, wakeboards, wake skates, or tubes.

All of these activities require a towboat with enough horses to get the rider to plane across the water. Once you're on plane, high speeds are neither necessary nor desirable. Running along at 15 miles an hour seems supersonic when you are at eye level with the water. Most inflatable toys are not rated for higher speeds. Also, be aware of local regulations regarding where towed water toys can be used. Many smaller lakes have speed zones for this sort of activity.

Riders of towed water toys must be wearing a Coast Guard–approved personal flotation device (PFD). Be sure the PFD really fits, especially with children. The force of moving water can tear an ill-fitting PFD off the wearer. Towed watersports are also not the place for inflatable PFDs, which may fail to inflate if the wearer falls unconscious. It is safe practice to have at least two people aboard the towboat. One drives while the other keeps an eye on the person riding the toy. Water-skiers have adopted a small red flag to indicate a "skier down" to other boats. This signal is required in Arizona, California, Colorado, Idaho, Missouri, Nebraska, Oregon, Texas, Utah, and Washington. New Jersey has mandated that a triangular flag be used for this purpose.

Towing a water toy puts quite a strain on the tow line. It's not a good idea to rely on a stern cleat. Instead, secure the towline to one of the stern eyes, which are bolted through the transom. Keep in mind that the drag of the toy will cause the towboat to be far less maneuverable than normal.

Many jurisdictions now require a quick-release device on all towable devices. This releases the toy instantly in an emergency. To avoid fouling your prop with the towline, use buoyant poly rope.

(Crest Pontoon Boats)

two-stroke engines to take advantage of the considerable torque at lower RPMs resulting from the power pulse on every downstroke. Four-stroke outboards, on the other hand, use a higher ratio because they have power pulses only every other piston downstroke. This means four-stroke engines need higher RPMs to produce the same torque.) Modern four-stroke engines typically use gear ratios of 2.4:1 or better which means they turn more than two revolutions for every rotation of their propellers. Changing the gear ratio increased hole-shot performance with only a slight sacrifice in top-end speed.

Another way to get more oomph out of an engine is to cram more air into the cylinder along with the fuel. One way to do this is with a supercharger, a mechanically-driven blower that compresses air.

Which Outboard Is Right for You?

The major brands offer pretty much the same choices in horsepower. As a consumer, you have to choose which outboard makes the most sense for you. How do you decide? Without doubt, the most important factor is the availability of parts and service. There's no advantage to buying whiz-bang technology if you have to drive 200 miles to buy a $20 part. Even the best machinery needs maintenance and the odd repair. You'll spend more hours on the water if you choose an outboard brand that has good local support.

Flexibility is the greatest asset of outboard engines. Outboards can be easily changed over the life of a boat. The same steering, shift, and throttle cables can be attached to a wide range of engine sizes provided you buy from a particular manufacturer. Outboard power allows the boat buyer greater leeway in choosing the horsepower and weight of engine. It is even pos-

sible to purchase a smaller engine and then move up to more power as the budget allows.

STERNDRIVES

Sterndrives, or I/Os (inboard/outboards), dominate the deckboat market and may soon become more important in pontoon boat sales. The sterndrive configuration combines an inboard engine (an engine that's mounted inside the hull) with a steerable lower unit like that of an outboard engine.

Until recently, few pontoon boats have been adapted for I/O propulsion because of the size and weight of the associated inboard gasoline engines. The 24- to 30-inch diameters of pontoon logs do not provide enough internal clearance for an engine block. MerCruiser's new Vazer engine, however, is a lightweight, 100-horsepower sterndrive that solves space and weight problems. Installed below the deck and forward of the stern, it is said to provide better speed and maneuverability than outboards.

Sterndrives are not perfect. Power from the engine has to go through a universal joint and make two right-angle bends in order to reach the propeller. All of that bending and turning adds complexity, which means more parts to break or wear out. Even so, the I/O has

ADVANTAGES OF STERNDRIVES
■ Choice of automobile-derived engine
■ Greater high-end horsepower
■ Larger engines last longer
■ Allows for better weight distribution in boat

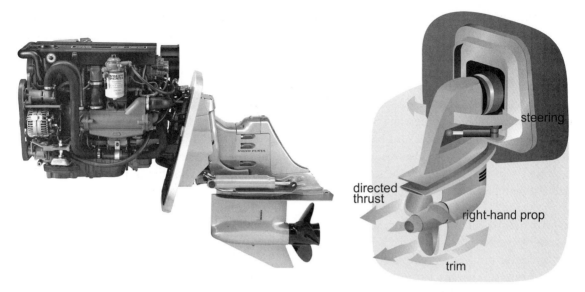

Sterndrive engine. Sterndrives combine a fixed interior engine with a pivoting external lower unit. When the steering wheel pivots the lower unit (right), the directed thrust from the prop will push the stern from side to side much like an outboard engine. The lower unit can also be tilted up and down to change the boat's trim. Just like outboards, most sterndrives have a right-hand prop. (left: Volvo Marine; right: Bob Sweet)

ALOHA 210

Although small enough to tow behind a compact SUV, this 21-foot Aloha 210 still has all the comforts of bigger pontoon boats. There's even an unseen ice chest tucked beneath the seats.

proven itself to be the most popular method for propelling powerboats under 30 feet in length.

A major improvement in sterndrive design was the introduction of contra-rotating propellers. In this type of lower unit, two propellers are mounted on the same driveshaft. They are geared so that one rotates clockwise, while the other rotates counterclockwise. This system was developed for torpedoes to cancel out *propeller walk* (lateral thrust created by the spinning propeller), but it had the happy benefit of more efficient performance. Contra-rotating propellers improve I/O boat performance at all speeds. Handling is easier because there is no tendency for the lower unit to "wander" as happens with single-prop I/O designs.

Safety Measures

Boat engines are marinized versions of gasoline engines developed for land vehicles. They share the basic block, crankshaft, and even pistons with their highway cousins. However, important changes are made to the bearings, lube oil system, cooling system, and exhaust manifold for boating safety and longevity.

There are three important safety areas in which marine engines differ from their automotive cousins: the fuel system, exhaust system, and electrical system. Gasoline fumes are both explosive and heavier than air. In a car, any fumes fall harmlessly to the ground where they dissipate. Not so in most boats, in which the hull collects fumes in the bilge where they become an explosion or fire hazard. To prevent trouble, marine engines are designed to eliminate any source of ignition as much as possible. Marine carburetors are designed not to leak gas into the boat for obvious reasons. The familiar paper automotive air cleaner is replaced with a metal marine flame arrestor. This device prevents a backfire from igniting either stray gas fumes or the boat itself. Fuel injection systems are also modified so they will not spray gasoline in the event of a malfunction.

An inboard boat's "wet" exhaust system is the second main safety difference between marine and automotive engines. Exhaust gases from an engine are extremely hot. The tailpipe of a car glows dull red after hard use. This is hot enough to set fire to wood or fiberglass. To avoid this obvious fire danger on boats, hot manifolds are water-cooled. Additionally, cool water is injected into the stream of hot exhaust gas at a specially-designed "elbow." The shape of the elbow prevents water from being sucked back into the cylinders. Cooling the exhaust also causes the hot gas to contract thus reducing engine noise.

The third difference involves using spark-protected electrical parts in marine engines so as not to ignite gasoline fumes. It has been estimated that half a teacup of gasoline has the explosive force of eight sticks of dynamite. That is why U.S. Coast Guard regulations require all electrical components to have spark protection. Marine electrical parts cost more than their automotive counterparts, but don't be tempted to save a few dollars by using lower-cost car parts on your boat's engine. It can be a dangerous and costly decision.

Cooling System

Boats do not have radiators. Instead, they use the water around the boat to keep the engine from overheating. Two different systems have evolved. The simplest is *raw-water cooling*, which draws water from outside the boat and circulates it through the engine. This system works fine in the clean, fresh water of lakes and some rivers. The majority of I/O deckboats (and all outboard-powered boats, including most pontoons) use raw-water cooling.

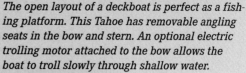

TAHOE

The open layout of a deckboat is perfect as a fishing platform. This Tahoe has removable angling seats in the bow and stern. An optional electric trolling motor attached to the bow allows the boat to troll slowly through shallow water.

Operating a raw-water-cooled boat in salt water, however, creates corrosion problems that can shorten the life of the engine. Silt can also plug the cooling passages of inboard motors. So-called closed-system cooling (sometimes erroneously called "freshwater cooling") evolved to solve these problems. Coolant is circulated through a heat exchanger where it cools the engine. This coolant is a biodegradable version of the coolant used in cars.

Inboard Engine Size

Deckboat companies offer several power options for each boat model. As a general rule, the midrange engine is the best all-around choice. The manufacturer often installs the lowest horsepower engine simply to meet a specific price point. In most cases, the result is an underpowered boat. On the other end of the spectrum, it is possible to install too much engine. Despite the extra horsepower, an oversized engine may be too heavy for the boat, and it might not perform any better than the midsized engine anyway.

Engine Controls

Widespread calls for more efficient automobile engines have benefited boaters. Fuel injection and computerized engine controls originally developed for the highway are now standard on the latest generation of boat engines. At first, old timers feared these new ideas would not stand up to the marine environment. The reverse has proven to be true. Computerized and fuel-injected engines are now preferred because they do not need extended warm-up periods, they burn less fuel, and they often produce more horsepower out of the same basic block.

PROPELLERS AND PROPULSION

Swedish-American inventor John Ericsson developed the modern propeller in 1839. One of the most successful applications of his so-called screw propeller was the U.S.S. *Monitor* during the American Civil War. At the time, it

PROP TALK

Propellers—like anything else in boating—come with their own terminology.

PITCH AND SLIP

Pitch is the theoretical distance a prop will move forward in the water during one revolution. A 24-inch pitch prop should push the boat forward 24 inches, but no propeller is that efficient. *Slip* is the difference between the theoretical 100 percent forward motion and the actual distance the boat moves forward.

DIAMETER

This is the width of the circle described by the outer tips of the blades as they rotate. The maximum diameter a boat can handle is determined by the distance from the prop shaft to the underside of the anti-ventilation plate of an I/O or outboard lower unit.

CUPPING

Some propeller blades are slightly dish-shaped by a process called *cupping*, which adds performance. Typically, cupping a prop causes a decrease in engine RPM, but results in better speed or better thrust for heavy loads.

side. As the prop rotates it draws water in from the front and expels it out the back. Moving this stream of water creates forward thrust. Water being drawn into the prop is called the *suction current* while the water pushed out the back is the *discharge current*.

Props are described by two numbers, the first being the diameter and the second the pitch. A 13 x 9 prop has a 13-inch diameter and 9-inch pitch. Any prop that has the same diameter as pitch, say 24 x 24, is called *square*. (You might hear that *square props* are best, but that's just a sea story.)

One propeller may not answer all of your needs. If you normally cruise with your whole family in your deckboat, you'll need a *power prop* with lower pitch. This allows your engine to develop maximum output. The downside is that the lower-pitch prop moves the boat forward less distance with each revolution, so the boat does not reach its maximum potential speed. If you want to go for speed, you'll have to leave some of the people and all of that picnic gear behind to lighten the load. Now, a more aggressive, deeper pitch will boost boat speed while still keeping the engine within its red-line limit.

was believed the propeller worked by screwing through the water like a common wood screw pulls itself into timber. The name stuck and propellers on ships and boats are still called screws even though the term is technically incorrect.

Propellers, or props, actually work by creating high- and low-pressure areas on either side of their foil-shaped blades. Low pressure is created on the forward-facing side, while a corresponding high pressure builds on the back-

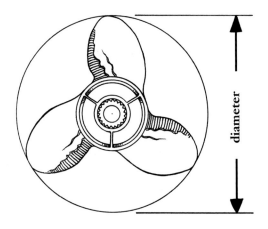

Prop diameter is measured as shown. (Christopher Hoyt)

Carrying two different propellers is not a far-fetched idea. Every boat should have a spare prop just in case. The spare does not need to be identical to the main prop. One could be a power prop for those times when you're carrying heavy loads. The second might be a *speed prop* for high performance. Either will get you home if the other one breaks. In addition to a spare prop, it pays to carry a spare thrust washer, propeller nut, and locking device. Some engines also require a specialized prop removal tool.

Aluminum Propellers

The propellers that come part and parcel with many outboard motors are inexpensive, aluminum castings that give reasonable performance on a variety of boats and under different loading conditions. Skippers who operate in snag-infested waters where damage is unavoidable usually prefer aluminum props that cost less to replace. Otherwise, aluminum props are not the best choice for larger outboards. The blades of an aluminum prop actually flex under strain, causing a loss in performance. This is particularly true of props either pushing a heavily loaded boat or trying to stand up to a high-horsepower engine.

Stainless Steel Propellers

This stronger metal holds its shape under strain, making it the metal of choice for most applications. As a rule, stainless props give greater bow lift on heavier boats, resulting in better overall performance. Virtually everyone can benefit from upgrading to a better aluminum or to a stainless steel propeller. Better performance, however, isn't cheap. Stainless props can cost two or three times as much as similar aluminum props. Outboards of 100 horsepower or more are best served with stainless propellers.

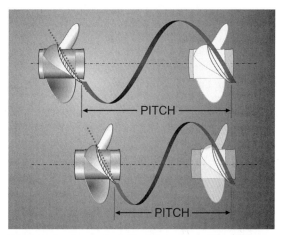

Pitch is the theoretical distance a propeller moves forward in one revolution. Here, the upper prop has a deep pitch for higher speed, while the lower prop has a shallow pitch to gain maximum power. (Bob Sweet)

It's important to note that the mass of a stainless propeller spinning through water puts considerable strain on the lower unit's gears. To compensate for this, engineers have built the shifting mechanisms to handle the strain, or *preload*, caused by heavier props. If, however, you're using a lightweight aluminum prop, the shifting mechanism won't experience pre-load and hard shifting may occur, particularly when shifting from forward to neutral.

ENGINE SIZE AND POWER RESTRICTIONS

Anyone who has ever tinkered with hot rods immediately equates the cubic-inch displacement of an engine with speed and power. While larger displacement engines do produce more horsepower, the relationship of cubic inches to speed on the water is not as direct as on land. The output of the boat's engine must be coupled into the water through a set of gears and the propeller. Even though a boat may have a monster V-8, it may not be able to get out of its own way if the transmission gear ratio and propeller are wrong. Factors that influence boat performance include:

- Weight of the hull, engine, and occupants
- Shape of the hull beneath the waterline
- Horsepower produced by the engine at various RPMs
- Diameter and pitch of the propeller
- Underwater appendages such as rudders, shafts, or struts
- Water conditions (smooth, choppy, etc.)
- Ambient air temperature, pressure, and humidity

Complex mathematical formulas are used by naval architects to determine the correct engine, gear ratio, and propeller for a specific hull. Fortunately, you do not need to know calculus or have a supercomputer to make good boat-buying decisions. Almost all of the number crunching will have been done by the boatbuilder before you walk into the dealer's showroom.

Capacity Plate and Safe Loading

Bigger is better only to a point. Horsepower is heavy. Excessive outboard engine weight causes an equivalent loss in weight capacity for people and gear.

Every boat has a maximum safe weight that it can carry and a maximum safe horsepower for the engine. Overloading and overpowering are two main causes of capsizes and other accidents, particularly in smaller craft. For this reason, the U.S. Coast Guard requires that builders of monohull boats under 20 feet in length mount yellow-and-black capacity plates

in a location where the operators can see them from the helm. (This regulation does not apply to pontoon boats.) The plate specifies the maximum load both in terms of the number of adults, and the total weight of people and cargo. The plates on boats with outboard engines must also display the maximum safe horsepower. Many people forget that every time they add a cooler full of ice and a set of water skis, the additional weight is lowering their passenger capacity. On an overnight trip with food, ice, soft drinks, sleeping bags, and other gear aboard, the safe number of people may be half of what's shown on the plate.

It may be foolhardy to carry too many people or install an overly large engine, but it is not illegal under federal regulations. State laws, on the other hand, are stricter. Most states prohibit overloading or excess horsepower based on the data shown on the capacity plate. Insurance policies, too, often require boatowners to operate within the safe capacity and loading data

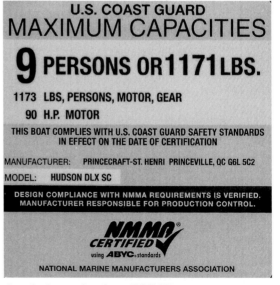

A typical capacity plate. (NMMA)

U.S. COAST GUARD WEIGHTS (IN POUNDS)
OF OUTBOARD ENGINES AND RELATED EQUIPMENT

Boat Horsepower Rating	Engine Weight	Battery Weight	Full Portable Fuel Tank	Total Weight
Up to 2	25	n/a	n/a	25
2.1 to 3.9	40	n/a	n/a	40
4.0 to 7.0	60	n/a	25	85
7.1 to 15	90	20	50	160
15.1 to 25	125	45	50	220
25.1 to 45	170	45	100	315
45.1 to 60	235	45	100	380
60.1 to 80	280	45	100	425
80.1 to 145	405	45	100	550
145.1 to 275	430	45	100	575
275.1 and up	605	45	100	750

shown on the plate. Carrying too many people or pushing the boat with an overly large engine can be reason enough for an insurance company to refuse to pay a claim.

Vessels over 20 feet in length are not required to display capacity plates. However, this does not mean they are immune from accidents caused by excessive horsepower or carrying too many people. As a rule of thumb, never carry more people than the boat can accommodate in the fixed seating arrangements installed by the builder.

Horsepower Restrictions

Smaller lakes and many municipal reservoirs often have legal restrictions on the size of engines, typically limiting engines to under 10 horsepower. (This explains why so many 9.9-horsepower outboard motors exist.) If you plan to boat in one of these restricted lakes, your engine options will be limited. Fortunately,

pontoon boats up to about 20 feet in length can be handled by one of those ubiquitous 9.9-horsepower outboards. Such a small engine isn't the most satisfactory power arrangement, but it is workable. A deckboat with its big inboard engine and outdrive cannot legally operate its main propulsion system on horsepower-restricted waters. Instead, it must have its propeller removed from the inboard or I/O and be fitted with an outboard motor that meets the horsepower limit.

BOOSTING FUEL ECONOMY

As powerboats go, pontoon and deckboats are not particularly fuel thirsty. A few gallons of gas can provide hours of fun on the water. Still, nobody wants to spend more at the gas dock than necessary.

Savings Add Up

Fuel consumption can't be cut in half by flipping a switch or changing some obscure engine part. Getting better fuel economy is an incremental process. The first place to look for fuel savings is the engine. Today's engines run so well that it's easy to forget they require periodic maintenance. In the old days, ragged performance told when an engine needed tuning. Modern computer-controlled engines can accommodate for lack of tune. No matter what the age of an engine, however, an out-of-tune engine decreases fuel economy from 10 to 30 percent.

Mechanical fuel injectors should be serviced during any regular tune-ups because dirty injectors increase fuel use. Even worse is a leaking injector that does not completely shut off fuel flow. This allows unburned gasoline to wash lubrication off the cylinder walls and even dilute the lube oil, causing rapid bearing wear.

Spark plug wires on gasoline engines should be inspected regularly. Do this in the dark to see any telltale spark trails caused by leaking high voltage. The marine environment is notoriously hard on plug wires. Cracks in brittle insulation might not cause a problem in a car, but the moist air around the water allows high-voltage current to leak away. The resulting weaker spark at the plug translates into wasted gasoline. Wires with more than three seasons of use are candidates for replacement.

Changing oil more frequently will save a little fuel, especially if you switch to one of the new synthetic oils. Fresh lubricant lets internal parts roll and slide with less energy-robbing friction. The fuel savings are small, maybe a percent or two. However, you get big savings from not having to overhaul the engine as the result of premature wear.

Make sure the flame arrestor is clean. As mentioned earlier, U.S. Coast Guard regulations require all gasoline engines in boats to be equipped with metal flame arrestors. The honeycomb holes in arrestors are meant to trap backfires, but they're equally good at filtering grease and dirt from the air. A dirty arrestor starves the engine for air, causing a marked decline in fuel economy. Remove the flame arrestor and take it ashore for cleaning. (Never operate the engine while the arrestor is removed.) Aerosol-spray brake cleaner works well to degrease the honeycomb. Be sure to wear eye and hand protection, and don't smoke, as this cleaner is highly combustible. You could also take the arrestor to an auto shop that has a parts washer. Dry the clean arrestor thoroughly before reinstalling it on the carburetor.

Estimating Fuel Use

As a rule of thumb, conventional four-stroke inboard gasoline engines burn in gallons about 10 percent of the horsepower being developed. If, for example, you're burning about 7.5 gallons per hour, your engine is making about 75 horsepower. This fuel/horsepower relationship applies to developed horsepower and not to the maximum power output of the engine. A boat might need those 75 horses to go 20 miles per hour. Fuel burn goes up substantially for modest speed increases. Increasing this hypothetical boat's speed to 30 miles an hour might require the engine's full 150-horsepower output, burning 15 gallons per hour. Those additional 10 miles per hour represent a 50 percent increase in speed, but they have doubled the consumption of fuel. This is why the best way to save gasoline is to pull back on the throttle.

Sweet Spot

Each boat/motor combination has a "sweet spot" that produces the best speed for the least

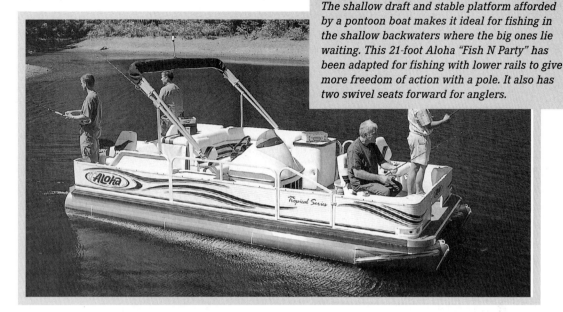

ALOHA "FISH N PARTY"

The shallow draft and stable platform afforded by a pontoon boat makes it ideal for fishing in the shallow backwaters where the big ones lie waiting. This 21-foot Aloha "Fish N Party" has been adapted for fishing with lower rails to give more freedom of action with a pole. It also has two swivel seats forward for anglers.

fuel burn. Finding the sweet spot is easy if you can monitor fuel flow in real time. The latest engines have built-in fuel management systems that constantly monitor fuel consumption. Earlier-model boats can be retrofitted with fuel-flow meters that serve the same purpose. These meters are easily installed, but caution is always advised when working on gasoline fuel systems. Do not allow gasoline to run into the bilge. Be careful with electric lights and other spark-producing equipment. And be sure there are no fuel leaks when you are done.

Once the fuel-flow meter is working, make a series of test runs at various combinations of trim tabs (see page 57), engine trim (see page 89), and engine rpm. Write down the details of each test run for comparison. Typically, you will see fuel flow increase rapidly until the boat comes out of the hole, but it will decrease once you hit the sweet spot. Fuel guzzling goes up rapidly as speed is increased above that.

The sweet spot varies with water conditions, atmospheric pressure and humidity, and the weight in the boat. Recording data from each trip over a season will give you a pretty good idea of what's best. Also, keeping records will let you compare fuel use trip by trip.

Prop Tuning

Even a well-tuned, well-oiled engine is only as efficient as its propeller. Upgrading from a standard to a top-shelf prop can produce surprising results. However, it isn't necessary to go to the expense of a super-high-quality propeller to increase economy. Improvements can be obtained by having your stock propellers tuned for best performance. If your propeller has ever struck an object, minor nicks and dings might not be the only problem; a blade may have been knocked out of pitch. Boats typically pick up a full mile an hour more speed after having their props restored to factory pitch and balance. Sometimes the speed improvement is 5 miles an hour or more. That's only part of the good news. This extra speed usually comes with a slight reduction in fuel consumption. Now that's a win–win deal.

Drag and Weight

A dirty bottom or too much unnecessary gear can steal money from your wallet.

What most people call *drag* is really a combination of frictional resistance and wave-making resistance. Naval architects have found that under ideal conditions about 25 percent of the total resistance to forward motion of a planing hull comes from friction with the water. Even the smoothest hull imparts energy into the water through friction. The boat drags along the molecules closest to the hull. These molecules in turn transfer energy outward. A 30-foot boat operating at displacement speed has been found to drag a band of water about 5 inches thick at its stern. Moving all that water is expensive. A smooth bottom reduces the friction that pulls water along with the boat. A rough, multilayer coat of bottom paint can increase friction. So do barnacles. Even a few weeks' worth of algae growth on the bottom can have a noticeable effect on boat speed.

Also take a good close look at your boat wake. How big is it? Remember, moving water

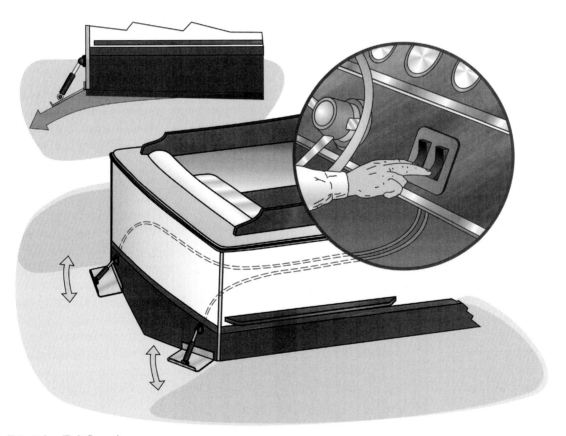

Trim tabs. (Bob Sweet)

costs money. The bigger your wake, the more money you are putting into churning the lake instead of moving your boat. This is why it's important to get a powerboat fully on plane and not to "mush" along.

Excess weight inside the boat also steals fuel. Simply pumping the bilge before each trip can cut your gas bill; you'll lose more than 8 pounds with every gallon of bilgewater sent overboard. Look around your boat for clutter that doesn't need to be there. Oversized tool kits, canned goods from last year's cruise, and full holding tanks all add unnecessary weight.

Trim Tabs

When used correctly, trim tabs (see illustration on facing page) can help get a boat on plane quicker and stay on plane at lower speeds. The potential fuel savings are obvious. Too much tabbing, however, increases drag. The goal is to apply only enough tab to operate at the most efficient attitude, or angle of bow to the water. The same is true when altering the angle of the lower unit of an outboard or I/O drive.

A zero-degree angle (or negative angle) of the boat to the water puts the entire bottom of the boat in contact with the water. This increases wetted area and, hence, surface friction. Most standard hulls run best at about a 4-degree upward trim by the bow. Deep-V hulls usually need about 6 degrees. The amount needed varies slightly with hull design, but the correct angle is critical for best fuel economy.

Don't confuse the trim angle of the outdrive or outboard with the trim of the boat. You may need 10 or more degrees of trim on the outdrive to run the boat at an attitude of 6 degrees to the water. There is an interrelation between the two, but the angles are separate entities.

Trailering

Deckboats and trailers are such a natural combination that it is hard to think of one without the other. Now, thanks to innovative trailer design, pontoon boats can also be easily towed from one boating area to the next. Trailering also allows you to avoid slip fees and storage costs by storing your boat in your back yard. Plus, when repairs or maintenance are needed, your tools will be nearby.

By putting wheels on your boat, a trailer widens your horizon to lakes and rivers across the country. Trailered boats can also be kept at home, avoiding storage and marina charges.

To get your boat down the highway successfully, however, you'll need both a good tow vehicle and a proper trailer.

TOW VEHICLE

It is no secret that bigger SUVs, vans, and trucks burn more fuel than small sedans. Few people can afford to own a big truck for the sole purpose of pulling a boat. So, they choose the largest tow vehicle they can afford to drive to work on an everyday basis. The size of your vehicle determines the weight of the boat and trailer that can be safely towed. Here are typical towing capacities for different types of vehicles:

- **Economy car**—under 1,000 pounds tow capacity
- **Mid-size car**—1,000 to 1,500 pounds tow capacity
- **Minivan**—1,500 to 3,000 pounds tow capacity
- **SUVs**—3,000 to 5,000 pounds tow capacity

- **Truck**—up to 10,000 pounds tow capacity

Weight limits are established by the car-maker and published in the owner's manual. They can also be obtained from a new car dealership. Each vehicle has several different limits based on different criteria.

- **Gross Combined Weight Limit**—GCWL includes the weight of the passengers and gear inside the car and the weight of the boat and trailer. GCWL is the maximum limit for all the weight of every kind that a tow vehicle can handle.
- **Gross Vehicle Weight Rating**—GVWR is the total amount that the tow vehicle can weigh when loaded with people and gear.
- **Allowed Trailer Weight**—The manufacturer sets the maximum trailer weight that a vehicle can tow. This limit varies depending upon the car's engine, transmission, suspension, and brakes.

Just because a car is rated for a 3,500-pound trailer does not mean it is always safe to tow that much weight. The reason for this is that the GVWR and the towing capacity may add up to more than the GCWL, which must never be exceeded.

Towing Package

Vans, SUVs, and trucks are usually available with so-called towing packages. When ordered on a new car from the factory, these packages usually cost less than upgrading an existing car. Some items, like oversize brakes, may not be available as an aftermarket upgrade. A typical towing package might include:

- **Larger radiator**—Keeps engine cool under the extra load of the trailer

Modern trailer hitches bolt to the frame of the vehicle and are not supported by the bumper. The hitch receiver accommodates a drawbar with ball. This allows the same hitch to be adapted to different trailers.

- **Transmission oil cooler**—Prevents burned fluid in an automatic transmission
- **Stronger suspension**—Improves handling and prevents broken rear springs when towing
- **Better brakes**—Larger diameter or double-thick rotors help stop extra load of trailer
- **Trailer light connector**—Prewired plug for connecting trailer lights to the car's electrical system
- **Lower rear-axle gear ratio (rear-wheel drive vehicles only)**—Provides more torque to pull a heavy boat.

There are two drawbacks to many factory-installed towing packages. The major disadvantage to towing-equipped rear-wheel-drive vehicles is that they often cost more to operate than the standard version because towing pack-ages usually include a lower gear ratio than the

TRAILER SPECS BY CLASS

Trailer Classification	Minimum Ball Diameter (Inches)	Maximum Trailer Weight
Class I	1⅞ inches	up to 2,000 lbs.
Class II	2 inches	up to 3,500 lbs.
Class III	2 inches	up to 5,000 lbs.
Class IV	sized to provide strength required for load	up to 10,000 lbs.

standard version of that vehicle. A low ratio helps the engine handle the load of the trailer, but it also reduces overall fuel economy—even when the car is not towing. A second disadvantage is a stiff ride caused by the heftier springs and shock absorbers. When not towing, the ride is usually less comfortable.

TRAILER HITCH

With the exception of a few SUVs and trucks, most vehicles must be fitted with an aftermarket trailer hitch receiver. This is a bracket that is bolted to several points on the car's frame. The receiver accepts a separate drawbar, which is sized according to the weight of the trailer. A hitch ball mounts on the drawbar. Balls come in sizes ranging from 1⅞ to 2⁵⁄₁₆ inches in diameter.

TRAILER COUPLERS

Mounted on the tongue of the trailer is a ball-shaped socket called a coupler, which drops over the hitch ball to make a universal joint between the tow vehicle and trailer. Couplers are stamped with the size ball they require. A latching mechanism prevents the coupler from popping off the ball under rough driving conditions.

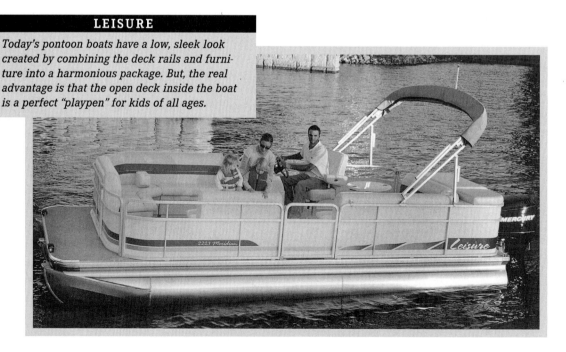

LEISURE

Today's pontoon boats have a low, sleek look created by combining the deck rails and furniture into a harmonious package. But, the real advantage is that the open deck inside the boat is a perfect "playpen" for kids of all ages.

DECKBOAT TRAILERS

Although the trailer stays behind when you leave the dock, it is still vital to your day of fun on the water. Undersized or poorly made trailers can damage your boat, or be downright dangerous on the highway. Consider the types of ramps you will be using. Is there enough underwater roadway to accomodate a drive-on trailer? Or, do you need to winch the boat out of the water? How much weight will the boat put on the trailer frame, axles, and tires? Do you need a galvanized trailer for protection against salt water? Your safety and enjoyment depends on finding the right answers to questions like these.

Drive-on or Winch-on?

The earliest boat trailers were all of the winch-on style. The boat had to be hauled from the water by cranking a manual winch or by using an electric winch.

With larger craft, there has been a switch to drive-on trailers. Their rollers, bunks, and guides are arranged such that the boat can power itself from the water onto the trailer. There's no doubt that drive-on trailers make the end of a boating day a lot easier. Unfortunately, not all ramps have the right slope or sufficient water depth to allow full use of a trailer's drive-on capability. Often, the boat stops a foot or so short of the winch stand. This is why even most drive-on trailers are equipped with a winch to haul the boat those last few inches into position.

Another option is a tilt-frame trailer. Tilt-frame trailers have sections that swing up or have pivoting bunks that help ease the boat off when launching. These tilting sections also make retrieving easier. A trailer with some sort of tilt mechanism should be considered for any boat over 18 feet in length. Tilting trailers are the most versatile because they automatically adapt to different launching-ramp angles.

Weight Capacity

Like cars, trailers have weight capacities. This information is printed on the certification label affixed to the tongue. Manufacturers establish the gross axle weight, which is the maximum weight an individual axle can carry. Adding axles is the standard method to increase load capacity. This is why there are so many two- and three-axle boat trailers.

Trailer prices go up with weight capacity. First-time buyers are often tempted to scrimp by purchasing the minimum-size trailer for their new boat. Dealers often encourage this sort of cost saving as one way of containing the price of the total boat, motor, and trailer combination. Sadly, undersized trailers always result in more frustration than fun. An undersized trailer is more likely to experience mechanical troubles. It also makes it harder to launch and recover the boat.

Trailer weight limits are determined by the diameter and construction of the tires, the weight rating and number of axles, and the size of the metal in the frame. A common mistake is to match the trailer's capacity to the published weight of the boat. In the real world, boats always weigh more than their so-called dry weight. Published weights do not include outboard engines, fuel, water skis, and anchors—all of which add weight to the load. A full 30-gallon fuel tank, for instance, adds 222 pounds.

Fitting the Trailer to the Hull

Bunks are padded boards that support the keel or flat sections of the hull. Rollers ease the job of getting the boat on or off the trailer, and they may help support the keel. Different hull configurations require a variety of bunk and roller placements. A trailer that does not properly support the boat can actually damage the hull.

The majority of trailers use rollers to support the keel of the boat. These rollers must be aligned so that none are too high or low. A high roller will push the hull up, while a low roller will allow it to sag. Worse, either condition makes it hard to launch or retrieve the boat. Any long, straight object such as a 2×4 or length of metal pipe can be used to help align the keel rollers. Obviously, the boat must be off the trailer to do this work. The roller brackets are slotted to fit over mounting bolts. Loosening these bolts allows rollers to be adjusted up or down.

Lateral (side-to-side) support comes from bunks, which should be located out near the chines of the boat. (Chines are the sharp edges where the sides of the boat meet the bottom.) Bunks can be simple boards over which the boat slides, or they can be elaborate roller devices. Both types should be adjusted so that the boat sits level on the trailer. The hull should receive equal support the full length of each bunk. A special synthetic material resembling outdoor carpeting is used on board-style bunks. It is slippery when wet, so the boat slides easily, but is also impervious to rot. Bunk carpet wears out and must be replaced every few years as part of regular maintenance.

The weight of the engine is largely centered over the stern. Be sure to provide the back of the boat with enough support. The stern should not extend beyond the last rollers or bunks, but instead should be supported where the transom meets both the keel and the chine. Many trailers also have individual rollers midway between the keel and chine for additional stern support.

Construction

Galvanized steel trailers have proven durable in both salt and fresh water. If you plan on trailering to coastal waters, the extra cost of a galvanized trailer is money well spent. Otherwise, a less-expensive painted steel trailer is satisfactory for use in rivers, lakes, and other freshwater bodies.

The downsizing of American cars has led to an overall reduction in towing capacity. Trailer manufacturers have responded with all-aluminum products. The cost of an aluminum trailer is greater than painted steel, but a lightweight trailer saves on fuel.

Welded construction is generally preferred to bolted connections, especially on trailers purpose-built to fit individual boats. Welding allows the trailer frame to be customized to the boat without a reduction in strength. Road vibration, however, can cause welds to crack, necessitating a welder for repairs. Bolted trailers, on the other hand, are a bit easier to repair. Loose bolts can be fixed with a wrench and a little elbow grease. Bolted trailers are also less expensive. Plus, boat dealers can configure them to a variety of hull shapes. For these reasons, bolted trailers dominate the market for boats under 25 feet in length.

Tongue Weight

The amount of weight that presses down on the hitch is called "tongue weight." Many people make the mistake of reducing tongue weight to make it easier to push the boat around the garage. However, an improperly loaded trailer wanders down the road like a drunken sailor. Newcomers to boat trailering are often unaware that 55 to 60 percent of the load should be forward of the axle (or axles). Placing too much weight behind the wheels causes "fishtailing," a condition in which the trailer sashays from side to side with increasing force.

Too much tongue weight can be equally dangerous. Without a load-equalizing hitch, it pushes down on the back of the tow vehicle. This could take too much weight off of the vehicle's front wheels, making steering a dicey proposition.

Adjust tongue weight by changing the position of the boat on the trailer. Moving the boat forward increases tongue weight, while moving the boat back decreases it. When the proper location is found, adjust the winch stand against the bow of the boat and tighten it. Thereafter, pulling the boat against the winch stand automatically puts its weight in the correct location for safe road operation.

Finding exactly the right amount of tongue weight may require several rounds of adjusting the boat and winch stand. As a rule of thumb, the tongue weight should be between 5 and 7 percent of the total weight being pulled (boat, motor, and trailer). For most boats, the correct tongue weight is too much for one person to lift comfortably. Given a 3,000-pound load, it works out to between 150 and 210 pounds.

MEASURING TONGUE WEIGHT

The easiest way to measure tongue weight is to set the coupler on a bathroom scale. This works fine with smaller boats, but few household scales have the capacity to measure tongue weight directly when the load is more than 5,000 pounds. To do it, you'll need to get a little creative. Find a brick (or something equally solid) that's the same thickness as the scale. As the illustration on the following page shows, set a 4×4 timber across the two so it rests on short sections of pipe set a measured distance apart. (The pipes' round shape prevents an erroneous reading on the scale.) If you place the tongue

The winch stand on a trailer provides a mounting place for the winch and it also serves as the stop against which the bow of the boat can rest. The winch stand can be moved to adjust the trailer's weight balance.

TYPICAL TONGUE WEIGHTS
(5 TO 7 PERCENT OF TOTAL LOAD)

Load Weight (lbs.)	Tongue Weight (lbs.)
1,000	50 to 70
1,500	75 to 105
2,000	100 to 140
2,500	125 to 175
3,000	150 to 210
4,000	200 to 280
5,000	250 to 350
7,500	375 to 525
10,000	500 to 700

measuring tongue weight

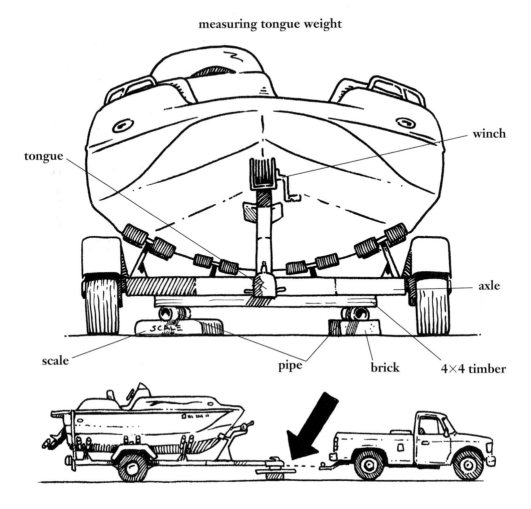

tongue

winch

axle

scale

pipe

brick

4×4 timber

Proper tongue weight is essential to proper tracking on the highway. A bathroom scale can be used to measure tongue weight. If the weight is beyond the range of the scale, the arrangement above will allow you to get an accurate measurement. With tongue centered on the timber, the scale reads exactly half the tongue weight. The scale must be as high off the ground as the hitch of the two vehicles for accuracy. (Christopher Hoyt)

of the trailer in the middle of the 4×4 timber, the scale will show half of the tongue weight. Or, divide the distance between the pipes in thirds and place the tongue one third of that distance from the "dead" end of the timber. Now, the scale will read one third of the tongue weight.

Make sure you place the trailer's coupler on the scale or the 4×4—don't use the crank-down jack stand wheel. This is located several feet behind the actual coupler, so you lose the lever arm represented by the length from the jack wheel to the coupler. The result is an inaccurate measurement.

PONTOON-BOAT TRAILERS

Basic information about deckboat trailers (above) applies to pontoon boat trailers as well. The only exception is the lack of centerline keel rollers. Instead, trailers for pontoon boats have double sets of bunks designed to cradle the 'toons. These bunks run the full length of the boat and are generally covered with slippery synthetic carpet. Small trailers have the same winch stands as deckboat trailers.

If the launching-ramp angle is correct, a pontoon boat can be driven onto the trailer right up to the winch stand. Otherwise, it is necessary to winch the boat the last few feet.

Pontoon boat trailers are recognized by their parallel sets of long bunks to cradle the pontoons. The bunks should be padded with low-friction carpeting for ease of launching.

WINCH POWER

All boat trailers are equipped with either a manual or power winch. There is always more friction when winching a pontoon boat because the logs present more surface area to the bunks. Therefore, an electric winch is more desirable if you have a pontoon boat. Barring that, pontoon-boat trailers should at least be equipped with a dual-speed manual winch. The higher-speed gear is used to haul the boat most of the way up the trailer. Switching to the low-speed gear eases the work of pulling the boat those final inches to the winch stand.

Manual winches are equipped with flat nylon webbing, synthetic rope, or steel cables for hauling the boat. Webbing is mostly used on smaller craft, rope on midsized, and steel cable on the largest. It is rare for a new rope or cable to break under load because of the roller system of the trailer. However, worn and frayed cables have been known to snap, causing injuries to anyone within range of the backlash. For safety, pull the cable off the winch drum at the beginning of each season and examine it for wear. Replace it if it's questionable.

Electric winches were introduced to allow easy trailering of boats in excess of 25 feet in length. Today, they are popular even on smaller craft simply because operating a switch is less

TYPICAL MANUAL WINCH GEAR RATIOS

Load (lbs.)	Gear Ratio
500	3:1
1,500	4:1
2,000	5:1
2,500 and up	5:1 high 12:1 low

work than cranking. All electric winches are powered by 12-volt DC from the tow vehicle. Because they draw so much current, it is necessary to have heavy-gauge feed wires directly from the car battery. Some people install these wires permanently in the vehicle. Others choose to have long leads on the winch with battery cable clamps at the ends to connect to the car's battery. Here are some things to keep in mind when wiring an electric winch:

- Never use the tow vehicle's lighting circuit to supply power to an electric winch.
- Route the winch feed wires well away from hot surfaces on the tow vehicle, such as exhaust manifolds and mufflers.
- Properly install a wiring harness on the tow vehicle. Support the wires by attaching nylon wire ties to the car's frame every 12 to 18 inches.
- Install the heavy-duty circuit breaker supplied with the electric winch at the battery end of the feed wires.

Most electric winches are operated by someone standing next to the trailer. Recently, electric winches have been equipped with remote control devices that work much like a garage door opener. All electric winches come with a manual crank just in case something goes wrong.

SPECIAL SAFETY EQUIPMENT

Weight-Distributing Hitches

Vehicle manufacturers usually specify the use of a weight-distributing hitch for towing the vehicle's maximum permitted loads. A weight-distributing hitch spreads the total weight of the load over the trailer and frame of the tow vehicle. Both axles of the tow vehicle share the weight of the trailer, so the back of the car will not sag and cause the front wheels to lift off the ground. The result is better steering and increased control, especially when going downhill or in high winds. Most people notice the improvement most when being passed by a big 18-wheel truck. Without a weight-distributing hitch, the blast of air from a truck can create some interesting driving conditions.

Antisway Control

Sway is unwanted side-to-side movement of the trailer. A variety of sway-control methods are available on weight-distributing hitches. The least expensive are friction systems that apply resistance to the trailer's wheels. These systems resist sway, but they do nothing to prevent swaying from developing in the first place. To make matters worse, manufacturers of these simple antisway systems usually recommend releasing the friction in the event of rain or snow—just the conditions when control is most needed. A better option is dual-cam antisway control. These cams are specially designed pivots that create a rigid connection between trailer and tow vehicle when going straight down the road. This prevents swaying. When the tow vehicle turns, however, the cams disengage and thus permit full maneuverability. Two cams are necessary, one for each side of the trailer.

Trailer Brakes

Lightweight trailers can be handled without brakes. Starting at about 1,000 pounds, however, the addition of trailer brakes makes for a safer ride. Check your tow vehicle's specifications to determine the weight at which trailer brakes become a requirement. No matter what

A surge brake mechanism. State regulations call for brakes on larger trailers. Most common on boat trailers are surge brakes that use the momentum of the trailer to actuate the brake cylinder. The surge brake mechanism is totally contained in the coupler on the tongue of the trailer.

the car can handle, however, most states require brakes on a trailer with a loaded weight of more than 1,500 pounds. In addition, the trailer must have a breakaway switch that activates the brakes if the trailer breaks free from the tow vehicle.

There are two popular types of trailer braking systems.

- Surge brakes are independent hydraulic brakes that are powered by a master cylinder built into the trailer coupler. As the tow vehicle slows, the "push" of the trailer against the hitch ball causes the master cylinder to activate the brakes. Surge brakes are self-compensating for changes in trailer load.
- Electric brakes have an electronic con-

troller in the tow vehicle that activates the trailer brakes whenever the driver applies the brake in the tow vehicle.

Both systems have proven reliable. Still, many experienced boatowners prefer surge brakes because they do not rely on electrical connections to activate the brakes.

Note that it's illegal to directly connect the tow car's hydraulic brake system to the trailer brakes. If you have a multi-axle trailer, some states will require brakes on all axles, while other states only require brakes on one axle.

Whether intentionally or not, trailer wheels are often submerged when launching or retrieving a boat. This can cause rust and corrosion in the brake system. Trailer brake systems should

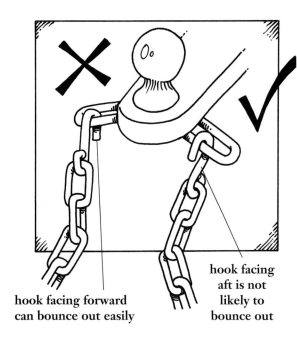

hook facing forward
can bounce out easily

hook facing
aft is not
likely to
bounce out

Every trailer must have safety chains connecting it to the tow vehicle. In the event of a breakaway, these chains keep the two vehicles connected so the rig can be brought to a safe stop. Be sure to hook the chains under the eyes, not over. (Christopher Hoyt)

be cleaned and lubricated (where necessary) at the start of every boating season. If the wheels get wet on a regular basis, it may be necessary to check them more often.

Safety Chains

Trailer couplers have been known to come loose from the tow vehicle. All states require safety chains connecting the trailer to the tow vehicle just in case the unthinkable happens. Trailer manufacturers equip these chains with hooks that clip into eyes on the trailer hitch. There should be some sag in the chains to allow the trailer to pivot during turns; however, the chains shouldn't be so long as to drag on the ground. Be sure to cross the chains under the coupler.

Trailer Lights

Federal law requires trailers to display taillights, brake lights, side marker lights, and turn signals just like cars. In addition, trailers must be provided with rear reflectors. Manufacturers know the regulations and equip their trailers accordingly. The job of the boatowner is to maintain what the manufacturer installed.

The number one reason for trailer-light problems is either a broken or weak ground wire. The ground wire forms the return path for electricity from the various lightbulbs. If it is not working properly, the electricity will find a way to complete the circuit. This can cause some strange problems. For instance, the right taillight may go out when the brakes are applied. Or the amber marker lights may blink opposite to the left turn signal—but not the right. The rule when troubleshooting trailer lights is "check the ground wire first."

The standard trailer-light connector is a flat rubber plug with four terminals. The pigtail lead from the tow vehicle has the female connector, while the male connector is on the trailer.

Lightbulbs shatter if they are submerged when hot. This is why experienced trailer boaters always unplug the trailer connector before backing down the launching ramp. Of course, that opens the possibility of forgetting

---

TRAILER WIRING CODE

- **White**—Common, or "ground" wire.
- **Yellow**—Left turn signal/brake light.
- **Green**—Right turn signal/brake light.
- **Brown**—Taillights, amber marker lights.

to reconnect the lights for the return trip. To avoid both burned-out bulbs and human forgetfulness, trailer manufacturers have begun adopting so-called waterproof light fixtures.

Some boatowners fashion a light bar that is temporarily affixed to the stern when trailering. This bar not only carries the trailer lights, but is also part of the tie-down system. Straps from the bar to the trailer keep the boat in place on the highway. Because the trailer lights are removed for launching the boat, they never get wet. A simple 4-pronged plug connects the bar to the trailer wiring.

Newest to the market are LED (light-emitting diode) trailer lights that are always cool to the touch and may put an end to water-induced light burnout.

Breakdown Kit

Boat trailers are generally reliable, but things occasionally go wrong. A breakdown kit includes items to either get back on the road, or protect your rig until help arrives. Items that should be carried include:

- Spare tire mounted on a wheel and filled to the correct air pressure
- Jack suitable for changing a trailer tire (The jack for the tow vehicle probably won't work on the trailer.)
- Large lug wrench sized for trailer's lug nuts (The wrench for the tow vehicle is probably the wrong size.)
- Spare trailer lightbulbs
- Reflective triangle and/or road flares to warn approaching motorists

If you are going on an extended road trip, it is probably a good idea to include a spare set of wheel bearings in your emergency kit. Be sure to get both the outer and inner bearing sets.

ON THE HIGHWAY

Boats probably cover more distance on the highway in the United States than they do on

TAHOE

While most deckboats are I/O powered, some like this 19-foot model from Tahoe are designed to take advantage of today's powerful new outboard motors.

the water every year. These millions of trailer miles are proof that there's no need to have white knuckles on the road to a boating adventure. Trailering is not difficult if done correctly. You have to keep in mind, however, that hauling a boat down the road has a lot in common with big-rig trucks. You'll experience slower acceleration, wider turns, and increased stopping distance.

Hitching Up

It's an exciting moment to back the car up to a boat for the first time. But don't let the thrill overcome common sense. It's your responsibility to make sure everything is road-worthy before the tires cross the curb. To do so, make sure you've satisfied the following requirements:

LUG NUTS ON TRAILER WHEELS MUST BE TIGHTENED TO THE CORRECT TORQUE

Perhaps the most overlooked safety items are the lug nuts on the trailer wheels. These should be checked prior to every trip. Don't be surprised if a few need tightening. (The author knows this first-hand, although seldom discusses the day his trailer tire passed him on a four-lane highway.)

HITCH COUPLER MUST BE CLOSED AND SAFETY CHAINS ATTACHED

The latching mechanism inside the trailer coupler won't always catch the hitch ball properly on the first try. Physically inspect the connection to be sure that the ball is properly seated and the latching mechanism has closed. Insert the locking pin if one is supplied with the coupler. Make sure the hooks on the safety chains are fully inserted into the hitch eyes.

THE TRAILER LIGHTS SHOULD FUNCTION PROPERLY, INCLUDING THE BRAKE LIGHTS AND TURN SIGNALS

Trailer lights can be finicky. Do not assume that the turn signals work if the brake lights function correctly. Checking trailer lights is a two-person job. One person sits in the tow vehicle and operates the lights, turn signals, and brakes. The other person stands behind the trailer and checks that every light is working correctly.

THE AIR PRESSURE IN ALL TIRES SHOULD BE CORRECT

Carmakers, in an effort to give their cars a smoother ride, will often spec their tires at a lower than optimal air pressure. When towing, however, higher pressure is required. Check your owner's manual for the correct air pressure when towing. Trailers need to be checked, too. Trailer tires can lose air while sitting idle. Check and equalize the pressure in all trailer tires prior to every trip. Low pressure is one of the biggest reasons for trailer tire blowouts.

THE SIDE-VIEW MIRRORS MUST PROVIDE A CLEAR VIEW DOWN BOTH SIDES OF THE TRAILER

Most trucks and larger SUVs are equipped with side mirrors that provide a clear view around a boat. Smaller tow vehicles, on the other hand, may require auxiliary mirrors. Aftermarket mirrors can be clipped onto the car's front fenders without scratching the paint.

THE BOAT MUST BE SECURED TO TRAILER WITH TIE-DOWNS

Every year people forget to tie down their boats and launch them into traffic on the highway. The rollers and slippery bunks of a trailer are designed to let the boat slip off, not to keep it in place, so tie-down straps are of the utmost importance. The stern should be secured either with a strap that goes all the way over the boat, or with two straps from the transom eyes to the trailer. The winch cable is not a reliable bow tie-down. Leave the cable hooked to the bow eye, but reinforce it with a strap secured to both the foredeck deck cleat and the trailer.

EVERYTHING CARRIED INSIDE THE BOAT MUST BE PROPERLY STOWED SO IT WILL NOT BLOW OUT AT HIGHWAY SPEEDS

Drive down any highway that leads to a popular boating area and you'll see cooler lids, bait buckets, and seat cushions strewn along the median. These items were not discarded; they were blown out of the boat. This sort of unintentional littering is easily prevented by spending a few minutes to secure such items prior to the trip.

BRIEFLY INSPECT THE BOAT AND TRAILER DURING EVERY STOP ALONG THE WAY

Take a moment or two during each routine bathroom or snack break to perform a quick walk-around safety check of the tow vehicle and trailer. Be sure that:

- Hitch coupler and chains are secure
- Trailer lights still work
- Trailer wheel bearings are not hot
- Trailer tire tread is not overheated
- Boat contents are not blowing around

Trailer wheel bearings and tire treads should get warm as they roll down the road. They should not be too hot to touch. A hot bearing indicates lack of lubrication or unusual internal wear. Bearing problems can seize wheels or, on rare occasions, break an axle. Hot tire tread indicates that something is wrong with the tire. It could be low air pressure, or the tread could be separating from the tire.

Hourly walk-arounds are suggested during long trips. The exception comes at the very beginning. The first safety check should be done about 20 to 30 minutes after departure. This first stop catches any problems or any safety procedures that were overlooked.

AT THE LAUNCHING RAMP

A properly designed launching ramp has four distinct areas. The first is a staging area where you can prepare your boat to go into the water. The second is the actual ramp into the water. The third is the parking lot for tow vehicles and trailer. The fourth is another staging area for tying down the boat after it is retrieved from the water. Even if the ramp does not have these four divisions, they should be kept in mind. It is impolite to block a ramp lane while you untie the straps or load supplies.

Pre-Launch Preparation

Prior to launching, you should take these steps:

- Insert the boat's drain plug
- Remove tie-down straps
- Unplug trailer lights
- Move lunches, water toys, and other items from car to boat
- Attach bow and stern lines
- Rig fenders
- Double-check that the drain plug is in place

Backing a Trailer

There is a trick to backing a trailer straight down the ramp. The trailer goes in the opposite direction of the tow vehicle's front wheels, so, when backing, put your hands on the bottom of the steering wheel. By steering from the

Launching ramps can be public or private. Learn proper ramp etiquette. Prepare your boat before backing down the ramp to keep time to a minimum. When retrieving, haul the boat up to the tie-down area before preparing it for the road. (U.S. Army Corps of Engineers)

bottom of the wheel, you will find that the trailer moves in the same direction that your hands move.

Back the boat down the ramp until the trailer's tires are almost touching the water. Have a crewmember take the bow line in hand. (The rope should be long enough to allow this person to stay safely away from the car as the rig is backed down the ramp.) The trailer should only back deep enough into the water so that the boat will float off easily. The line handler then moves the boat to the dock while the driver takes the car and trailer up the ramp to the parking lot.

One hazard lurks at every ramp. It's the thin covering of slime over the concrete just where it disappears underwater. This slime is so slippery it makes wet ice seem like sandpaper. Remind everyone working around the trailer to

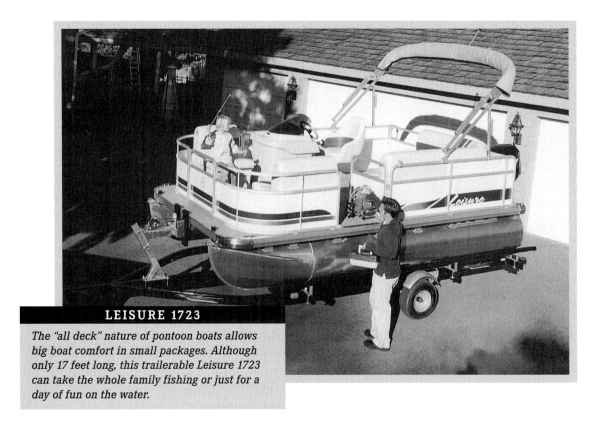

LEISURE 1723

The "all deck" nature of pontoon boats allows big boat comfort in small packages. Although only 17 feet long, this trailerable Leisure 1723 can take the whole family fishing or just for a day of fun on the water.

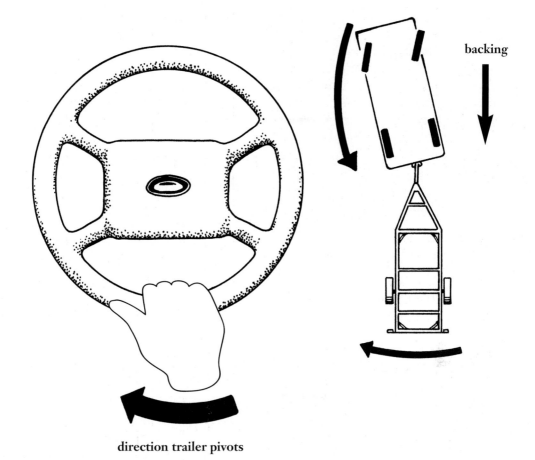

backing

direction trailer pivots

When backing a trailer it is helpful to steer from the bottom of the wheel. The trailer will back to the left when the bottom of the steering wheel is turned left. If you steer from the top of the wheel, you can easily be confused by having to turn right to back left. (Christopher Hoyt)

beware of the slime. The driver of the car must be ready at all times to stop the rig if someone disappears. This slime can trip up a rear-wheel-drive tow vehicle as well. Back tires can lose all traction on that slime, and it's not unusual for the whole rig to slide slowly underwater. Always keep the tow vehicle's tires on dry ground.

Never allow anyone to wade into the water barefoot to help guide the boat off the trailer. A person in the water can be most helpful, but the area around a boating ramp is not a swim beach. Broken bottles, pieces of jagged metal, and other hazards can lie beneath the surface. Anyone who goes into the water should wear rubber-soled canvas shoes to protect against lacerations.

If you need to exit the vehicle to launch the boat, be sure to shift into park and set the parking brake before getting out. Once you're outside, place chocks under the rear wheels of the tow vehicle.

Retrieving the Boat

It's harder to get the boat back on the trailer than it is to launch it. This is particularly true if there's wind blowing across the ramp. Unless the trailer is designed for the purpose, trying to drive the boat onto the rollers can turn into a major disaster. Usually the boat can be centered on the trailer using bow and stern lines and a boat hook. Have someone walk down the trailer on the catwalk to secure the winch cable to the boat's bow eye. Winch the boat into place on the trailer. Drive to the tie-down area to get the boat ready for the highway.

Once there, perform these steps:

- Attach all tie-downs
- Plug in trailer lights and check operation
- Remove drain plug
- Secure all items in boat that might shift or blow out

Back Home

Look for a flat place to uncouple the trailer. Place blocks in front of and behind at least one wheel before disconnecting the trailer from the tow vehicle. Adjust the height of the crankdown front wheel so that water in the boat will run out, and remove the drain plug. Place the trailer-light pigtail in the car under the mat in the trunk or protect it from damage in some other manner.

TRAILER RULES AND REGULATIONS

All trailers must display license plates. As a rule, however, no other special permits are required for a trailer under 10,000 pounds and no more than 102 inches wide. Most states require trailer brakes on loads over 1,500 pounds. Some states do not allow surge brakes. Be aware of special width, height, or weight limits on specific roads or bridges along your route. Propane gas and other volatile fuels are banned from tunnels. Because of these limits and bans, you may need to choose a different route to reach the water. Drivers towing more than 10,000 pounds total weight require a commercial driver's license (CDL) even if used for recreation.

Boat Handling
and Seamanship

Learning brush techniques does not necessarily make one an artist. Similarly, learning boat handling skills doesn't necessarily grant seamanship. Seamanship, in its broadest sense, encompasses all actions—maneuvers, decisions, and precautions—from the moment you board your boat to the moment you leave it. Seamanship includes boat handling (casting off the dock lines, motoring away from the dock, making turns, crossing wakes, changing speeds, and returning home), but it encompasses much more. Navigating and reading the

Driving a boat is unlike an automobile. Boats steer from the back end rather than the front and they don't have brakes. (Triton Industries, Inc.)

weather are parts of seamanship. So are the rules of the nautical road, anchoring, handling rough water, and much more.

You can keep on improving your seamanship as long as you keep on boating—that's part of what makes boating endlessly fascinating—but you can learn the fundamentals of boat handling in an afternoon. We'll start our exploration of the art of seamanship there.

BOAT HANDLING

New boaters mistakenly transfer their car skills to the water—boats do not accelerate, steer, or stop like cars. Children often pick up boat-handling skills faster than their parents because

Single-lever controls combine shift and throttle. This lever also has a thumb switch for adjusting the trim of the lower unit. The operator's hand stays on the control for three different operations.

adults often have to unlearn driving skills. The result is frustrating and can be comical to watch.

Controls

STEERING

An adult's misconception that boats operate like cars is initially reinforced by the steering wheel. Just like driving a car you turn the wheel clockwise to turn right, or counter-clockwise to turn left. But that's where the similarities end. We'll examine the differences now.

THROTTLE

New boaters may be surprised to notice that their boat lacks both gas and brake pedals. Instead of a gas pedal, a hand lever controls the throttle. There is no corresponding brake lever because boats do not have brakes. Instead, you slow or stop forward motion by shifting the engine into neutral or reverse.

Depending on the boat, engines and transmissions can be controlled by a single lever that combines both functions, or a pair of levers that control the engine and transmission separately. Some boats have two engines. In this case, each engine will have its own lever—or pair of levers. (Few deckboats or pontoon craft have twin engines, however.)

Single levers are most popular because their operation is intuitive. Pushing the lever forward shifts the transmission into forward. The farther you push the lever forward, the more throttle is applied and the faster the boat goes. The same action occurs going into reverse.

Separate levers often confuse beginners who find that rapid hand motions required from one lever to the other are difficult when docking or in other close-quarters situations.

TRIM

Trim and tilt control switches are often built into the knob at the top of a single-lever con-

Every boat has different handling characteristics that must be learned for safe operation. The ability of a boat to track straight is often at odds with quick maneuverability. (Forest River Marine)

trol. These switches allow you to adjust the trim angle of a sterndrive or outboard engine while underway and to raise it to keep it from scraping the highway when trailering the boat. This is called *tilting*. The universal joint inside a sterndrive can bend far enough to tilt the lower unit out of the way for trailering; however, the angle required is too sharp for the universal joint to transmit power. That is why I/O engines have an interlock or other safety device to prevent operation in the tilted position.

Steering

Steering wheels on boats and cars may look the same, but the actions they control are very different. When steering a car, turning the wheel causes the car's front wheels to pivot and pull the car in the desired direction. The result is you steer the front end of a car *toward* your destination. However, a boat's steering action takes place at the stern. For instance, when the wheel is turned to starboard, the stern swings to port. This means that in a boat you really do not so much point the bow toward your destination as you do point the stern away from it.

Pivot Point

The *pivot point* is a theoretical location along the boat's centerline around which the hull pivots during a turn. Each boat has a different pivot point, but on most boats it is about one-third of the boat's length aft of the bow when running at dead idle speed. At higher displacement speeds, the pivot point tends to move forward to about one-quarter of the way aft from the bow. The location of the pivot point at planing speeds can be less than one-quarter of the way aft. In reverse, the pivot point moves almost to the stern of the vessel.

The location of the pivot point closer to the front of the boat means the stern swings a wider arc when turning than does the bow. This creates a phenomenon called *stern kick*, which accounts for the first mistake made by many first-time boatowners when they leave a dock. Thinking he's in a car, the novice skipper turns the helm away from the pier and shifts into forward. He is expecting the "front wheels" to pull the boat safely away from the dock. Instead, the

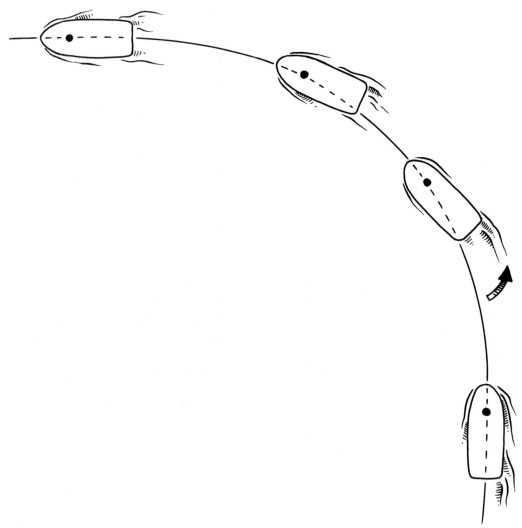

Boats turn on a pivot point. The pivot point changes depending on speed and whether the boat is in forward or reverse gear. At harbor speeds when moving forward the pivot point on most boats is one-quarter to one-third of the way aft of the bow. You must determine this point's exact location on your boat by observing how it handles with various amounts of steering and speed. Knowing your boat's tendencies will help you judge how much of an arc your boat will make in a turn. (Christopher Hoyt)

back of the boat swings toward the hard concrete supporting the gas pumps. A sudden "whump" announces that the stern has slammed into the pier.

A more experienced skipper knows to swing the stern away from the pier before attempting to leave. This can be done in several ways, but the simplest is to turn the steering wheel hard in the direction away from the pier. Then, back away.

Advance and Transfer

After you initiate a turn, the boat continues to travel on its original course for a short time even though the hull is moving slightly sideways. The distance the boat travels along its original course after the wheel is turned is called *advance*. Eventually, though, the boat's stern swings in a wider arc and the boat begins to take a circular path. The distance the boat swings in the direction of the turn before it steadies on its new heading is called *transfer*. Advance is measured in the direction of the original course while transfer is measured at right angles to the original course.

The amount of advance or transfer varies with the shape of your boat's hull, the steering angle, and boat speed. Monohull boats under 30 feet in length, like most deckboats, pivot quickly and exhibit the least advance before beginning to transfer in the new direction.

Pontoon boats are different. Their long, narrow 'toons resist rotation of the bow, so the boat advances farther before it begins to curve in the new direction.

Boats become more sensitive to small changes at the steering wheel as speed increases. For most people, boat handling at planing speeds becomes more like driving an automobile. Keep in mind, however, that a boat does not have any hard contact to slow it down

quickly, like rubber tires on roads. Instead, a boat slides over the top of relatively frictionless water. It is important to keep up to 10 times more distance between boats and other watercraft than you would between cars on the highway. The same tenfold safety factor should be applied to stationary objects such as piers, breakwaters, or buoys.

Tracking

A boat's ability to hold a straight course is called *tracking*. Conventional powerboats that track best have a deep underwater profile. Maine lobster boats and other single-screw inboard workboats are perfect examples. While renowned for their tracking, such boats have too much wetted surface to have the sparkling speed that marks a deckboat. Instead of a deep hull, deckboats are built with a shallower underbody capable of higher speeds because it has less water resistance. Speed helps with towed watersports like skiing and tubing.

Tracking can be adversely affected by prop walk: deckboats with traditional single-propeller I/O units have a tendency to wander at slow speeds, which requires the driver to make constant adjustments of the helm. Most people adapt quickly to prop walk and find that after a time they are no longer aware of making these small course adjustments. One way to avoid this wandering is to choose an I/O lower unit that features two contra-rotating propellers. Torque created by each of the two props cancels out the torque of the other because they are spinning in opposing directions. This results in almost total elimination of wandering at slow speed.

Single-screw boats often steer slightly harder one way than the other. If your boat fights turning to one side, a small adjustment may help. Some larger outboard motors have an anti-torque tab located beneath the anti-ventilation

---

SWAMPING

Be careful when throttling back. If you slow too quickly, it is possible for the boat's stern wake to catch up to the transom, spill over the gunwale, and fill the boat with water. Swamping may also cause an engine to stall. A stall in open water is generally of no consequence. However, the same engine failure while docking is always followed by the sickening (and expensive) sound of a boat crunching into a pier.

---

plate. The tab rides in the discharge current of the propeller. To cure a boat that fights turning to port, turn the back edge of the tab to port. Turn the back edge of the tab to starboard if the boat resists going to starboard. Make a small adjustment and try each new setting before making another change. It is easiest to make these adjustments with the boat on shore, but you can do it in the water. Tie your tools to your wrist to prevent making a contribution to Davy Jones' Locker.

Adjusting the trim angle of the lower unit can also lighten the helm. Moving the drive leg away from the transom (out) should reduce steering effort. Beware that adjusting it out too much may result in some loss of directional control. Also, keep an eye on the tachometer to make sure you are not over-revving your engine when the lower unit is trimmed out.

Stopping and Backing

Stopping a boat requires more time and a longer distance than you might think. There are no brakes on a boat and momentum keeps watercraft in motion whether the propeller is engaged

or not. The best way to slow the forward momentum is to shift into reverse and apply a short burst of reverse thrust. Inexperienced skippers fear shifting their boats into reverse; as car drivers they know that shifting into reverse while speeding down the road would grind their transmission to pieces. Nothing like that happens in a boat so long as the shifting is done at the engine's idle speed (which, if you're using a single-lever throttle, is the only way you can shift gears). Simply pause in neutral for a few seconds before shifting to reverse; this will let the engine and gears spool down to idle speed and prevent any transmission damage.

GETTING UNDERWAY

Leaving the dock involves a lot more than starting the engine and cranking the throttle. Be sure to follow all of the steps described below.

Pre-Trip Inspection

Pilots always inspect their planes before takeoff. Why? Because pilots know that hull or engine problems cannot be fixed mid-flight.

The same is often true of boating.

It takes only a few minutes to make a similar pre-trip inspection of your boat. Few things can do more to ensure your fun on the water. Make a list of the specific items you need to

---

PRE-DEPARTURE INSPECTION

- ❏ Explosive fumes in bilge?
- ❏ Excessive bilge water?
- ❏ Adequate engine fluids?
- ❏ Adequate fuel quantity?
- ❏ Proper safety gear?

---

check on your boat. Then, follow this list the same way airline pilots perform their preflight checks. As skipper, don't let anyone else board the boat until you are certain everything is safe.

BILGE FUMES

If you have an I/O deckboat, you must check for explosive fumes in the hull prior to every trip. Any gasoline that has leaked from the carburetor will not dissipate; instead, the fumes become trapped in the bilge because they're heavier than air. A stray spark can set off an explosion and fire. This sort of disaster is easily prevented by using nothing more complicated than a human nose: extinguish any smoking materials prior to checking and then simply open the engine compartment and sniff. An outboard engine is much safer in this regard; the engine is mounted outside the hull, so fumes won't be trapped inside the boat.

SHAKEDOWN CRUISE

Whether you're a first-time boater or an old salt, you need to take a shakedown cruise whenever you acquire a new boat. You'll want to know that everything is functioning, but you also need to figure out how your new boat handles. On your first outing, motor out to open water away from other watercraft. Run the boat at harbor speed and gently turn the wheel one way and then the other. Increase the speed and continue to test maneuvers until the boat is operating at full throttle. Once you have learned how your new boat responds to throttle and helm, come back into the harbor to practice docking and other close quarters maneuvers.

STARCRAFT STARFISH 246

Low sides and long stretches of rail make a pontoon boat an ideal fishing platform. The position of the anglers in this 24-foot Starcraft Starfish 246 clearly indicate why pontoons are often called "four-corner boats."

Mechanical or engine smells are normal. If, however, you smell a gasoline odor that is so strong you instinctively recoil, the vapors have reached an explosive condition. Get everyone as far away from the boat as possible. This includes people on surrounding boats in the marina. Seek professional help by calling the local fire department. Even if the smell does not make you recoil, any strong odor of gasoline must be treated with respect. Move people away from the boat. Open all hatches, doors, storage compartments, and windows to air out the fumes. Have a trained mechanic find the source of the leak and fix it before starting the engine.

BILGEWATER

While sniffing, deckboat owners should also check the bilge for excessive water. An inch or so of water is not a problem. Virtually every boat will have a small amount. But any more than this is a sign that something is leaking and should be fixed. One often-overlooked source of bilgewater in a deckboat is a cracked or worn outdrive bellows. This is a rubber gland that seals the transom while allowing the outdrive to steer and tilt. Over time the rubber loses its resilience and begins to crack. If a worn bellows is not replaced, the cracks can let water into the boat. On nearly all deckboats, the bellows is below water when the boat is tied up at the dock.

OIL LEVEL

Oil does more than lubricate the internal moving parts of an engine; it also helps prevent engine overheating. Maintaining proper oil level is vital to the long life of every engine, but particularly the new four-stroke outboards. Those engines must never run low on oil. Check

Keep the crankcase topped off with clean oil. Boat engines are under constant load, making lubrication extremely important. (Nigel Calder)

the dipstick prior to every trip. Add oil as necessary, but don't overfill. Too much can create excess oil pressure and damage engine seals.

COOLING SYSTEM

Outboard engines on pontoon boats are raw-water cooled, meaning they use outside water to cool the engine. The only pre-trip check necessary is to look for the telltale stream of water that indicates the water pump is working. The inboard engines common to deckboats are also raw-water cooled; however, there is no telltale stream of water. Instead, keep an eye on the engine water temperature gauge as the machinery warms up.

Some deckboat engines have closed cooling systems that recirculate engine coolant through a heat exchanger. These engines have a radiator cap on the cooling system expansion tank. Coolant level should be checked *only* while the system is cold—removing the filler cap while the engine is hot can cause scalding-hot coolant to spray out.

FUEL AMOUNT

Running out of gas is the number one reason that boaters request on-the-water assistance. Defy the statistics by checking the fuel level before every trip. Even better, never leave home port without filling the tanks. Also, it can be helpful to envision your tank's contents divided into thirds: one third of the fuel is reserved for going out; one third is for returning; and the final third is reserved for emergencies.

SAFETY EQUIPMENT

Visually inspect all required safety equipment. Vandals have been known to discharge fire extinguishers, steal distress signals, or tie anchor lines into knots. Safety gear is all intended to help you get out of an emergency. You don't want to discover your extinguisher is empty

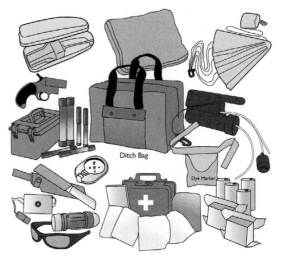

The U.S. Coast Guard and state watercraft agencies mandate that boats carry specific safety equipment. This gear ranges from PFDs to distress signals and fire extinguishers. The exact requirements are determined by the overall length of the boat. (www.mirtoart.com)

when you have a fire, or that your anchor can't be used when the engine quits. Most important, make sure you have one properly sized PFD for each person aboard.

Engine Startup

Older two-stroke outboards and sterndrives equipped with conventional ignition systems must be warmed up for five minutes or so before leaving the dock. This prevents stalling when you shift gears to maneuver out of the harbor. Newer computer-controlled engines technically do not require a warm-up period at all. Their computers can catch a stall before you know it's going to happen. However, a short warm-up period gives you time to observe that everything is operating correctly.

During the warm-up period, keep an eye on the oil pressure gauge with the intention of shutting everything down if pressure does not come up in a few seconds. On both inboards and some outboards, check the ammeter for alternator output. If the ammeter indicates continuous discharge, the alternator is probably not working. The meter should show charging after startup until the battery is replenished, then the meter should come to the center position indicating the alternator output is equal to the load on the electrical system.

Boarding

The relatively wide, flat design of deckboats and pontoon boats make both particularly stable for boarding. They are still boats, however, and improper boarding or loading can create dangers.

It's easiest to load and stow picnic supplies and other gear before people come aboard. Be sure heavy items are properly distributed to maintain proper balance of the boat.

Once your gear is loaded, break out the PFDs and pass them ashore so your passengers can don them before boarding. Children should wear PFDs whenever they are near water as falls from piers or seawalls are more likely to occur

---

PASSENGER ORIENTATION

Once everyone is aboard, it's a good idea to share safety tips with your passengers.

- Show the locations of PFDs (if you haven't already distributed them)
- Show the location of throwable PFDs in case someone falls overboard
- Show the location of the fire extinguisher
- Remind everyone to remain seated while the boat is underway

---

than boating accidents. Wise parents carry their children's PFDs in the car so the kids can put them on before leaving the parking lot.

Deckboats are usually boarded by stepping down into the cockpit from the pier. An agile adult should enter the boat first to assist the others, especially children. Only one person at a time should come aboard and they should sit down before the next person steps onto the boat. Passenger weight should be equally distributed so the boat does not list (lean to one side). Discourage kids from running and jumping while aboard.

The decks of pontoon boats are usually about the same height as the pier. Boarding is so easy that some people never realize they're afloat until the boat leaves the dock. Even so, the rules of safe boarding still apply. No more than one person should step aboard at a time, and passengers should sit down quickly. Safe distribution of passenger weight is as critical on a pontoon boat as on a deckboat.

DEPARTING

The maneuvers for leaving a dock vary with the physical situation and the wind or current conditions. What follows is only a basic outline of the process. For a full discussion of maneuvering in harbors see Bob Sweet's *Powerboat Handling Illustrated*. No matter what techniques you use to leave the dock, however, the Rules of the Road governing getting underway are always the same:

- A boat leaving a dock or pulling out of a slip does not have right of way. It must give way to boats operating in the main channel. From a practical standpoint, this means that you must stay docked until traffic is clear.

All vessels from ocean liners to deckboats are required to sound a prolonged blast on their whistles before leaving a dock or slip. Few pleasure boats do this, but you should be aware of the requirement and the reason it exists. This blast of sound alerts everyone (including an approaching boat that you may not have noticed) of your intentions. It gives the other boat a chance to sound a similar blast to warn you not to back into an accident.

Don't be shy about recruiting passersby for assistance at the docks.

Getting away from a dock is easiest when the wind and current are carrying you away. Untie the lines and give a shove. Let the wind and current carry the boat far enough away to avoid problems with stern kick. Shift into gear and have fun. Life doesn't get much easier or better.

Most of the time, however, the wind or current won't cooperate. If wind is holding the boat against the pier, you can employ a bit of seamanship called *motoring on a line*. First, be sure to place a fender between the boat and the dock to prevent damage. Next, untie all dock lines except one leading aft from the bow. Turn the steering wheel toward the pier. If you are docked on the starboard side, turn to starboard.

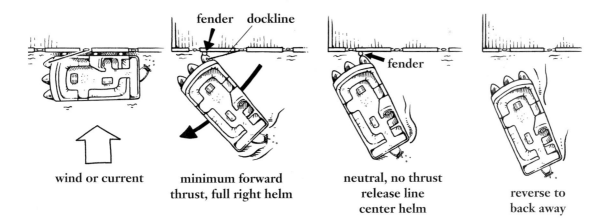

wind or current	fender dockline	fender	
wind or current	**minimum forward thrust, full right helm**	**neutral, no thrust release line center helm**	**reverse to back away**

When wind is pushing your boat against the dock, use a dockline and your engine to redirect the boat for a smooth departure. (Christopher Hoyt)

Shift into gear at dead idle speed. The stern will slowly swing away from the pier. When it is clear, release the last dock line and back into clear water.

Motoring on a line must be done with care. Never use more than idle speed as excessive force can break the rope or pull a cleat out of the boat. Injuries are possible in either case.

Departing a Slip

The majority of marinas require boats to dock with their bows toward shore. When departing, this requires the operator to back out of the slip, turn in the channel, and then motor out of the harbor. Learning how to use wind, current, and prop walk to advantage can be a daunting task to the beginner. As with any skill, practice makes perfect.

NO WIND OR CURRENT
Without wind or current, a single-engine I/O or outboard boat will naturally back slightly to port. This is because of the side pressure created by the propeller. Turning the helm a bit to the right will counteract this tendency, allowing the boat to back a straight line. Increasing the throttle will pull the stern to port more than it will

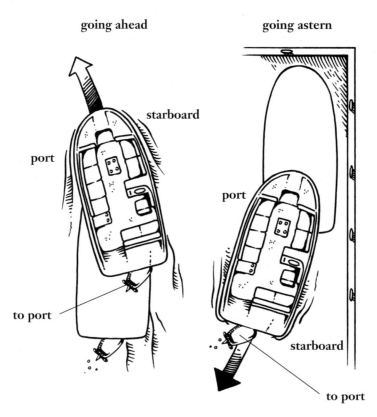

In forward gear, when the lower unit of an I/O or outboard is turned to port, the bow steers to port. Note the outward swing of the stern to the starboard. In reverse, the stern is pulled to port, while the bow follows without the pronounced outward swing. (Christopher Hoyt)

RAFTING UP

A *raft* is a group of anchored boats tied side by side such that people can move freely from one boat to another. Rafting is common on lakes and rivers where wave action is not likely to cause problems. Formation of a raft starts with one boat setting a large anchor. Additional boats come alongside until the raft is built with an equal number of vessels on both sides of the anchored boat. If the raft is to stay together for several hours, the outermost boats set out anchors at 45-degree angles to the original anchor line.

Before you approach a raft, prepare your boat. Rig at least two fenders and bow and stern lines on either side of your boat. That way, you can tie up port or starboard side as needed. Get specific permission from the owner of the boat that you will tie alongside. Work out with that skipper the placement of fenders and tie-up lines. If fenders are not rigged, boats in a raft can be tossed against each other by the wake of a passing boat. It will take a bit of trial and error to tie the lines so the raft will hold together without squeezing the fenders out of position.

If you are inside the raft with boats tied to either side of you, it won't be easy to leave. Give everyone plenty of time so that plans can be made for rebuilding the raft once you depart. Untie only when enough hands are available to assist.

---

increase reverse speed. So, the throttle becomes part of the equation when steering in reverse. A short, small burst of throttle can often be used to straighten the boat if the stern is cocking to starboard in the slip. When wind and current are not a problem, it is easiest to turn to port after exiting the slip.

CROSSWIND OR CURRENT

Expect the boat to slide sideways faster than it moves backwards when wind or current is across the slip. The solution is to apply enough helm, or steering, to pull the boat toward the upwind side of the slip, but not enough to cause the bow to crash into the downwind side. This can be all but impossible to accomplish in lightweight pontoon boats or deckboats. Judicious fending off by your crew is usually the only answer. Avoid fending off with bare hands as injuries are common. Instead, have your crew use boat hooks (long poles with special fittings to assist docking) to push against objects. If something gets crushed against the boat, it will be an aluminum pole and not somebody's fingers.

As a boat backs out of a slip, the bow constantly swings in response to the wind or current. Good boat handling is dictated by what the boat wants to do and not what the skipper has in mind. Never fight the boat. It is best to give the boat its head and find somewhere to turn around if you need to go in the other direction.

Cleanup Crew

Designate one member of the crew to tidy up the boat after it's out of the dock. This person should start by coiling up all dock lines so they can't get caught in the propeller. Next, all fenders should be removed and stowed. Fenders flying alongside the boat are not only unsightly, but they can cause worn spots in the paint or gelcoat. Also, they have a tendency to detach themselves and become lost at sea.

TAHOE

At first glance, this deckboat appears to be a family runabout. But, a closer look reveals dual mounts for removable fishing seats on the fore-deck. The square hatch on the starboard bow conceals a folding ladder for when the bow is being used as a swim platform.

No-wake zones are marked by buoys and signs. Speeds in such zones are limited as a safety measure and to prevent wave damage to boats docked in the area. (NOAA)

OPERATING SPEED

Harbors and No-Wake Zones

Your speed in harbors and designated no-wake zones should be the slowest at which the vessel can safely maneuver. This is known as *bare steerageway*. Bare steerageway can be somewhat faster in strong winds or currents, but is always as slow as the boat can be safely maneuvered. Keep watch on the wake produced by your boat. In most cases, you are responsible for any damage it does to persons or property.

Maintaining a straight course at bare steerageway takes concentration. All boats tend to wander off course, and this tendency is somewhat greater with I/O propulsion. (The big exception is a contra-rotating, dual-propeller lower unit.) Don't worry about small variances in the boat's track. Correct only large movements, and then use the smallest amount of steering possible. Beginners try to correct every little wander, forgetting the boat will probably swing back on its own accord. A small wander to port followed by an equal wander to starboard averages out a straight course. Nothing needs to be done unless a big wander threatens to take the boat into danger.

"Steer small" is age-old advice to helmsmen. It means to apply the smallest amount of correction that will get the job done. Make a small correction, then another if necessary. Oversteering to correct a slight change in course will result in a greater divergence from course on the other side. This will then require a larger correction than the original. Pretty soon, the boat is visibly zigzagging.

Another skill to be learned is "meeting" the swing of the bow. In a car, you straighten out coming out of a turn by letting the steering wheel slide through your fingers. This technique won't work on a boat. To stop the bow from swinging too far, a skilled helmsman applies a small amount of counter-helm just as the boat reaches the desired heading. If, for instance, you've turned to starboard, you'll apply enough helm to port to stop the rotation of the bow, but not enough to start it rotating left. Knowing how much counter-helm to apply takes practice.

In addition to no-wake zones, many states and localities have speed restrictions. Some are specified as miles per hour, a difficult standard to meet in a boat without an accurate speedometer. Others allow faster than no-wake speed, but prohibit boats from operating at full planing speeds. Florida, in particular, has regulations aimed at protecting the manatees that live in shallow coastal waters. Virtually all states have laws limiting speeds near shore or other on-water structures such as swimming floats.

Open Water

Nothing beats the sense of freedom that comes from letting 'er rip across open water. Like all freedoms, however, high speeds and open water demand respect. Make sure your passengers are ready before you increase the throttle. Take a second look around for other boats that could be rocked by your wake or collide with you. Remember that just because there's water up ahead doesn't mean you can go there. A sandbar, submerged rocks, or even an old house (common in artificial lakes) may lie just below the surface waiting to catch your propeller and lower unit. So make sure the open water is also deep water.

It is wise to get your boat on a plane quickly. Once on plane, it is possible to throttle back for maximum fuel economy. Savings of up 10 to 20 percent over full-throttle operation can be achieved by finding the best combination of throttle and trim. Finding the right combination is easiest if you have both a tachometer and speedometer. The goal is to reduce engine rpms as much as possible without causing any serious reduction in boat speed. The exact settings of throttle and trim will vary from trip to trip as you change the number of people and amount of gear in the boat.

Passengers should remain seated whenever the boat is operating at planing speeds. A sudden change in the location of passenger weight can result in the bow unexpectedly veering off course. Also, the inevitable bouncing and swaying of the deck can cause an unwary person to lose footing and tumble overboard. Slow down if it becomes necessary for someone to move about.

Engine Trim and Speed

Trim refers to the angle of the lower unit relative to the transom of the boat. *Neutral trim* means that the vertical axis of the lower unit is parallel to the transom. Changing the trim of

NIGHT OPERATION

Night brings both a special magic to boating and special dangers. Human eyes are adapted primarily for daylight. This is because our species relies so much on color vision. The color receptors in the retina are not as sensitive to low light as those receptors that see only in black and white. Because of the way human eyes work it is necessary to learn how to see in the dark and to accept the limitations of night vision.

Sailors, hunters, and anyone who must work at night under just starlight know a vision trick. Because color vision is centered in the retina, they know dark objects disappear from view when looked at directly. Instead, they look slightly to one side of the object to gain the advantage of those black and white receptors at the edges of human vision. By looking to one side, above, or below an object they are able to see it with greater clarity. The problem with this trick is that it goes against human nature. It has to be practiced until you can do it well. And, you must continuously remind yourself how to use your eyes at night because it is so easy to fall back into daylight habits.

Night vision depends upon a process called *dark adaptation*. After several minutes in the dark you really can see better than immediately after coming out of bright light. Dark adaptation takes time to build, but can be wiped out by a flash of bright white light. When operating at night, the driver must be protected from exposure to bright lights. This means light from video games, flashlights, and even cigarette lighters. Red instrument lights have been found to be less damaging to dark adaptation, although very dim white light is nearly as good.

Because of the limitations of human vision, the first thing to do after dark is pull back on the throttle. Slowing down allows

the lower unit has a corresponding effect on the way the boat rides. *Trimming in* brings the lower unit closer to the transom and causes the bow to come down. Trimming in too much causes the bow to plow through the water. When this happens, the boat is hard to steer and has a tendency to *yaw*, or swing rapidly to one side of its course or the other.

Trimming out moves the lower unit away from the transom. As the lower unit is trimmed out, the bow tends to rise. This reduces yawing, but too much outward trim will cause the propeller to ventilate, or suck air. This results in over-revving of the engine and reduced speed and control. Quite obviously, the goal of the operator is to find the right angle of trim for

the best ride, fastest speed, and greatest steering control.

Until you learn your boat, start at idle speed with neutral trim. As you advance the throttle, trim the lower unit out. Don't overdo things. Watch the tachometer and listen to the sound of the engine. Overtrimming will result in rapid rise in rpms and engine noise, but no increase in speed. Never let the engine over-rev as this can cause permanent damage. Once the boat reaches maximum throttle, trimming in just slightly should allow the throttle to be closed slightly without a reduction in boat speed. Proper trim can reduce fuel consumption by a significant amount. The right setting is never constant, but varies with water conditions.

more time to assess dangers. Remember, you will be considerably closer to danger at night because it will take you longer to perceive the situation due to the limitations of night vision.

Navigation lights can sometimes make finding buoys and harbor entrances easier at night than during the day. This is only true where urban sprawl has not created an explosion of street lights, house lights, neon signs, and the like. Many times it can be virtually impossible to sort out critical navigation buoys or lights from the mass of shore illumination.

Distance judgment is seriously compromised at night. Even skilled sailors find it difficult to judge distances with acceptable accuracy. People have actually driven into shorelines that were in clear sight, but which were perceived to still be some distance away. Distance judgment is particularly difficult when looking at a single light such as on a buoy. The same is true of moving boats where all you can see are the navigation lights. As a rule, if you can see the hull of another boat at night, you are close enough that there is danger of collision.

Spotting floating dangers such as logs is difficult to impossible at night. Sometimes, they show up as dark spots in a patch of glistening water caused by moonlight. Slowing down makes the job easier. Some people turn on docking lights or use spotlights to help find floating dangers. This technique works, but destroys night vision. As a result, objects outside the illumination of the bright white lights are effectively hidden from perception. If you use docking lights or spotlights, speed must be reduced so that you can stop within the distance illuminated by those lights. And, keep in mind that other boats will be that close before you see them, so be prepared to maneuver quickly to avoid collision.

Remember that jerking the throttle all the way back from full speed can swamp a boat or stall the engine. Make sure you reduce power gradually, letting the wake fall away behind the boat as it comes down off the plane and enters displacement mode.

ENTERING HARBOR

Many marinas are entered via a channel that runs between protective breakwaters. While still a hundred yards or so offshore, line up so you can see clearly all the way into the harbor. Then, enter on a straight line up the channel. This allows you to see other boats in the channel as well as any inconsiderate operators who appear suddenly around the harbor entrance. By lining up your boat well outside the channel you will have time to avoid an accident, which is your primary job as skipper.

Once inside the harbor, the crew member who tidied up the lines when the trip began should now begin replacing those fenders and preparing dock lines. It is critical that dock lines be attached outside of stanchions and railings, but then led back inside the boat for coiling. Never allow a line to trail astern. Otherwise, it is almost certain to become tangled in the propeller as you maneuver to the dock.

Skilled operators learn to use neutral to their advantage when docking or performing other slow-speed maneuvers. When a pontoon or deckboat is coasting in neutral, bursts of thrust can be used to induce prop walk to turn the boat in the desired orientation. For instance, you might approach a dock to port at an angle, but the final docking requires the boat to be broadside to the pier. A skilled operator sets up the approach angle and speed while in gear. As the bow nears the dock, the operator shifts the engine into neutral and turns the wheel toward the pier. A burst of reverse-directed thrust walks the stern toward the dock and slows forward speed. Done properly, this maneuver stops the boat broadside to the pier at exactly the right place.

It's common for the boat to come against the pier when docking. Hard impact can cause

Fenders are used to protect the boat's hull from damage against piers when docked.

damage, so there is a tendency to want to fend off by pushing with hands, arms, and feet. This is a dangerous practice that can lead to crushed fingers or broken bones. Never put any part of your body between a solid object and a moving boat. Although a boat is moving slowly, it contains a great deal of momentum, often more than human muscle can handle. To avoid injuries, always rig fenders before you approach docks. Teach your crew that it's better to dent the aluminum or scratch the gelcoat than make a trip to the emergency room. Parents must keep careful watch on children who enjoy dangling fingers into the water.

SEAMANSHIP AND PONTOON BOATS

Seamanship of pontoon craft is in a class by itself. For starters, pontoon boats do not have any hulls at all, but float on two (or three) airtight cylinders. The initial stability of a pontoon boat can lull inexperienced skippers into making bad decisions. While capsize accidents are extremely rare, it is possible to cause a boat to roll over. As with conventional monohull boats, capsizes of pontoon boats are the result of overloading, improper use, and operator error.

Weight Limits

It cannot be stressed enough that operators must know the weight limits of their craft. Pontoon boats are not required to display a safe loading sticker, even if under 20 feet, but many manufacturers provide them anyway. (If your boat does not have a weight or passenger limit sticker, see the weight limit calculations in the appendix.) It's often hard to know just how much weight you have onboard, but there are a few rules of thumb that will help you to determine—at a glance—if you're safely loaded.

1. No boat should leave the dock with more passengers than permanent factory-installed seats. This isn't a comfort issue; the number of seats indicate what the boat's designer thought was safe capacity.
2. No pontoon boat should leave the dock if less than half of each log is visible above the waterline.

That said, the amount of weight a pontoon boat can support is astounding. While the 'toons may not look impressive compared to a regular boat hull, they contain a large volume of air, which, in fresh water, produces 62.4 pounds of buoyancy per cubic foot. Nonetheless, it is unsafe to load the boat to its maximum buoyancy. Safe loading requires that considerable reserve buoyancy be maintained to prevent capsize.

Stability

Stability refers to a boat's ability to tolerate load shifts from port to starboard. Within reason, the wider the distance between the 'toons, the greater the stability. Most pontoon boats are intended for trailering on the highway, which limits them to a maximum beam of 8'6". This highway limit also restricts maximum stability. Under ABYC standards, the boat must be able to support the passenger weight moved all the way to one side without submerging the low pontoon.

A complete stability test of a pontoon boat includes moving passenger weight both fore and aft to simulate people crowding into either end of the boat. Neither end of the pontoons should submerge. From a practical standpoint, few boats have problems keeping the bows of their 'toons above water with the weight moved forward. This is because of the counterbalancing weight of the outboard engine. Things change dramatically when passenger weight is moved aft. The weight of the outboard now becomes a

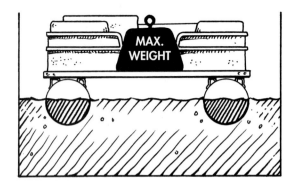

The pontoon boat stability test done by manufacturers calls for placing a weight equal to the combined weight of the people, engine, and other gear on the centerline. The weight is then moved to one side. To pass, the low pontoon must not submerge. (Christopher Hoyt)

liability, helping push down the 'toons. The safe allowable weight must be reduced until both pontoon sterns come above water.

Bow-Up Trim

Pontoon boats are no different than other watercraft in that they operate best with a slight bow-up trim. As we'll discuss later, the height of the deck above the water at the bow is also a critical safety factor in rough water. Boat manufacturers know the importance of trim, and adjust the weight of the engine and furniture to give a slight rise to the bow when the boat is empty. It is up to the skipper to adjust the weight of passengers to maintain the slight bow-up orientation.

Handling Waves

Without doubt, 'toons provide more fun for the dollar than any other watercraft, but only if they are used on the proper waters.

A pontoon boat in good operating trim rides with the bow slightly high. If the bow is too high, the boat "mushes" and wastes fuel. If the bow is too low there's a risk of submerging the bow into an oncoming wave. The boat in this photograph is just right for one occupant. It's a little high now, but will come down with more passengers.

Pontoon boats do not respond well to rough water or high winds. The relatively narrow cylinders of pontoons react to waves quite differently than a traditional monohull such as a deckboat. Most of a conventional boat's hull is above water where it represents *reserve buoyancy*. The outward flare of a conventional bow flings spray aside and creates a bit more reserve buoyancy: when the flared bow of a conventional boat enters a wave, the wave pushes against the flare and helps lift the boat over the swell.

The narrow shape of each log on a 'toon means the bow has little ability to lift itself up and over waves. Instead of lifting over waves, the logs tend to slice through them. Therefore, the boat should not be allowed to encounter waves larger than the height of the foredeck. Most boats with 24-inch-diameter 'toons have a deck height of about 18 inches when the boat is fully loaded with people and gear. Such a boat can be expected to keep itself dry when running through 18-inch waves. If, however, you run into a bigger sea, those higher waves will wash onto the deck. An 18-inch wave sounds small, but in reality it represents the roughest conditions typically encountered on inland lakes and rivers.

BOAT WAKES

Wide-beam cruisers can produce wakes of four or more feet in height, especially when operating at full mush—the transition speed between displacement and planing modes. Wakes quickly lose their initial height and power, but they still travel for several hundred yards as a recognizable wave. While capsize is the ultimate danger of improperly catching a wake, the more likely outcome is to have passengers tossed about inside your boat. The result can be nothing more serious than bumps and bruises, or it can be a dangerous tumble overboard.

Many first-time powerboat owners are unaware of both the size of their wake and their legal responsibility for any damage done by it. Passing slower cars on highways is perfectly benign, but the same maneuver on the water can put other people's lives in jeopardy. As a pontoon boat operator, it pays to keep your head on a swivel when operating in heavy-traffic areas.

AVOIDING CAPSIZE

As with any boat, water rolling around on deck presents a capsize hazard to a pontoon boat. Water is heavy. A cubic foot of fresh water

FETCH

The distance that wind blows over the water is known as *fetch*. As a general rule, the longer the fetch, the larger the waves; however, waves can only reach a certain height for any given wind speed and it takes hours of exposure to wind to reach that maximum height.

The table below gives average predicted wave heights based upon both the duration of the wind and the distance, or fetch, over which it blows. The majority of pleasure boating is done in winds up to 12 miles an hour.

DURATION OF WIND AND LENGTH OF FETCH (ADAPTED FROM BOWDITCH)

Speed of Wind	Maximum Wave Height	Duration in Hours to Build Wave Height (Unlimited Fetch)			Fetch in Statute Miles to Build Wave Height		
		50% Maximum Height	75% Maximum Height	Full Maximum Height	50% Maximum Height	75% Maximum Height	Full Maximum Height
8–12 mph	2 feet	1.5 hrs	5 hrs	8 hrs	3.5	15	>29
16–20 mph	8 feet	3.5 hrs	8 hrs	12 hrs	11	33	>66
30–36 mph	19 feet	5.5 hrs	12 hrs	21 hrs	24	82.5	>165

Note: A statute mile *is the 5,280-foot mile used in the United States for highway distances and the like. Wind speeds on rivers and inland lakes are expressed in statute miles per hour. This is different from the conventional measurement of wind speed in knots or nautical miles per hour at sea. A nautical mile is a bit more than 6,000 feet long.*

Understanding the role fetch plays in the height of wind-driven waves is an important part of seamanship. Even on a windy day it is possible to find calm water along shore at the upwind side of a lake. For instance, prior to a cold front, the winds are typically from the southwest, making the northeast shoreline the rough side of the lake. After the cold front passes, winds are often blustery out of the northwest. This means that the southeast shoreline now experiences the largest waves, while in the northwest quadrant the water is dramatically calmer.

weighs 62.4 pounds. If the front 4 feet of a typical 8-foot beam pontoon deck is covered to the depth of just six inches (0.5 foot), the boat has 16 cubic feet of water on deck. This works out to an additional 1,000 pounds of weight.

$$4 \times 8 \times 0.5 = 16 \text{ cu. ft.}$$
$$16 \times 62.4 = 998.4 \text{ pounds}$$

To understand the significance of this weight, consider that the front 4 feet of a 24-inch diameter pontoon typically generates about that much buoyancy. Putting a thousand pounds of extra water on the foredeck has the same effect as eliminating the lift of one pontoon.

The worst-case scenario occurs when one corner of the bow dips underwater for some reason, such as plowing into a boat wake. Forward motion of the boat shovels water onto the deck so that the process becomes self-sustaining. The weight of water prevents the bow from rising while at the same time the low pontoon is pushed deeper below the surface. If the people aboard are also thrown to the low side, the result can be a sudden capsize.

When dealing with large waves it's preferable to let waves roll under the boat at a slight diagonal than take to them straight on the bow. When a wave comes broadside, it lifts one pontoon and rolls the boat away from the oncoming crest. The low pontoon submerges, changing its reserve buoyancy into active buoyancy to restore the deck to level. Some considerable rocking results, but the inherent stability of the pontoon boat should win the day.

When taking a wave from the side it is important for the skipper to his passengers to brace themselves. Caught unprepared, it is likely someone will be tossed to the low side of the boat. This sudden change in weight distribution comes just as the wave is doing its best to tip the boat onto its beam ends. The result is an increased chance of capsize.

Whenever a large wave approaches, the first thing to do is slow down to below planing speed. The reason is quite simple—to get rid of as much energy as possible. Impact from a large wake can divert the force of the propeller from

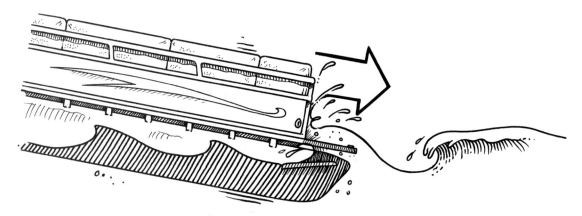

The worst situation for a pontoon boat occurs when the bow is buried in a wave. Forward motion of the boat forces additional water onto the deck and the boat quickly loses stability. A capsize is likely. Slowing down, changing the angle of the boat to the waves, or just staying out of rough water easily avoids this situation. (Christopher Hoyt)

STARCRAFT ELITE 246

A table umbrella gives a picnic appearance to this 24-foot cruising boat from Starcraft. The Elite 246 is a three-generation boat with room for the kids to play and for mom and pop to talk with grandma and grandpa.

moving the boat forward to contributing to a capsize. Reducing speed limits the amount of energy acting on the boat to only that contained within the wave. This allows your boat to maximize its natural righting ability. Slowing down also allows the versatility of shifting gears.

If you bury the bow and water is climbing onto the deck, you can shift into reverse to pull the bow out from under a dangerous load of water. To do this, shift into reverse and apply power smoothly. Keep the steering wheel centered if possible. If the boat begins to roll to one side, turn the wheel in that direction while reversing. The thrust of the engine will help counteract the roll. As the deck comes out from under water, ease the throttle back and shift into neutral.

Before getting underway again, check the boat for water damage after making sure all the people are safe.

HIGH WINDS

I'll discuss weather in greater detail in the next section, but for now let's just say that pontoon boats have such little lateral resistance that wind tends to blow them across the water like a leaf. Control in high winds can be nearly impossible. Instead of trying to run for port, *heave-to* and ride out the few minutes of high winds. A pontoon boat heaves-to by turning the back of the boat into the wind and then operating slowly in reverse. With careful throttle adjustment, the thrust of the engine can match the wind and you'll sit in one spot with the bow pointed downwind.

Heaving-to immediately reduces the buffeting and noise of the storm. Your crew will be visibly happier as a result of this apparent improvement in conditions. An aft curtain can be rigged to block wind-driven rain for even more comfort.

Sometimes you'll need to motor across a steady wind. Pontoon boats have been known to blow sideways almost as fast as they are moving forward, particularly at no-wake speed. In this circumstance it is necessary to steer a *crab course* to go straight to your destination. This means the bow is aimed upwind of the destination while the wind causes it to drift to leeward. As a result, the boat makes good the desired course. The amount of "crab" to apply depends upon the wind and current.

WEATHER

Everyone knows a story about the big storm that "came out of nowhere." These are wonderful tales of mayhem and survival. Most are true except for one detail—weather doesn't come out of nowhere. How and where storms occur is reasonably predictable if you pay attention to the signs and information available to you.

For starters, use your eyes. The majority of weather systems in North America move from west to east. Keep your eye on the western horizon, and you'll almost never get caught unaware.

Weather Information

Reliable weather information is everywhere today—newspapers, radio, TV, and the Internet. NOAA Weather radio stations cover most of the country with around-the-clock forecasts and data. There is really no excuse for not knowing the general weather trends for the next 24 to 36 hours. By watching weather trends over time, it is possible to get a good sense of what you will face over the coming weekend or longer. Remember that your boating area may not experience the same weather you have back home. If

Learning to look up from time to time can prevent you from getting caught in foul weather. The way clouds build tells an experienced skipper a great deal about what will happen in an hour or two. (NOAA)

you have a cottage at a distant lake, you'll want to zero in on forecasts for that area.

INTERNET

When it comes to finding weather information needed to plan your day, nothing is easier or more useful than the Internet. Hundreds of websites carry everything from the current NOAA regional forecast to live radar and satellite imagery for your specific location. Here are just a few examples:

> www.nws.noaa.gov
> www.weather.com
> www.wunderground.com
> www.accuweather.com

NOAA WEATHER RADIO

Once you leave home, stay updated by listening to National Weather Service information on the chain of all-weather NOAA radio stations. These broadcast on channels 1 through 10 of the VHF marine radio band. Many ordinary AM/FM receivers can also access weather radio stations. Carrying a battery-operated weather radio receiver gives continuous access to the latest weather information even when you are on the water.

TELEVISION WEATHER

Near large metropolitan areas some of the best weather information comes from the trained meteorologists working for TV stations. They often have local knowledge to put all of the data into a form you can understand. The bad thing about TV weather is availability. In most areas a full weathercast is carried only in the morning, at noon, and during the evening broadcasts.

The *Weather Channel* broadcasts national and regional weather on a 24-hour schedule. Local coverage is spotty depending upon the cable company providing service.

COMMERCIAL RADIO STATIONS

Thanks to automation, commercial radio stations are not the primary sources of weather information that they once were. Nowadays, many stations operate for extended periods without any weather announcements. Weather information is generally included inside news programs carried on the hour and half hour. Even if you're not receiving quality information from a broadcaster, the radio can still provide forecasts: unusual bursts of static on the AM band may indicate approaching thunderstorms.

Weather Maps

Lots of different maps are prepared by NOAA weather forecasters. Of these, the most useful for small-boat skippers show isobars of barometric pressure. An *isobar* is a line drawn on a map linking locations with the same barometer readings. Localized areas where the pressure is greater than the surrounding territory are called

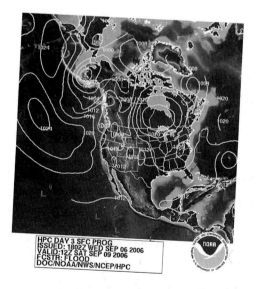

Weather maps can appear intimidating. The wavy lines are called isobars *and indicate areas of equal pressure. Expect high winds if the isobars are close together in your location. (NOAA)*

highs, while areas of low pressure surrounded by higher pressure are called lows. The actual barometric pressure is of less importance than the relative difference between high and low pressure.

The spacing of isobars indicates what meteorologists call the *pressure gradient*. When the lines are close together, the gradient is described as *steep*. Conversely, widely spaced lines indicate a *shallow* pressure gradient. As a rule, a steep gradient is associated with high winds, while shallow gradients indicate lower wind velocity.

HIGH-PRESSURE AREAS

Areas of high pressure are associated with fair weather. Almost dead-calm winds and clear skies are common when a high is directly overhead. On the fringes of a high-pressure area, cool or cold weather and often blustery winds are typical. The rate of movement is usually about 400 to 600 miles per day. During the summer months, however, high-pressure areas

Fronts *are lines along which there is a marked change in temperature and pressure of the air. Generally, a warm front brings deteriorating conditions, while a cold front comes with fast-building thunderstorms. (NOAA)*

often stall out for periods of time. They become *blocking highs* that prevent the normal movement of both storms and good weather.

LOW-PRESSURE AREAS

A falling barometer has long been known to precede bad weather. This is because storms and rain are associated with low-pressure areas, also known as *depressions*. These are the weather-makers. A fully formed low-pressure system looks somewhat like an upside-down check mark on a map. To the east, there is a warm front with its large area of rain. Trailing to the west is the curving stem of the check in the form of the cold front with its thunderstorms.

FRONTS

A *front* is nothing more than a boundary between two different air masses of different temperature and relative humidity. A warm front indicates that warm, moist air is displacing the existing cool, dry air. The opposite is a cold front, which displaces warm air. Each type of front brings with it specific changes in the local weather. Of the two, the warm front is less violent. The really nasty summertime weather is associated with cold front passages. In the normal order of things, a warm front precedes a cold front.

Weather Dangers

THUNDERSTORMS

Few people venture out when winds and waves are high, but boating conditions are often ideal—a calm lake and light winds—just before thunderstorms develop. Warm and moist surface air is sent rapidly aloft, causing the formation of classic anvil-shaped cumulonimbus clouds. These storms are most often associated with cold front passages. The greater the temperature drop across the front, the greater the likelihood of violent thunderstorms.

Isolated thunderstorms also pop up on hot, sultry afternoons during mid- to late summer without an approaching cold front. The particular spot where one develops is hard to predict, but the pre-existing sultry atmospheric conditions that spawn these storms are obvious. On such days, the weather forecasts almost always contain the warning: "possibility of afternoon thunderstorms." These storms are most common in the late afternoon and early evening.

MICROBURSTS

An unseen danger in thunderstorms is a phenomenon known as a microburst. This is a rapidly moving downdraft of air that spreads out in all directions when it slams into the water's surface. Localized winds of more than 100 miles an hour are common for a few minutes, explaining why so many boats are capsized or damaged. There is no way to see a microburst coming. Nor is it possible to know which thunderstorm will produce a microburst and which will not. Safety lies in avoiding thunderstorms by staying in port when they are expected in your area.

LIGHTNING

The rapid updrafts and downdrafts within a thunderstorm generate enormous amounts of static electricity, the precursor to lightning. A single discharge can produce millions of volts in less than a second. An electrical storm on the water is particularly dangerous because lighting tends to strike the highest object around—a dangerous reality to a boat on open water. Avoidance is the only safe way to cope with electrical storms.

- Don't go out if lightning threatens.
- If you are out, return to the closest place of refuge when you hear thunder or spot the first flash of lightning.

- Do not stay in your boat unless necessary. Seek shelter inside a building or other permanent structure ashore.

Running to safety from lightning is possible, but you needn't return to your launch site. If returning to the launch site means heading toward the storm, take a moment to determine if the storm is too close. Count the seconds between the flash and the resulting thunder, then divide that number by five. The resulting number is the approximate distance, in miles, between you and the lightning strike. If the storm is too close, you're much better off finding a nearby refuge. Thunderstorms usually don't last very long. In an hour or so you will probably be able to resume your trip.

FOG

Fog is nothing more than a low-altitude cloud. Clouds are formed when warm, moist air is cooled to its dew point. On rivers, fog forms when warm, moist air is chilled by cooler water below it. Expect river fog during the early morning and late evening hours as well as at night. It dissipates when the sun is high enough in the sky to penetrate into the river valley, or when the wind at water level is strong enough to blow the fog away. The biggest danger of river fog is unpredictability. A boat can be experiencing clear visibility, come around a bend, and suddenly find itself in near-zero-visibility fog.

Navigating in river fog is risky business even with radar. Most hazards do not show up on a radar screen. The prudent action in river fog is to move outside the commercial shipping channel if there is enough depth of water. Hang off the bank or anchor as necessary until visibility clears.

On small lakes, fog burns away in the sun or blows away in the lightest of breezes. Larger lakes, however, can experience advection fog, the scientific name for true marine fog that occurs when a warm, moist air mass moves over the colder surface of the water. This moving air brings with it a steady supply of moisture, so the fog persists even in a strong breeze. And lake fog doesn't always burn away in the sunshine.

SEVERE SUNSHINE

It's hard to believe that a perfect boating day with clear skies and calm waters brings any danger, but more people are injured by the sun than by high winds and lightning. Sunburn and related injuries are common because the water magnifies the sun's intensity. Sunscreen with a high SPF factor should be used by everyone, but particularly by children and people with fair skin. Wear protective clothing during the most intense periods of sunshine: 10:00 A.M. to 2:00 P.M. Keep in mind that parts of the body that do not usually get sunburned ashore, like under the chin, the upper arms, or behind the knees, can get burned when you're on the water. The sun's reflection on the water can direct the rays to the areas you least expect.

Eyes can be "sunburned" as well. Never venture on the water without sunglasses that provide full ultraviolet protection. Wearing a ball cap with a bill also helps protect the eyes. Unlike burned skin, ultraviolet damage to the lens of the eye takes decades to develop. It is believed that exposure to ultraviolet light is a primary cause of cataracts in people over 60 years of age.

Rules of the Road

The Rules of the Road book, the *International Regulations for Preventing Collisions at Sea*, was written to help prevent collisions on the water. The first international Rules were written in 1864 as a reaction to the advent of steamboats. At that time, the United States was torn apart by the American Civil War. Even so, safety at sea was considered so important that delegates from both the Northern and the Southern states signed the treaty. The international Rules were updated in 1948 and in 1960. These updates were followed by a major revision in 1972, which has become known as 72 COLREGS. The current Rules consist of 38 individual rules governing maneuvers, lights, and signals. An international treaty gives nations the right to modify the Rules to cover specific needs on their inland waters.

THE U.S. INLAND RULES

The U.S. Inland Rules govern federal waters: coastal waters, the major commercial rivers, and the Great Lakes. On the state level, all 50 states have adopted the Inland Rules nearly word for word to govern the nonfederal waters within their boundaries.

There are 36 individual rules and five annexes within the Inland Rules. In theory, they apply equally to the smallest fishing boat and the biggest oceangoing oil tanker. From a practical standpoint, however, only a few of the rules have direct bearing on everyday pleasure boating. Only these rules will be discussed here.

Terms to Know

To understand these rules it is necessary to know the terms used to describe different types of boats and ships.

- **Vessel**—Every description of watercraft, including nondisplacement craft and seaplanes, used as a means of transportation on water.
- **Power-Driven Vessel**—Any vessel propelled by machinery.

- **Sailing Vessel**—Any vessel under sail provided that propelling machinery (if fitted) is not being used. A sailboat with its engine running is nothing more than an ordinary power-driven vessel under the Rules.

- **Vessel Engaged in Fishing (Fishing Vessel)**—Any vessel fishing with nets, lines, trawls, or other fishing apparatus which restricts maneuverability. *This does not include a vessel fishing with trolling lines or other fishing apparatus that do not restrict maneuverability.*

Three other terms that do not refer to types or classes of vessels must be understood to properly interpret the Rules.

- **Underway**—A vessel that is not at anchor, made fast to the shore, or aground is *underway*. A vessel can be underway in either of two ways. It can be underway and *making way*, or it may be underway and *not making way*. A vessel is making way whenever it is propelled by its machinery or sails. It is not making way when the boat is adrift on the current or wind.

- **In Sight**—Two vessels are *in sight* only when both skippers can see each other. Sometimes conditions are hazy or vision is slightly obscured and, while one boat can see the other, the reverse is not true. Such one-way visibility does not qualify as in sight. This is an important distinction because there are rules that apply to

Angling with rod and reel may be "fishing," but boats engaged in sportfishing get no special consideration under the Rules of the Road. Only commercial fishing vessels with large nets or trawls that prevent maneuvering are given special privileges. (Godfrey Marine)

vessels in sight of one another, while other rules apply only when they are not. If you are uncertain that another boat can see you, the Rules require you to operate as if you are not in sight.

- **Restricted Visibility**—This is narrowly defined as a meteorological event such as rain, snow, or even blowing sand. Darkness is not considered restricted because it's a normal daily event. (Naturally, darkness places certain limits on human vision which must be taken into account when boating.)

Responsibility

Let's skip to the heart of the Rules of the Road: Rule 2 spells out the responsibilities of the people aboard vessels, while making it clear that vessels must depart from the Rules when necessary to avoid collision.

> **RULE 2**
> *RESPONSIBILITY*
>
> (a) Nothing in these Rules shall exonerate any vessel, the owner, master, or crew thereof, from the consequences of any neglect to comply with these Rules or of the neglect of any precaution which may be required by the ordinary practice of seamen, or by the special circumstances of the case.

This rule is often called the "Rule of Good Seamanship." There is no specific definition of good seamanship, since it covers such a broad variety of topics; however, it is generally agreed that a good seaman must:

1. Obey the Rules.
2. Take action to avoid collision.
3. Take action to lessen the effects of collision.
4. Use radiotelephone properly (Bridge-to-Bridge Radiotelephone Act).
5. Keep a proper lookout.
6. Display proper lights.
7. Use radar if aboard.

Court decisions have brought a large number of additional factors into the definition of good seamanship. These include carrying the appropriate charts and pilot books, having a copy of the Rules of the Road (on boats over 39 feet), and making sure the operator and crew are trained in their duties.

> **RULE 2**
> *RESPONSIBILITY*
>
> (b) In construing and complying with these Rules due regard shall be had to all dangers of navigation and collision and to any special circumstances, including the limitations of the vessels involved, which may make a departure from these Rules necessary to avoid immediate danger.

Historically, situations not specifically covered by any of the other Rules fall under Rule 2(b), which is called the "General Prudential Rule." This rule also warns against too rigid an interpretation of the Rules. No one is ever required to steam into a collision. Vessels may (or, in some cases, must) depart from the Rules of the Road under the following circumstances:

1. *In extremis*—This occurs when the action of one vessel alone will not avoid the collision. The term comes from Latin meaning "in extreme circumstances," but in this context has come to mean situations in which avoiding collisions is virtually impossible, so one

or both vessels maneuver "to take a glancing blow."

2. **Physical conditions**—These may make obedience impossible. For example, rocks may prevent a vessel from turning to starboard away from collision.

3. **Situation not covered by the Rules**—For example, when three or more vessels are present. The Rules only cover situations involving two vessels where danger of collision exists, because it was impractical to draft rules for every possible scenario involving three or more vessels.

4. **Both vessels agree** to depart from the Rules.

While Rule 2(b) authorizes departure from the Rules, such a departure is fraught with legal dangers because the two vessels may be doing things contrary to the published maneuvering requirements. If one of the vessels misunderstands, the result can be a collision.

A Proper Lookout

The Rules require keeping a "proper lookout" at all times. This requirement may seem obvious, but there are some important details in the regulation that are often overlooked. A skipper cannot be his own lookout unless there is 360-degree visibility from the helm station. Most pontoon and deckboats provide this all-around visibility. Even so, a skipper operating as his own lookout must operate with increased caution.

Another aspect of keeping lookout is that

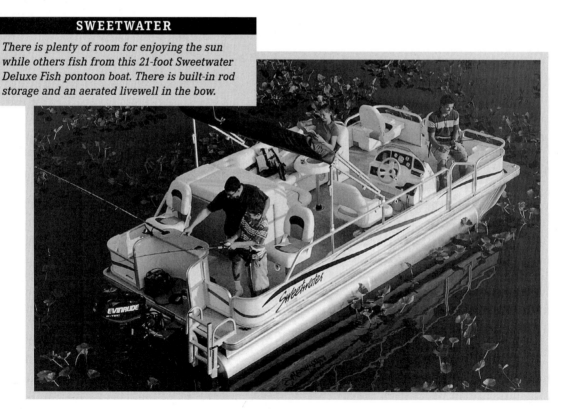

SWEETWATER

There is plenty of room for enjoying the sun while others fish from this 21-foot Sweetwater Deluxe Fish pontoon boat. There is built-in rod storage and an aerated livewell in the bow.

just opening your eyes is not enough. You must also listen for the whistle signals of other boats. Also, if your boat is equipped with radar, the Rules require that you use it for collision avoidance even during clear weather in daylight.

Collision Avoidance

The purpose of the Rules of the Road is to prevent collisions. One problem its authors faced when writing the original anticollision regulations was a three- or four-boat situation. Commercial harbors in the 1860s were as crowded with commercial vessels as today's waters are filled with pleasure boats. The writers of the Rules wisely understood that it is impossible to sort out three-, four-, or five-boat situations. So, they set up the Rules to cover only risk of collision between two vessels. When any more than two boats are involved, it becomes a *special circumstance* under which nobody has right-of-way. All of the vessels involved must give way or maneuver to avoid collision.

MEETING, OVERTAKING, AND CROSSING

Vessels can approach each other in any of three ways. The Rules outline specific actions for each vessel in situations where risk of collision exists.

Head-On The simplest situation occurs when two boats approach head to head. Neither is given the right-of-way. Instead, both vessels must turn, slow, or stop to avoid collision. The Rules instruct each boat to turn to starboard so they pass port-to-port just like cars. Unlike on the road, however, vessels sometimes find it advantageous to pass starboard-to-starboard. In such a case, the Rules do not expect or require boats to cross in front of each other when maintaining the initial starboard-to-starboard situation is safer.

KEEPING LOOKOUT

- **By sight**—Have someone posted to look for and report other vessels and dangers to navigation.
- **By sound**—Be listening for the whistle signals of other vessels, bridge tenders, or lockmasters.
- **By radar**—If your boat is equipped with radar, you must use it in fair weather or foul, day or night, to give advance warning of collision.
- **By radio**—If your boat has a VHF marine radio, you are required to monitor it for safety information. Channel 9 is now the small-craft hailing channel, but commercial vessels monitor Channels 16 and 13.

Radar units are now available for boats under 20 feet in length. If you have radar, however, the Rules require that you use it at all times. (Icom America)

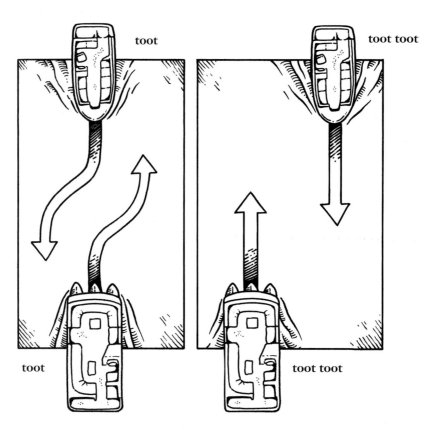

When two boats approach head-on, both are instructed to alter course to starboard so as to pass safely port-to-port. If the two vessels agree by radio or whistle signals, it is permissible to pass starboard-to-starboard. (Christopher Hoyt)

Overtaking On rivers and in narrow channels it is typical for one boat to overtake another. In this situation, the vessel being overtaken has full right-of-way and continues on its course and speed. The faster boat doing the overtaking must keep clear of the slower boat at all times. Commercial vessels invariably sound the required whistle signals. A barge tow that does not want to be overtaken signals five short blasts. In such a situation, the overtaking vessel must stay clear by slowing down and waiting for a better time to pass.

The same signal requirements apply to smaller pleasure boats, but are seldom observed on the water. Even so, it is wise to remember that that when you are overtaking another boat you are always responsible for staying clear. There are no requirements for the boat being overtaken to get out of the way of the faster vessel. On many waterways it is customary for slower boats to go to the right side of the channel to give faster vessels more room, but this is a courtesy not required or encompassed by the official Rules. The Rules also do not address the damage a faster boat's wake may do when it overtakes a slower boat. Even when the slower boat

RESPONSIBLE DRINKING

It's no secret that most parties involve adult beverages. This is true afloat as well. Never forget that a boat is a motor vehicle, and there are strict prohibitions against operating while intoxicated. Always have a designated driver.

The U.S. Coast Guard has done studies showing that drinking while boating is more dangerous than driving drunk on land. The motion, vibration, engine noise, sun, wind, and spray all cause fatigue, which increases impairment when drinking. Many a day has been ruined by alcohol, even in amounts that the person could have handled ashore.

One of the major causes of boating deaths is falling overboard. Alcohol causes a loss of coordination, judgment, and reaction time. Passengers who have been drinking are far more likely to tumble over the side. A skipper who has been drinking is significantly less able to turn around and rescue someone who has fallen overboard.

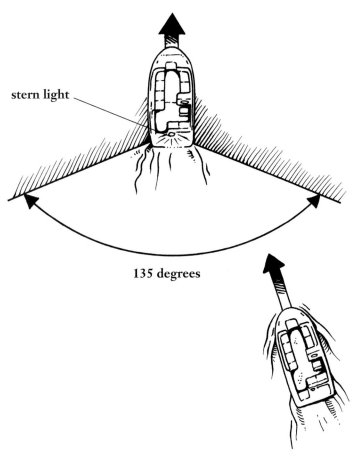

stern light

135 degrees

An overtaking vessel has full responsibility for staying clear of the boat it's passing. An overtaking situation exists until the faster boat is "past and clear" of the slower one. (Christopher Hoyt)

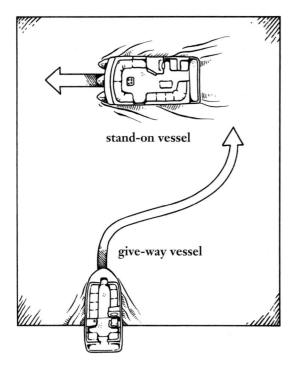

If a boat is approaching you from your starboard side, you are required to give way and maneuver to avoid collision. Speeding up to pass ahead of the stand-on vessel is specifically prohibited. The stand-on boat keeps its course unless it becomes obvious the other vessel is not maneuvering as required. (Christopher Hoyt)

gives permission to be overtaken, the faster craft is still responsible for its wake.

An overtaking situation is defined by the angle of visibility of the overtaken vessel's stern light. A stern light shines through a 135-degree arc. By day, if you are approaching another vessel in that same 135-degree arc, you are overtaking; practically, this means if you can see the other boat's stern. When in doubt, assume you are overtaking and give way to the other vessel.

Crossing When two vessels approach in any manner that is not defined as either an overtak-

ing or as a head-on situation, they are deemed to be crossing. In this situation, the boat that has the other on its right is the *give-way vessel*. The boat that has the other on its left side is the *stand-on vessel*. Under the Rules, the stand-on vessel maintains its course and speed. The give-way boat turns, slows, or stops.

When maneuvering to avoid collision, all vessels are instructed to turn to their right, or starboard. Turning is almost always the most effective means of avoiding collision. The Rules discourage making a series of small maneuvers. Instead, they want a single large turn, which is easily visible to the other vessel. The give-way vessel is not to speed up in order to pass in front of the stand-on vessel.

The stand-on vessel must maintain speed and course until it becomes concerned the other boat is not taking appropriate anticollision action. At that moment the stand-on vessel is authorized to turn right, speed up, or slow down. If for any reason a situation develops where the give-way vessel cannot avoid the collision by its maneuver alone, then the stand-on vessel must do whatever is necessary to avoid collision, or at least to take a glancing blow.

The Rules never require you to drive into a collision!

WHISTLE SIGNALS

All power-driven vessels of every size are to give and answer sound signals. When the first Rules were written in the 1860s, these signals were made on steam whistles, and they remain known as "whistle signals" today, even though they are more likely made with an air or electric horn. The unfortunate truth is that few pleasure boat operators know or exchange these signals. As a result, you cannot be certain that another boat will understand "whistle talk."

Signals are divided into short blasts of

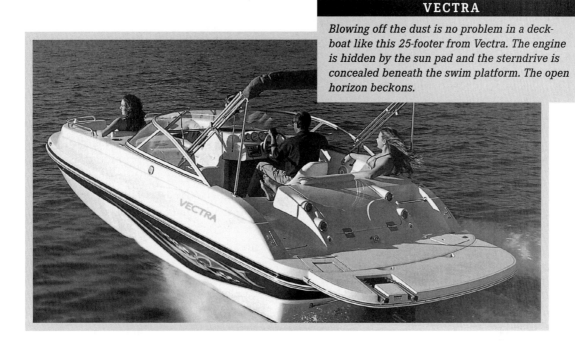

VECTRA

Blowing off the dust is no problem in a deckboat like this 25-footer from Vectra. The engine is hidden by the sun pad and the sterndrive is concealed beneath the swim platform. The open horizon beckons.

about 1-second duration, and prolonged blasts of 4 to 6 seconds. In general, short blasts are used for maneuvering signals, while prolonged ones are reserved for warnings. The following signals are authorized under the U.S. Inland Rules, which cover the major rivers, Great Lakes, and other federal waters. Most states require these same signals on their lakes and streams.

- **One Short**—"I intend to pass you on my port side."
- **Two Short**—"I intend to pass you on my starboard side."
- **Three Short**—"I am operating my engine in reverse."

Note that the one- and two-short-blast signals indicate intent. These signals must be acknowledged by the other vessel. If in agreement, the other boat signals the same signal. If in disagreement, the other vessel sounds the danger signal (see "Five Short" below) and both vessels must slow, stop, or maneuver to avoid collision until agreement is reached. By contrast, the three short blast signal simply indicates that the vessel is backing up. It is a signal of action which does not require an answer from any other vessels.

- **Five Short**—Indicates danger or doubt. (May be five or more short blasts.)
- **One Prolonged**—Announces the presence of your vessel to other boats that you may not see or that may not see you. Situations include leaving a dock or coming around a bend in a channel where oncoming traffic is obscured. Any vessel in the vicinity should answer with a similar prolonged blast. Then, when the two boats are in sight of one another they may exchange passing signals.

FOG SIGNALS

Whenever visibility is limited by fog, rain, or other weather conditions, power-driven vessels that are underway and making way must sound a single prolonged blast at intervals of no more than two minutes.

- **One Prolonged**—Power-driven vessel making way. The two-minute span between blasts is meant to allow your ears to recover from the loudness of your own boat's whistle. The intention is to listen intently for another boat's signal during the quiet period.
- **Two Prolonged**—Power-driven vessel not making way.
- **One Prolonged and Two Short**—Vessels with special rights. There is no right-of-way in fog, but vessels that may gain right-of-way when in sight have fog signals designed to indicate their special status. Sailboats, fishing vessels, and tugs

The Rules require boats to operate at a safe speed. This means a speed at which each boat can successfully maneuver to avoid collision. Safe speed does not refer to no-wake speeds in harbors or other posted areas.

engaged in towing all sound a prolonged blast followed by two short blasts. Pontoon and deckboats are power-driven vessels. As such, they must give way to sailboats and other vessels with special rights.

Unless in a designated anchorage area or well outside an area where other boats normally operate, a boat that anchors in a fog should ring a bell for five seconds every minute. If you do not have the correct apparatus to make the required signals, the Rules do not permit total silence. You must make some sort of fog signal, even it is nothing more than beating on a frying pan with a hammer.

SAFE SPEED

The Rules of the Road require you to maintain a safe speed at all times. This should not be confused with the no-wake speed laws established by local authorities on channels or in harbors. Remember, the Rules are only to prevent collisions between two vessels on open water. So, *safe speed* means any speed at which the boat can safely maneuver without colliding with any other vessels. Safe speed may be full throttle on waters where other vessels are seldom seen. In crowded conditions or fog, safe speed may be only bare steerageway—slower than the maximum speed in a no-wake zone.

The Rules do not specify a number of miles per hour. Instead, they suggest factors that must be taken into consideration:

- The state of visibility. Is it clear or foggy? Is it day or night?
- The number of other vessels around. In dense traffic you are expected to slow down.
- The ability of your vessel to turn and stop. Some boats are more maneuverable than others.

- The size of the waves, the strength of the wind, or the speed of the current, which may make it difficult to maneuver. Also, consider any nearby navigational hazards which may limit your maneuverability.
- Your draft (i.e., the depth of your boat) in relation to the available depth of water.
- At night, the presence of background lights on shore, which may make it difficult to pick out the navigation lights of other boats.

Boats equipped with radar are required to use it for advance warning of approaching vessels. The Rules require that you know the limitations of your equipment and remind you that not all boats may be detected in time to prevent collision. Small fiberglass boats can be extremely hard to detect, especially when waves are causing "sea clutter" on the screen.

Steering Clear of Commercial Barge Tows

Whether steel hits fiberglass, or fiberglass hits steel, it's always bad for the fiberglass. An important part of small-boat safety is steering clear of commercial traffic, especially the barge tows on the major rivers. Towboat skippers know and obey the Rules or they lose their jobs. It's the pleasure-boat driver who is at fault in most incidents involving a pleasure boat and a barge tow. Even when the towboat captain was wrong, the small boat usually missed the last opportunity to avoid disaster.

STAY OUT OF THE WAY

The phrase "not to impede" means just what it says—stay out of the way. The problem is that inexperienced boat skippers seldom realize that they can be impeding a barge tow that is still

SWEETWATER

This 19-footer parked in the driveway is a real kid magnet. The boat can be towed behind a compact SUV, but it is big enough to handle eight passengers and up to a 75 horsepower outboard.

RULE OF TONNAGE

Although it is not contained in the official Rules, there is one hard-and-fast maxim: in a collision the big boat always wins. It is a matter of physics, not law. Whether you have the right-of-way, or if the barge does, no pontoon or deckboat can stand up to the mass of a dozen or more loaded barges pushed by a triple-screw towboat.

The Rules are written to give commercial towboats the right-of-way on rivers. Rules 9(b), (c), (d), and (f) are specific.

- Fishing vessels and boats under 20 meters (~65 feet) in length are not to impede the passage of vessels that rely on a narrow channel or fairway for safe navigation.
- Boats crossing the channel are not to impede vessels that are restricted to operating in the channel.

- Everyone must avoid anchoring in a narrow channel except in a true emergency.

(U.S. Army Corps of Engineers)

hundreds of yards away. It can take a large tow a mile or more to come to a stop. When a towboat captain is concerned that an accident may occur, expect to hear the danger signal of five short blasts. Do not ignore this signal or assume it is intended for someone else. Take action to move clear of any tow that is sounding the danger signal. Better safe than sorry.

Navigation

In navigation there are three basic goals: 1) to know where you are; 2) to know how to get where you want to go (whether outbound or homeward-bound); and 3) to know the locations of rocks, dams, and other obstructions you need to avoid. On rivers, the only tool you really need to accomplish these goals is a good chart. On lakes, reservoirs, and sheltered coastal waters, you should have a chart and a compass—preferably an installed compass but a hand bearing compass will do. And with GPS receivers so cheap and easy to use, you may want one of these aboard as well.

CHARTS AND PUBLICATIONS

A variety of government publications contain the official body of knowledge about major waterways and larger lakes. These include pilot books, light lists, and charts. Any map specially designed for on-water navigation is properly termed a *chart*. Two U.S. governmental agencies

Being captain of your own boat brings with it the responsibility of safe navigation. You must always be aware of where your boat is and where it's going.

publish charts suitable for use in federally navigable waters. The National Oceanic and Atmospheric Agency (NOAA) is responsible for charts covering coastal waters, the Great Lakes, and some rivers and canals. The U.S. Army Corps of Engineers publishes charts for waters under its jurisdiction such as the Western Rivers and some artificial lakes.

Navigation Charts

Charts are special maps intended for water navigation. Like all maps, they are pictorial representations of a limited area on the surface of the globe. On land, you need a map showing highways and their route numbers to get from city to city. If you are hiking, you need topographic information to identify hills, ravines, and cliffs. On the water, the most important things are the shape of the shoreline, the nature of the bottom, and the location of aids to navigation and other landmarks. This is the information you need to avoid damage to your propeller or boat by going aground.

As a boater, your first choice should always be a NOAA (National Oceanographic and Atmospheric Administration) chart made for marine navigation. Unfortunately, the waters most popular for pontoon boats and deckboats are lakes and rivers not covered by traditional marine charts. Equally good charts of the Western Rivers (the Mississippi River and its tributaries) are published by the U.S. Army Corps of Engineers.

Finding a chart with underwater information can be difficult if neither type of government chart is available. A good alternative can be maps prepared for anglers. These can be found in bait and tackle stores. Topographic maps produced for hiking and other land activities are available for most areas of the United States. These are detailed maps with regard to mountains and valleys, but they do not contain information about the water other than the contours of the shoreline.

Like highway maps, nearly all navigational charts of lakes and bays are oriented with north at the top of the page. This may not be the case with river charts where it's normal for the long, narrow profile of a river to be oriented to the long direction of the printed page and not to true north. Confirm the direction of north on the chart by looking for the north arrow. Some charts use just an arrow with the letter "N." On navigational charts look for a "compass rose"—a concentric set of two circles showing both true north on the outer circle and magnetic north on the inner circle. True north is the direction of the geographic North Pole. Due to the nature of the Earth's magnetic field, compasses point to the magnetic north pole, which is currently in the Arctic regions of Canada. On a marine chart, the difference between true and magnetic north is called *variation*. On topographic maps prepared for hikers on land, this difference is labeled *declination*. Later in this chapter we will examine how the difference between true and magnetic north affects using a compass.

Navigating and driving are two separate jobs. The driver must keep vigilant for other boat traffic and for snags or deadheads in the boat's path. This requires 100 percent attention. The navigator handles the chart and keeps watch for landmarks or distant aids to navigation. If you must both steer and navigate, take time to stop the boat before studying the chart. Even a few seconds of distraction can be enough time for an accident to take place.

Charts are most often used for two purposes on inland lakes and rivers. The first is to orient yourself—for example, to determine if the nearest gas dock is upstream or downstream of your present location. The second is to gain knowledge of changes in the bottom that may pose a danger to your boat. In both cases, the chart is typically folded to a convenient size to lay in the lap. From time to time the navigator orients the chart with the shoreline to get a quick visualization of what is around the boat.

If you are crossing a lake or large bay, orienting the chart is easiest done by finding two prominent landmarks at several miles' distance from the boat that are also marked on the chart. Sight across the chart at these landmarks, rotating the paper until the printed marks align with the real world.

Now that the chart is oriented, you can get a quick estimate on your boat's location. With practice it is possible to quickly locate yourself to within a few hundred feet using this procedure.

On a river, the best way to orient the chart is parallel to the flow of the water. Look for mile markers on shore and match them up with printed mile numbers on the chart. Sometimes a large structure like a highway bridge, a dam, or the smokestacks of a power plant are helpful in determining where you are on a particular stretch of river.

NOAA Charts

NOAA charts contain information about water depths, the nature of the bottom, and geographic features of coastlines. They also show the locations of aids to navigation, such as harbor lights and coast lighthouses, and the locations of buoys and other floating aids. (Mariners are advised that the location of these aids may drift somewhat due to wind or current.)

Nautical charts also display the latitude/longitude grid and a compass rose indicating the variation in magnetic directions from true north.

SMALL-CRAFT CHARTS

Until recent times, NOAA nautical charts were constructed primarily for big commercial ships and military operations. Full-size charts are intended for big ships with chart tables. As a result, they are cumbersome to use on pontoon or deckboats. To solve the problem of handling full-size charts on small boats, NOAA has published special small-craft chart books covering popular coastal boating areas.

CHART SCALES

The scale of a chart does not refer to the size of the paper it is printed on, but to the amount of detail shown on the chart. Small-scale charts show only the largest of details such as the general shape of the coastline. Ships use small-scale charts to help them navigate between ocean ports—Boston, Massachusetts to Portland, Maine, for instance. Large-scale charts show small details—down to individual docks within a harbor—with great clarity.

- **Coast Charts**—Medium scales of 1:50,000 to 1:150,000. These are for inshore navigation leading to bays and harbors of considerable width and for navigating large inland waterways. Few deckboats and almost no pontoon boats navigate on waters covered by coast charts.
- **Harbor Charts**—Larger-scale charts (e.g., 1:10,000, 1:20,000), for harbors, anchorage areas, and the smaller waterways. This scale of chart covers waters most frequented by pontoon and deckboats.

CHART SYMBOLS There are too many chart symbols to cover at length in this book. (A U.S. Coast Guard publication titled *Chart Number 1* contains a key to the chart symbols used by

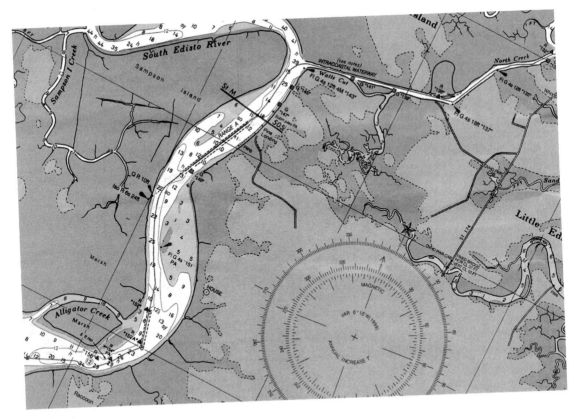

Deep water shows white on a chart. Tinted areas indicate shallow water. Look for printed depths and contour lines for indications of the slope of the bottom. (NOAA)

NOAA and other agencies.) It is imperative, however, to learn how to read water depths and bridge clearances on a chart.

Deep water is shown on NOAA charts as white areas. Blue-tinted areas are shallow water. As the depth decreases, the tinting transitions from light to darker blue. Areas that are swampy or may uncover at low water are tinted green. Land areas are shown in a distinctive buff color. Water depths on charts used by small boats are usually given in feet, or feet and fathoms (1 fathom = 6 feet). A few U.S. charts printed primarily for use by incoming foreign ships now give depths in meters.

The distance from the surface of the water to the underside of a bridge is known as *clearance*. Fixed bridges are given only one clearance, while bridges that open for water traffic are given both their closed and open clearances. Do not rely on the charted numbers. High water during flood season can significantly reduce the available clearance from what is shown on the chart.

Army Corps River Charts

There are more than 8,200 miles of navigable rivers in the United States maintained by the Army Corps of Engineers. In all, you can visit 22 of the 50 states on the nation's river system.

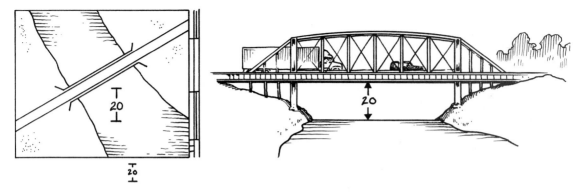

Bridge clearances published on charts are for "normal" conditions. The actual height available may vary if the water level is above or below chart datum. Checking the water level gauge on a river is a wise precaution before going under a low bridge. (Christopher Hoyt)

Charts for the nation's rivers can be obtained either electronically from the Corps' website, by mail order, or from marine stores serving major river-boating areas.

River charts are less complex than their deepwater navigational cousins. The river is shown in blue, while the commercial shipping channel is light blue. Land is shown in white, while swampy areas are tinted green. Charts are available for the following rivers:

MANITOU LEGACY

The bow of this 22-foot Manitou Legacy illustrates the creative design touches being applied to modern pontoon boats. Molded units at the corners of the foredeck contain the red and green running lights, docking lights, and the horn. The center boarding gate makes it easy to handle dock lines on the foredeck.

Huntington District
- Kanawha River
- Ohio River

Louisville District
- Ohio River
- Kentucky River
- Green River

Nashville District
- Tennessee River
- Cumberland River

Pittsburgh District
- Allegheny River
- Monongahela River, including Youghiogheny River and Tygart Valley River
- Ohio River, including Beaver River

St. Louis District
- Upper Mississippi River
- Minnesota River
- St. Croix River

Illinois Waterway

Tennessee-Tombigbee Waterway

River charts produced by the Corps of Engineers are intended primarily for commercial barge traffic. These charts show the width of the river at a condition known as "full pool." In times of flood, the river will be considerably wider than during low water times. The resulting changes in the shoreline can be confusing to anyone unfamiliar with the area. The locations of buoys shown on river charts are approximations. River channels are constantly in motion, requiring buoys to be relocated to reflect these changes.

On Corps of Engineers charts, most named sloughs, chutes, and cuts are generally safe for small boats. Outside the 9-foot deep commercial navigation channel, however, hazards may exist. All submerged features cannot be shown with precision because depths and hazards change from time to time.

Topographic and Local Maps

Inland lakes and rivers that are not considered "navigable" under federal law are often uncharted. However, state agencies often publish topographic maps primarily for use by farmers and hunters, but with considerable information of value to boat operators. Topographic maps are not generally sold at marinas and boat stores. Look for them in shops that cater to hunters and hikers.

Some states produce so-called "fishing maps" for artificial lakes and impoundments. These often display bottom information about groves of trees, old houses, or barns remaining from when the bottom was dry land prior to construction of the lake. Fish find these structures attractive. While not intended for navigation, such maps can be valuable for both orienting yourself on the surface and avoiding underwater obstructions.

Navigation Publications

Several agencies of the U.S. government, as well as various states, publish information for use by mariners. Most of these publications are aimed at commercial operators, but the information is just as useful to the pleasure-boat skipper. In addition to government publications there are a variety of private guidebooks aimed at pleasure boats.

COAST PILOT BOOKS

The National Ocean Service (NOS) office of Coast Survey, National Oceanic and Atmospheric Administration (NOAA), publishes nine different *Coast Pilot* books. These cover the Atlantic, Gulf, and Pacific coasts as well as the Great Lakes.

1. Eastport to Cape Cod
2. Cape Cod to Sandy Hook
3. Sandy Hook to Cape Henry
4. Cape Henry to Key West
5. Gulf of Mexico, Puerto Rico, and Virgin Islands
6. Great Lakes and Connecting Waterways
7. California, Oregon, Washington, and Hawaii
8. Alaska: Dixon Entrance to Cape Spencer
9. Alaska: Cape Spencer to Beaufort Sea

Coast Pilot books are meant to supplement the navigational information found on NOAA nautical charts. These books describe channels, anchorages, bridge clearances, current information, specific dangers, and small-craft facilities. Most of the waters covered by *Coast Pilot* books are outside the areas normally cruised by pontoon and deckboats. However, the detailed information on some rivers and the Intra-Coastal Waterway may make one of these editions particularly valuable to you.

LIGHT LISTS

These books are really catalogs of all the buoys, beacons, daymarks, and lights maintained by the U.S. Coast Guard. Each aid is given its unique number. The books describe the characteristics of aids and give their locations. Light Lists are divided by Coast Guard districts so they do not follow the division of *Coast Pilot* books.

1. Atlantic Coast: St. Croix River, Maine to Shrewsbury River, New Jersey
2. Atlantic Coast: Shrewsbury River, New Jersey, to Little River, South Carolina
3. Little River, South Carolina, to Econfina River, Florida
4. Gulf of Mexico
5. Mississippi River System (and tributaries)

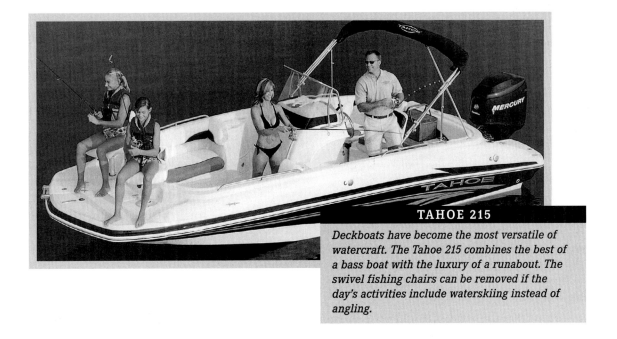

TAHOE 215

Deckboats have become the most versatile of watercraft. The Tahoe 215 combines the best of a bass boat with the luxury of a runabout. The swivel fishing chairs can be removed if the day's activities include waterskiing instead of angling.

6. Pacific Coast and Pacific Islands
7. Great Lakes

Of the seven Light Lists, Volume No. V, covering the Mississippi river system, is most valuable to inland cruising. The book covers all of the Western Rivers. Aids are listed consecutively going upriver on the Mississippi. Tributary rivers are listed separately.

QUIMBY'S GUIDEBOOKS

Privately published guidebooks contain information specific to pleasure boats. On the Western Rivers, the most widely respected is *Quimby's Cruising Guide* (formerly *Quimby's Harbor Guide*). Updated annually, it covers 9,436 miles of water on 24 rivers and the Gulf of Mexico Intra-Coastal Waterway. This book has been revised and updated every year since 1962. Starting in 2005, *Quimby's* has also been broken down into three smaller books for those who do not need the full version. These cover the Mississippi River, the Ohio Valley, and the Southern Region.

WATERWAY GUIDE

This series of publications is primarily aimed at larger boats cruising the East Coast and Great Lakes. However, the Great Lakes edition covers the Hudson River, the Erie Canal, the Champlain Waterways, and Canada's Trent-Severn and Rideau Canals. This book also covers the Illinois Waterway from Chicago to the Mississippi River, and the Tennessee-Tombigbee Waterway.

AIDS TO NAVIGATION

Aids to navigation are the fixed lights, buoys, and daymarks installed by government agencies and private individuals to guide boats. Until 2003, three different systems were in use on U.S. waterways, but the situation was far less confusing than it sounds. All three systems were based on the same concepts. Currently, the Uniform State Waterway Marking System (USWMS) is being merged with the U.S. Aids to Navigation System. You may encounter the older system for some years to come during the transition period.

Buoys and Beacons

Buoys are floating aids that come in a variety of shapes and sizes. They are moored to the bottom with concrete sinkers and a chain, so they wander a bit depending upon wind or current. Buoys convey information by their shape, color, light characteristic, number, and in some cases sound. Some coastal buoys have bells or gongs actuated by wave action.

Beacons are permanently fixed structures. They range from lighthouses to small single-pile structures. They may be located in the water or on land. Lighted beacons are called *lights*, while unlighted beacons are called *daybeacons*. They carry red or green coloring to indicate lateral significance.

In all three systems, colored buoys or lights designate the side of a channel and indicate the side on which to pass them. Generations of mariners have learned the memory aid, "Red Right Returning." Red aids should be passed on your right side when returning to port or heading upriver. Likewise, green lights or buoys should be on passed on your left side when entering a harbor. (When leaving a harbor or going downriver, pass them on the othier side.) White or yellow buoys are informational, or serve some special purpose.

Uniform State Waterway Marking System (USWMS)

This simplified buoyage system was developed primarily for lakes and rivers outside federal

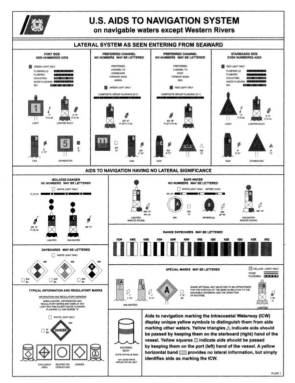

navigable waters. They are used to mark smaller inland lakes and impoundments. This system was officially discontinued on December 31, 2003, but continues to be seen, albeit with decreasing frequency as the older aids are retired. In USWMS buoyage, solid red aids mark the starboard side of the channel, while solid black aids mark the port as you enter or head upriver. Most older USWMS buoyage is being brought into conformance with the overall U.S. system by repainting the black buoys green.

State buoyage also used three Cardinal System buoys. A buoy with alternating vertical red and white stripes indicates it is not safe to pass between that buoy and the nearest shore. A black-topped white buoy indicates safe passage to the north or east of the aid, while a red-topped white buoy indicates safe passage to the south or west.

Buoys used on U.S. waters mark the sides of the channel. Red buoys with even numbers mark the right side of the channel when inbound or upriver. Green buoys mark the left side. Light colors generally match buoy colors, while the rhythms (flash patterns) indicate the purpose and importance of the buoy at night. (NOAA)

Regulatory Markers

These buoys are white spars with orange signs or symbols. A diamond inside a square indicates either a boat exclusion area (e.g., a swimming beach) or an isolated danger such as a rock. A circle inside a square is used to mark no-wake or slow speed zones.

Western Rivers Marking System

The Western Rivers are the Mississippi and all of its tributary rivers (the Ohio, Missouri, etc.) and connecting waterways. Although California's Sacramento River is "out west," it does not connect with the Mississippi, so is not a Western River. A special version of the U.S. buoyage system is used on these rivers. It is discussed in detail in Chapter 9, "River Cruising."

U.S. Lateral System

Port-hand marks are green, odd-numbered, and flat-topped if they are buoys. Green daybeacons are square. Starboard-hand marks are red, even-numbered, and buoys have a cone-shaped "nun" appearance. Various light rhythms (flashing sequences) are used so that no two adjacent buoys have a similar appearance. Buoy numbers start at the seaward entrance to a channel and increase as you go farther into the channel.

Preferred Channel Buoy

It is common on rivers for a secondary channel to split off the main fairway. When this happens the upstream buoy where the two channels meet has dual significance. It must be passed on one side for the main channel, but the other side for the secondary route. This has led to the development of the bifurcation or "preferred-channel" buoy, which is horizontally banded. The top and bottom bands show the color and lateral significance for the main channel. The middle band gives that information for the smaller waterway.

If a small channel comes off to the right while heading upstream, the preferred channel buoy will have red top and bottom stripes. This indicates you keep it to starboard while heading

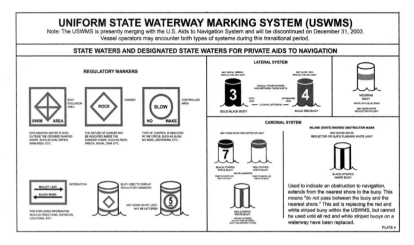

Regulatory markers are white pillar buoys with symbols and sometimes words marked on them. They indicate no wake zones, swimming areas, and dangers such as low-head dams. (NOAA)

	Fl = flashing
	Q = quick flashing
	Fl (2) = group flashing (2)
	Fl (2+1) = composite group flashing
	Mo(A) = Morse code "A"
	Iso = isophase (E Int)
	Oc = occulting

The characteristic flash of a light helps identify it at night. Lights that are on more than they are off are called occulting. Lights that show dark more than they are lighted are called flashing. The rhythm of the flashes helps identify the particular aid. The abbreviations (above right) are used on nautical charts. (Jim Sollers)

up the main channel. The middle band will be green, indicating you pass it to port when entering the secondary channel. At night, the preferred-channel buoy flashes either a green or red light in accordance with its topmost color band, marking the main channel. If the top band is red, the light will also be red and it will be kept on the right side when heading into a harbor or upriver. The pattern of flashing for these "bifurcation" buoys is always 2+1—two flashes followed by a single flash. No other buoy flashes this characteristic pattern. To remember this flashing characteristic think, "Two channels into one (2+1)."

Light Characteristics

Flashing lights on Coast Guard aids to navigation have specific patterns. These sequences of flashes help to identify the specific aid and to give some information about it.

- **Fixed**—A light that is always on and never flashes.
- **Flashing**—The duration of light is less than the duration of darkness.
- **Group flashing**—A sequence of flashes (two or three) followed by a period of darkness equal in duration to the time of the flashes.
- **Composite group**—Two flashes followed at an interval by a single flash. Used on preferred-channel buoys.
- **Isophase**—A light that is on and off equal amounts of time.
- **Morse A**—A short flash followed by a longer duration flash for Morse code letter "A."
- **Occulting**—Any light that is on for a longer duration than it is off.
- **Quick flashing**—A rapid sequence of flashes much like a strobe light.

Lights on aids to navigation may be red or green if they carry lateral significance. Lights on aids with no lateral significance may be white. Some fixed lights show sectors of different color to indicate off-lying dangers in the water. Generally, it is unsafe to operate your boat in a red sector displayed by a light on shore. Some fixed lights (lighthouses) show alternating white and either red or green. The white flash can be seen well offshore to guide you to the harbor, while the colored flash usually has lateral significance when entering.

Ranges and Range Lights

Whenever two objects on shore line up, one visually above the other, they are said to be *in range*. Hold a straight course by keeping them aligned. Steer toward the front range marker when the boat drifts off course. If the front mark appears to have moved to the left of the back, steer left to bring them back in range. Steer right if the front mark goes to the right. Official ranges installed by governmental agencies are only available on major waterways. These consist of two dayboards set some distance apart. The vertical lines painted on the boards make it easy to spot a small slide to one side or the other. Most navigational ranges have lights for night use. Pontoon and deckboat skippers operate on smaller waters where official ranges are rare. Still, the concept of two objects in range can be useful. A peculiar tree may line up with a distinctive radio antenna to provide a natural range to help you stay in the center of a channel.

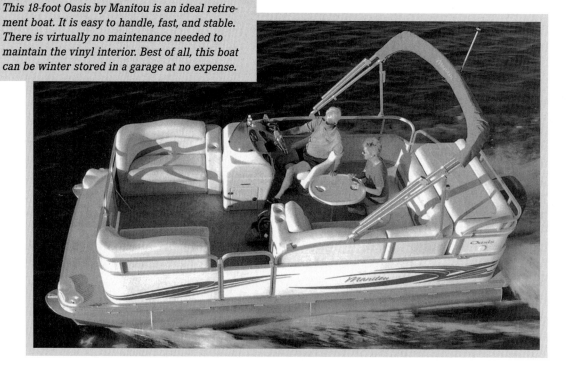

MANITOU OASIS

This 18-foot Oasis by Manitou is an ideal retirement boat. It is easy to handle, fast, and stable. There is virtually no maintenance needed to maintain the vinyl interior. Best of all, this boat can be winter stored in a garage at no expense.

Private Aids

These are buoys, daymarks, and even range lights put out by private individuals. Usually, they are maintained by a marina for the convenience of its customers. Private aids can be more useful than official government aids, or they can be totally misleading. The only way to sort out the good from bad is local knowledge. Never trust a private aid until you have full understanding of the intention behind its placement.

The compass remains the basic navigational tool despite modern electronic devices. (Ritchie Navigation)

MARINER'S COMPASS

The magnetic compass has been the mariner's trusted guide for nearly a millennium. Originally developed in China, it was the device that made possible the voyages of Christopher Columbus and other early European navigators. The idea is simple. A bar magnet suspended so that it is free to rotate will ultimately align itself with the Earth's magnetic field. Modern compasses use bundles of powerful magnets rather than a single bar, and they are suspended in low-friction liquid for smooth operation. Otherwise, they remain fundamentally the same as the ones used in Columbus's day.

Technology has developed a magnetic compass that does not require bar magnets pivoting inside a liquid. Digital, or *fluxgate*, compasses use an electronic sensor to measure the Earth's magnetic field. This measurement is then converted into either a digital numeric reading or a virtual rendering of a traditional compass display. Electronic compasses are considerably more expensive than a traditional mariner's compass.

Boats operating on narrow rivers usually do not carry compasses because a river has only two directions: upstream and down. The geographic orientation of the stream as it wanders across the land is incidental to the direction of flow. This does not mean that compasses cannot serve an important purpose on pontoon or deckboats operating on wider rivers such as the Mississippi at St. Louis. And they can be vital when boating on major lakes. Fog or rain can make familiar landmarks disappear, particularly at night. A trusty magnetic compass can help you get home when nothing else is visible.

COMPASS ERROR

The magnetic compass does not point to true north, but to the magnetic north pole, which is currently located northwest of Hudson's Bay in Canada. The magnetic pole wanders and will some day be in Siberia. The difference between the true north pole and the magnetic pole is the primary cause of a compass error known as *variation* to mariners and *declination* to those who navigate on land.

No matter what it is called, variation increases or decreases as you move around the globe. In the United States it fluctuates from almost nil to as much as 20 degrees. Charts intended for navigation show the magnetic variation at the center of each compass rose. Variation changes from year to year because the

SAILOR'S EYE

When crossing a river look for a landmark low on the far bank and a second one some distance upland behind it. Note the apparent horizontal distance between them. You are making *leeway* (moving sideways) if this apparent distance changes over a short period of time. Angle a bit more toward the distant object to adjust your leeway. Wait a few min-utes, then make a new observation and adjustment. Determining leeway in this manner is known as using a "sailor's eye." It works over a span of a few minutes only. Much longer and the boat's forward motion causes the objects to appear to grow apart because of perspective. But, over a few minutes this trick is a handy way to estimate and correct for leeway.

magnetic pole is moving. A correction factor to account for this change is also printed on the compass rose.

Magnetic materials inside the boat also cause compass errors. The iron block of the engine, magnets in radio speakers, and even pans in the galley can all cause errors in readings obtained from the boat's compass. These errors from inside the boat are lumped into the term *deviation*.

Compass errors cannot be ignored. A one-degree error over a mile of travel puts you a bit less than 100 feet off course. A 15-degree compass error crossing a 4-mile-wide lake can put you more than a mile away from your destination.

Plotting a Course

Advanced navigational techniques are outside the scope of this book, but we will touch on the basics.

For a fuller explanation see the book *Boating Skills and Seamanship* published by the U.S. Coast Guard Auxiliary. Both the U.S. Power Squadron and the U.S. Coast Guard Auxiliary offer excellent courses in small-boat navigation.

As mentioned earlier, courses are seldom plotted when cruising on a river. This is because there are only two directions: upstream and downstream. The need to plot a course comes only when you cross a wide lake or other larger body of water.

The first step to plotting a course is to consult your chart. Using a pencil, mark your starting point and your destination, then draw a straight line between them. (Naturally, landforms and hazards will often prevent you from drawing a straight line. In that case you would break the course into several *legs*. To keep things simple, however, let's stick to a single, straight line.) Once the line is drawn, you'll use the chart's compass rose or a hiking compass to determine what the course bearing is from your starting point to your destination. If the bearing is, say, 230° you'll steer your boat on a heading of 230° and—if winds and currents don't blow you off course—you should reach your destination without even looking.

It sounds simple—and it truly is—but there are a few complicating matters.

For starters, course lines drawn on a chart are expressed in the true geographic direction based on the north and south poles. The compass reading actually steered will be somewhat different because of variation and deviation. Applying corrections for compass error to true course produces a compass course by the mathematical process of *uncorrecting*. Conversely, mathematically converting from a compass heading to a true course on the chart is called *correcting*.

It is rare that any boat under 25 feet in length has a deviation table listing compass error on various headings. Without this table it is not possible to accurately correct or uncorrect courses or headings. Making the situation worse, most highway and fishing maps of inland waters lack accurate information about local magnetic variation. Not having variation or deviation numbers does not reduce the usefulness of the compass. It can still be used to orient yourself and augment or confirm what you can see with your own two eyes.

Global Positioning System

These days, a handheld GPS unit will not only give extremely precise positioning information (latitude and longitude coordinates), but it may also display your position on a map. A GPS receiver combines signals from several different satellites into geographic positioning information. Depending upon the receiver's software, it may also compute a boat's speed and direction, or keep track of where the vessel has been.

GPS receivers with built-in mapping capability are now quite common in vehicles. Some can provide the driver with turn-by-turn directions to their destination. Even small handheld units may contain maps of the whole country. While these maps are primarily designed for highway use, they are accurate enough to place your boat on a lake or river. Used in conjuction with available paper maps, GPS mapping offers benefits even on these uncharted waters.

On charted waters the Coast Guard has established a series of 55 land-based transmitter sites to improve the accuracy of of GPS receivers. These transmitters broadcast special corrections to be applied to the information obtained from the satellites. You'll need a special receiver in order to receive these ground-based radio signals; many units intended for land use lack this ability, but most marine GPS receivers will work. The ground-based signals cover all coastal waters of the United States as well as most of the Great Lakes and the Western Rivers.

River Cruising

No group of boatowners has more *esprit de corps* than "river rats." This spirit dates back at least to the mid-1800s. Sam Clemens, who would later adopt the name Mark Twain, wrote this in an 1866 letter to a friend: "The only real, independent and genuine gentlemen in the world go quietly up and down the Mississippi River." In his book *Life on the Mississippi*, Twain recalled, "A pilot, in those days, was the only unfettered and entirely independent human being that lived on the earth."

Every pilot is humbled from time to time. The course of a river is never straight, nor is the channel the same from day to day. Sandbars build and disappear. Trees wash down the banks to become lodged as snags. These age-old challenges are the same today as they were when Sam Clemens faced them. However, some things have changed for the better. The major Western Rivers are now controlled by dams that provide long stretches of clear navigation called "pools." Moving from one pool to another requires traveling through high-lift locks operated by the U.S. Army Corps of Engineers. "Locking through" is an experience Sam Clemens never encountered.

The term *Western Rivers* got its start back in the days when Sam Clemens was learning his trade as a river pilot. Prior to the Civil War, the Mississippi River was the western boundary of the United States. It really was "way out west" back then. To pilots like Clemens, *Western Rivers* meant the Mississippi and its tributaries. Today, the term encompasses many more waterways and some that simply didn't even exist 150 years ago:

- Mississippi River
- Missouri River
- Illinois River
- Ohio River
- Monongahela River
- Allegheny River
- Kanawha River
- Tennessee-Tombigbee Waterway

The term *Western Rivers* survives today even though the western boundary of the United States is the Pacific Ocean and the

Western Rivers are in the middle of the continent. U.S. rivers that do not flow into the Mississippi are by definition not Western Rivers. California's Sacramento River certainly qualifies as "out west," but by definition it is not a Western River. This is an important legal difference with regard to the Inland Rules of the Road (see Chapter 7).

Sometimes it's hard to tell where river boating ends and lake boating begins. Most of the large artificial lakes around the country are not really lakes at all, but rather impoundments of major rivers. As such, these lakes exhibit more of the characteristics of a river. The level of the lake rises or falls with the seasons, as does the stage of the river feeding each of these lakes. Also, impoundment lakes have slight currents created by the flow of water over the dams that created them.

The height of the water at any given moment is called the river's stage, *or sometimes its* gauge. *Both refer to the amount of water beneath your keel. "Normal" water level as given in the official datum height is simply an average of the highs and lows over the years. (U.S. Army Corps of Engineers)*

WATER STAGE

Boating on all rivers is much the same, although each waterway has a distinct personality. For example, the Hudson River exhibits tidal fluctuations all the way to Albany, about 150 miles north of New York City. The Ohio River, by comparison, does not have tidal variations even though it does exhibit wide changes in depth depending on the season. Most rivers have boisterous personalities in spring during winter runoff. Currents can double or triple in speed while sandbars and snags change hourly during flood season. In late summer, the same river may flow at a languid pace with a barely perceptible current.

River levels change constantly due to seasonal and daily variations in precipitation, evaporation in summer, and other factors. The height of the water at any given moment is called the river's *stage*, or sometimes its *gauge*. The terms are technically different, but from a boating standpoint both refer to the amount of water beneath your keel. The stage of a river is measured from the river's *datum*, or height of the surface of the river above sea level. Always keep in mind that datum is not "normal" water level, but an adjusted average of the highs and lows over the years.

Water is defined as high when the level is above datum, or low when it drops below datum. Flood stages are generally expressed in feet above datum. Depths printed on charts are based on this datum. If the river stage is high, you add the high water to the printed depth. However, if the water is low, you must subtract the difference from datum to get the depth of water in which you are floating. When the river stage goes below datum, be extremely cautious around wing dams, snags, sandbars, and other obstructions.

On many smaller rivers datums have either not been established or they're not easily obtained. Locals living near these rivers will have a clear knowledge of what they consider flood stage in their vicinity. And they will have a reasonably accurate estimate of the difference between the existing water level and local flood stage. They can also estimate if the river level is normal for that time of year.

Nothing guarantees that a river will be at its normal stage on any given day. Most marinas have water gauges to help boatowners judge the depth. These typically read in feet above the bottom of the river at the location of the gauge and may not indicate the official stage of the river. Government gauges are based on datum. It is necessary to learn the method of measurement used on any gauge in order to interpret the depth of water over or under datum.

Trailer boaters must be especially aware of water-gauge readings. Boat ramps can be unusable in fall or winter when the water level naturally drops, or when water in the lake has been drawn down for repairs to dams or other structures. In low water, the paved ramp may end several yards before the edge of the water. Worse, during spring flooding the ramp may be completely covered with rapidly flowing water.

Most major rivers have dams to provide a measure of flood control against spring floods. The stretch of river above a dam is called a "pool." Each pool has its unique datum, or "normal," level. Efforts are made to maintain pools at their published datums in order to provide commercial barge tows with deep water. Pool levels are maintained by reducing or increasing the flow of water over the dam as necessary. Even so, pool levels cannot always be maintained precisely. Pools are subject to fluctuation during abnormally wet springs or after a prolonged stretch of drought.

WESTERN RIVERS BUOYAGE

Like deepwater sailors, river rats have a nautical language all their own. This is an inland jargon built largely on the vocabulary of the nearby countryside.

Which Side?

Many laws, regulations, and sailing directions contain references to the side or bank of the river. This has led to an official system of naming the banks on rivers as either right or left. By convention, the right bank is on your right if you're heading downstream.

The New York State Canal System is slightly different. The right bank has been designated as the north side of the Erie Barge Canal. This puts the right bank on your right

The water level affects launching ramps. Many ramps are usable only in normal conditions. High water may flood parking lots, while low water may leave the ramp high and dry. (U.S. Army Corps of Engineers)

side when you head west from Albany to Buffalo. On the Champlain Canal, the east side is designated as the right bank.

Mileage

Locations on rivers are not established by latitude and longitude coordinates. Instead, the mileage upstream from the mouth of the river is used. Buoys and daymarks are identified by their mileage upstream as indicated on associated mile boards posted on the riverbank. Daybeacons normally have a mile board attached. Look for mile boards on bridges and other major structures. Locks and dams are also identified by their mileage numbers. In the Western River buoy system, navigation aids are not sequentially numbered as they are on coastal waters.

Crossing Daybeacons

A special navigation aid used only on rivers is a diamond-shaped dayboard. These marks do not have lateral significance, but instead mark locations where the navigation channel crosses from one bank to the other. Crossing daybeacons are always on the opposite side of the river. When you see one of these distinctive daybeacons along the river, you should steer for the diamond to stay in the channel. Treat the color of the daybeacon as a lateral channel mark. A red diamond is kept on your right side going upriver.

MANITOU OSPREY 20

No one can ask for a more stable casting platform than a pontoon boat. And, no boat can get into thinner water. Anglers are increasingly turning to boats like this Manitou Osprey 20 for the room they provide to swing a rod.

Special Marks

Isolated danger marks and safe-water marks are not used on the Western Rivers. Wrecks, hazards, and other obstructions may be marked with unlighted buoys that are not specifically identified in the Coast Guard Light List.

STATE BUOYAGE SYSTEMS

Rivers not part of the federal Western River system are buoyed and marked by state or local government agencies. Generally, the buoyage system closely matches that used on the larger, commercial rivers. However, buoys marking the deepwater channel are fewer and more widely scattered. Skippers are on their own when it comes to "reading" the river and finding the safest passage. Dams and other dangers in areas where boating traffic is heavy are the exception. They are usually well marked with white danger buoys.

The old Uniform State Waterway Marking System is still occasionally used on state waters. The main difference that may be encountered is the use of black paint instead of green on can buoys. A red and white vertically striped buoy advises that it is unsafe to pass between it and the nearest shore or bank.

BRIDGE LIGHTING AND SIGNALS

Bridges across federally navigable waters are required to display warning and informational lights. Bridges on state waters often follow the same pattern of lighting, but are not required to do so by Coast Guard regulation. On many tributary streams and small lakes, bridges do not carry any lights, so caution must be exercised at night.

Fixed Bridges

Red lights mark bridge abutments or piers to warn boats of these immovable objects. On fixed bridges, green lights mark the spans under which it is safe to pass. Boats should go between the red lights and beneath the green. If there is more than one channel through the bridge, the preferred navigation channel may additionally be marked with three white lights in a vertical line.

Drawbridges

Bridges that open for water traffic have slightly more complex lighting patterns. As before, red lights mark piers and abutments. Red lights also warn that the "draw," or opening part of the bridge, is closed. Only after the draw is fully open do these red lights change to green, indicating it is safe to proceed. Double-opening swing bridges may be lighted with three lanterns on top of the span structure so that when closed it displays three red lights to approaching boats. When open, this type of bridge displays two green lights.

Clearance Gauge

Many bridges are equipped with a vertical clearance gauge. This is a column of numbers indicating the distance from the actual waterline to the underside of the bridge. These gauges do not indicate river datum. The numbers are

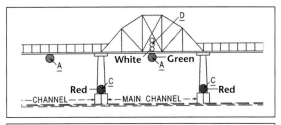

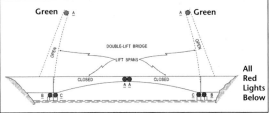

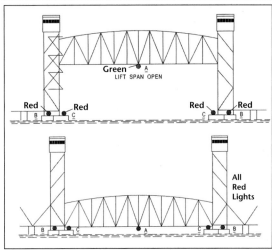

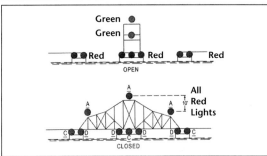

Bridges are marked with green lights to indicate where safe passage is possible. Red lights mark bridge abutments and closed sections of drawbridges. (NOAA)

placed exactly one foot apart, with the bottom of each number indicating the clearance. The spaces between numbers are 6 inches as well. If you see water at the bottom of the number "7" it indicates 7 feet of clearance from the surface of the river to the underside of the steel girders. If the waterline cuts the top of the "7" in half, the clearance is 6 feet 6 inches. It is possible to estimate vertical clearance to within 3 inches, or half the height of the numbers, using this type of gauge.

Opening Signals

A young attorney named Abraham Lincoln won the court case that allowed railroads to build bridges across federal rivers. This victory put him into the public eye. However, out of the Lincoln case came requirements that drawbridges must open for water traffic. Modern interpretation of this requirement requires bridges to open on demand for commercial traffic, but allows a more limited schedule of openings for pleasure boats. Bridges in urban areas typically open only on the hour and half hour for pleasure boats. Where there are several bridges in close proximity, these openings may be sequential so that only one bridge of the series is opened at a time. Information about bridge openings is posted on a sign attached to the bridge or its approach wall.

By federal regulation, you may request an opening only if your vessel will not fit beneath the span after you have lowered all "appurtenances not necessary to navigation." In simple terms this requires the lowering of radio antennas and other similar equipment. Starting in 2006, bridge tenders (the people operating the bridge) have been asked to report pleasure vessels that refuse to lower swing-down antennas or outriggers. Such refusal is a violation of federal regulations and the operator may be fined. Of course, there is nothing wrong with taking advantage of a scheduled opening to go through with a group of boats. The problem arises only when a solo boat improperly requests an opening to clear those "appurtenances not necessary to navigation." Fortunately, deckboats and pontoon boats can scoot under the majority of closed drawbridges without ever needing to signal for an opening. The exception comes during spring when high water significantly reduces clearance.

In this unlikely event, it's necessary to signal the bridge tender that an opening is desired. This can be done by whistle or VHF radio. If using a whistle, the standard bridge signal is a prolonged 4- to 6-second blast followed by a short 1-second blast. The bridge tender acknowledges receipt of this signal by responding with a prolonged and a short blast if the bridge will open or 5 short blasts if the bridge cannot open.

Most U.S. bridges monitor Channel 13 on VHF marine radio. Using 1-watt transmitting power, call using the exact name or description of the bridge and not just the words "bridge tender." Most rivers have two or more bridges in radio range, so there will be confusion unless you specify a particular bridge. This sort of confusion over which bridge was talking to what boat caused the Federal Communications Commission to authorize specific bridges in Florida and some parts of Georgia and South Carolina to monitor Channel 9 instead of 13. The channel the bridge tender monitors is posted on the bridge.

The bridge tender also sounds five or more short blasts if the tender must close the draw for some emergency while you are either approaching or passing through. If approaching, you should immediately stop or maneuver not to go through the draw. If you are already in the draw, you must clear the area as rapidly as possible with due regard for the safety of other vessels.

A word of thanks on the radio or a friendly wave of the hand after passing through a bridge is proper, especially if you have to pass through the bridge again on your way back later that day.

READING A RIVER

Rivers are constantly changing. Mud and sand scoured from the bottom by floodwaters may build a sandbar a hundred miles downriver. Trees floating downstream eventually become snags that await the unwary even in deep water. A river pilot quickly learns that just because there is water ahead doesn't mean it can be crossed safely in a boat. Depths as shallow as three inches look exactly the same from a distance as the main shipping channel with thirty times that much water.

Currents and Hazards

Every river has a main current where the bulk of its water flows. This main current increases during floods, and decreases in dry seasons. It may also decrease below a control dam when flow over the spillway is restricted. The main current picks the path of least resistance, which is generally the deepest part of the channel. Flow usually decreases in shallow waters close to the banks.

The constant flow of river current means that your boat is always in motion until you tie up or anchor. Even in neutral, your boat continues to drift downstream at the speed of the flow. Full understanding the role current plays in maneuvering is necessary when docking or entering confined waters such as locks. In most cases, it is easiest to dock when heading into the current. Ease the throttle back until your boat is virtually standing still. Turning the wheel toward the pier will bring the boat sideways into the dock almost as if by magic. The same trick in reverse can be used to depart a dock.

A savvy river pilot estimates the speed of a current by careful observation of the water. Currents less than 3 miles per hour have little visible effect. As the speed increases, buoys and other fixed objects in the stream begin to develop small V-shaped wave patterns (like a boat wake) pointing upstream against the current. Above 6 miles per hour, a floating buoy will "lean" downstream with the current. As the water speed increases, the buoy's V-shaped wake increases in size and its downstream lean becomes more pronounced until—on occasion—the whole buoy is dragged beneath the surface. Don't assume, therefore, that a missing buoy has been carried away; it may still be in position, but pushed underwater by strong currents or high waters. Here the buoy becomes an unseen hazard to your propeller. A fast current can also disguise other dangers such as snags and deadheads (see below).

It can be extremely difficult to maneuver a boat in fast-moving water. During a simple turn, the current can turn your boat sideways and push it downstream toward danger. Eddies and whorls often develop in strong currents. Skillful boat handling can overcome these dangers, but the risks are seldom worthwhile.

Natural Channel

The natural channel is not always in the center of the river. Rather, it tends to favor the outside

---

DOWN ON THE UPSIDE?

Here's an interesting twist: rivers don't always flow downhill. Certain rivers are heavily influenced by ocean tides and other factors. The Hudson River, for example, is tidal for 150 miles upstream to Albany. In Ohio, the Maumee and Portage Rivers temporarily flow uphill for six or more miles inland whenever the water level rises quickly on Lake Erie. For these reasons, anyone trailering to an unfamiliar stretch of river should seek local knowledge about such unexpected conditions.

---

of bends. Flowing water is an efficient earth mover. At a bend in a river, for instance, the more rapid current scours the bottom at the outside of a bend, while the slower-moving water along the inside of the bend drops silt and sand. This is why boats looking for deep water favor the outside of bends.

Bars

Sand and mud bars build up anywhere the river current slows enough to cause the suspended solids to precipitate. As mentioned above, bars are most often found along the inside bank of a bend in the river. They also tend to form downstream of islands. Expect bars to build wherever the speed or direction of the current changes. Conversely, expect them to disappear if current flow increases or changes direction. This is why bars shift or move around, often with surprising speed. A bar can form or be washed away in hours during flood season. Even in late summer when currents are slow, bars have been known to move over the span of a few days. This shifting character of bars makes it impossible to chart their location with accuracy.

Spotting a bar can be difficult. The surface of the water across one may be as smooth and unbroken as over deep water. More often, however, there will be subtle differences in the appearance of the surface. The pattern of waves over the bar may be different, or the water may appear smoother than the rest of the river. On some occasions the water may have a different color. The rolling swell of a boat wake often gives away the location of a bar by changing to a plunging whitecap on top of the shallow water. Standing waves are another tip-off. Any wave that appears to stand in one spot is a prime indicator of shallow water. Shore birds are another indicator. It is not unusual to see birds congregating in shallow water surrounding bars.

Deadheads are logs that point toward the surface like spears. Boats that strike a deadhead can be holed and sunk. This innocent-appearing chunk of wood is actually the butt of a section of tree more than 20 feet long.

Deadheads and Snags

Erosion of riverbanks is a natural geological process. Rivers often claim full-grown trees as a result. When a tree succumbs to erosion, it floats away with branches and leaves high. As time passes, however, the leaves are stripped away and twigs and branches break off. Eventually, only a waterlogged trunk remains. These trunks often float vertically with one end high out of the water. This end of a floating trunk is a *deadhead*. It can be extremely difficult to see by day and virtually invisible at night. Deadheads are a major hazard to high-speed boating.

Not all deadheads occur naturally. Keep a lookout for fence posts, utility poles, patio furniture, and even propane tanks on rivers in the spring or following a period of unusually heavy rainfall. A large number of factory-made deadheads wash away from homes and businesses during even a minor flood. River boating after a flood is best confined to daylight operation or curtailed entirely until the river's natural cleansing process gets things back to normal.

Snags are sections of trees, pieces of utility pole, or other objects that get stuck in the bottom. Over time, the force of moving water rotates them around so their upper ends point downstream with the current. The result is an unseen underwater lance with its butt anchored in the mud and its point aimed to puncture an unwary boat. In Sam Clemens's time, the majority of wrecks were caused by steamboats skewering their hulls on snags that smashed through their wooden hulls. Today, snags more often result in bent propeller blades and damaged lower units. Still, fiberglass pleasure boats have been holed and sunk by them. Snags are most common close to the banks or in other areas of shallow water.

Sand Boils

Sand boils are whirlpools that bring sand from the river bottom in an impressive upwelling. Less spectacular whirlpools can be found in the turbulent water below dams. Both can cause a boat to spin out of control or capsize. Sand boils and whirlpools can be spotted during daylight, but may be almost undetectable at night.

Wind and Waves

Air blowing across water experiences less friction than air blowing across land. This explains why winds and breezes tend to follow the course of a river. A boat going into the wind will have a pleasant, cooling breeze. This is because the speed of the real wind is added to the boat speed to give a higher apparent wind over the deck. Conversely, a boat will experience almost dead air if the wind is traveling at the same speed and direction as the boat.

When the wind opposes a river current, short choppy waves develop. These waves build quickly, often within a few minutes. When wind opposes current, the resulting waves can sometimes appear to stand still for extended periods of time. Or, the waves may move slowly downstream in opposition to the wind. While this type of wave seldom builds to dangerous heights, it can provide a bone-jarring experience to passengers in a boat running at high speed.

DAMS AND FLOOD CONTROL

All of the Western Rivers and most navigable nonfederal rivers have dams that provide deep water for navigation and serve as flood control.

Major rivers are controlled by dams to control flooding and allow for commercial barge traffic. Locks allow barges and pleasure boats to go safely around the dams. (U.S. Army Corps of Engineers)

Some dams have locks that move boats from one side to the other.

Many dams serve as hydroelectric stations; they are large, marked with warning buoys, and generally easy to spot. Other dams, however, are less apparent.

Wing Dams

Erosion control structures called *wing dams* protect the banks along many stretches of river. Wing dams are carefully noted on Corps of Engineers river charts, but may not be marked with buoys or lights. The rock or masonry walls of a wing dam are set at an angle downstream from the bank, but they do not extend into the navigable channel and they never completely cross the river. Wing dams are seldom solitary, but are found as a series of structures. Occasionally they are built in pairs, a dam extending from each bank, leaving only a gap in the middle for the channel. Paired wing dams help to force the current into the center of the river where it works to keep the shipping channel clear of silt.

Low-Head and Roller Dams

Many smaller rivers and tributaries still have hidden dangers left over from the days of water-powered gristmills. These are so-called low-head dams built to create millponds. In some places there are similar but more modern flood-control structures called roller dams. Both low-head and roller dams are often triangular-shaped structures built across the flow of the river. The pointed top is usually rounded for easier water flow. At low water these dams are visible, but easy to overlook. Both types sink beneath the surface during floods, at which time the smooth flow of water over these structures makes them virtually impossible to spot from upstream.

Unwary high-speed boats have literally launched themselves into midair by running over low-head dams. Worse, underpowered boats have been swept over the crests of these hidden dams despite the best efforts of their operators. Difficulty spotting low-head dams is one reason states like Pennsylvania require warning buoys upstream of the danger.

Approaching from downstream can be equally dangerous. Water pouring over a low-head dam creates powerful, unpredictable forces on the downstream side. A boat venturing too close to the roiling water below a dam can be pulled upstream under the waterfall. This almost always causes a capsize. People thrown into the water at the foot of a dam often drown. The force of the roiling water even overcomes a PFD. When approaching a roller dam from downstream, never move closer than several hundred feet.

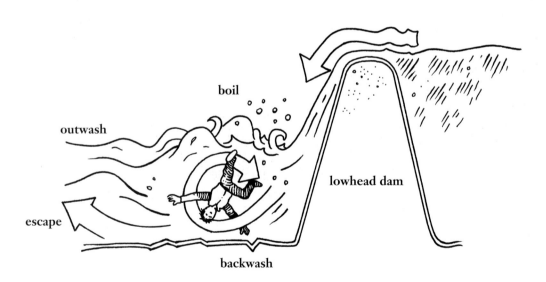

Hydraulic currents below dams can pull boats into danger and cause them to capsize. Even a PFD may not keep passengers from being pulled underwater. Look for warning buoys, but in any case stay well clear of all dams and similar structures. (Christopher Hoyt)

LOCKS

The hydraulic lock was one of the first inventions of the Industrial Revolution. The basic concept has not changed in more than two centuries. A lock is just a large concrete or stone chamber with opening gates at either end. The water level inside the lock can be raised by filling the chamber with water from the upstream side. Or, the level can be lowered by releasing water from the chamber at the downstream end. Boats or barges inside the chamber are lifted or lowered by the changing water level.

Lock gates are designed so that they can only open when the water levels on both sides of the door are the same. For instance, if the water is at the lower level, only the downstream gate is free to open to let boats enter the chamber. Once the downstream gate is closed, rising water in the lock chamber pushes the angled

Locks on major rivers are designed to serve commercial barge tows. The walls are rough and unfriendly to pleasure boats. Knowing how to rig fenders and secure your boat in a lock will prevent damage. "Locking through" is part of the adventure of river boating. (U.S. Army Corps of Engineers)

lower gates closed. The upper gates likewise remained pinned closed until the level in the lock reaches that of the upper river. At that

ESCAPE

Big fun comes in a little package from Escape. This 13-foot deckboat has seating for six and a canopy for sun protection. It is powered by a 48-volt electric motor for silent, pollution-free operation.

point, the upper doors are free to swing open and the boats are able to leave the lock on the upstream side.

The ingenious thing about river locks is that no mechanical pumps are needed to operate them. All of the work is done by gravity, relying on the principle that water seeks its own level.

Pecking Order

Some lock systems like Canada's Trent-Severn Waterway or Ohio's Muskingum River are used solely by pleasure boats. On the Western Rivers, however, pleasure boats share the water with commercial barge tows. The differences among the various types of vessels using the river forced the adoption of a pecking order for who gets locked through first:

1. Military, law enforcement, and government vessels
2. Vessels carrying U.S. Mail
3. Commercial passenger vessels
4. Commercial cargo vessels
5. Pleasure boats

The person in charge of the lock is the lockmaster. It pays to maintain the friendliest of relationships with lockmasters, as their decisions are final on who gets into their locks and when those boats get locked through.

Equipment Needed

The amount of special equipment needed to successfully lock through has decreased in recent years. The introduction of floating bollards (see below) has all but eliminated the need to carry long lock lines and rugged fenders. However, experienced river rats know that not all locks have been modernized and occasionally those bollards are out of service. So, they still carry fenders and a few extra lengths of rope just in case. Every boat entering a lock needs:

- **PFDs**—Every member of the crew handling lines must be wearing a life jacket. It should be a standard PFD, not an inflatable.
- **Work Gloves**—Blisters are likely when handling lock lines barehanded. Cotton or leather-palm work gloves protect hands from rope burns.
- **Air Horn**—A handheld air horn is needed for signaling the lockmaster. Built-in electric boat horns generally cannot be heard by lockmasters.
- **Fenders**—Lock walls are either concrete or stone, both equally destructive to fiberglass and aluminum. Stout fendering is needed.
- **Lock Lines**—Two lines at least 100 feet long are needed. One should be carried forward and the other aft just in case the lock does not provide a floating bollard system.

Approaching a Lock

Never approach a lock without first looking for commercial river traffic. Small boats and big barge tows have to share the same navigation channel in and out of locks. How close pleasure boats approach to the lock itself depends upon the waterway. On some rivers, pleasure boats are requested to stay 400 feet away from locks until signaled to enter. Other waterways require pleasure boats to dock at a designated location to announce their intention to lock through. If a whistle signal is required to indicate your intention, it is a prolonged blast followed by a short blast. Many small boat horns, however, are not loud enough to be heard by the lockmaster.

Some locks will have telephones, pull-chains, or signal buttons installed on the approach walls. If a telephone call box has been provided, this is the preferred method for small-craft skippers to contact the lockmaster. Instructions for using the telephone will be posted.

Operators at Corps of Engineers locks monitor VHF Channel 13. This channel is reserved for lock operations and commercial bridge-to-bridge radio traffic. Pleasure boats may hail locks on Channel 13 after monitoring to make sure there is no ongoing radio traffic. Use the exact name of the lock when you hail and identify your boat by name and radio call sign as well as a brief description and the direction from which you are approaching:

> Muskingum River lock number five, this is the pontoon boat *Silver Streak* approaching from downriver. I would like to request passage through your lock. Over.

Keep radio transmissions short and to the point. Your voice will boom into the small lockmaster's office. Wait a reasonable length of time for a reply. If a tow is passing through the lock all of the lockmasters may be busy and won't answer your call immediately.

Entering a Lock

Locks on the major rivers are equipped with colored signal lights to control boat traffic. These lights use the familiar red, yellow, and green lights of highway traffic lights.

- **Flashing red** tells approaching vessels to stay well clear of the lock and not to enter.
- **Flashing yellow** indicates it is safe to approach the lock at a no-wake speed.

Pleasure boats in a group should approach in single file. Do not enter the lock under a flashing yellow light.
- **Flashing green** means it is safe to enter the lock at a no-wake speed.

Some locks still use sound signals to indicate when it is safe to enter. Generally, five short blasts means to stay clear. One prolonged blast followed by one short blast means it's time to enter the lock chamber. Some locks use both flashing lights and sound signals. This is particularly true of tandem locks where two locks lie side by side. Whistle signals indicate which chamber to enter:

One prolonged whistle indicates that you should enter the lock closest to shore, or the *landward lock*.

Two prolonged whistles instruct vessels to enter the outer chamber, or *riverward lock*.

Boats always enter locks at idle speed. Before going through the lock gates have your crew don PFDs and stand by with lock lines ready. The lockmaster will instruct you where to tie up along the lock wall. Only after you enter do you know for certain on which side to rig fenders. To save time and aggravation, many experienced river skippers simply hang fenders on both sides of their boats.

Stone or concrete lock-chamber walls reflect sound, creating an echo-chamber effect. The sound of boat engines bouncing around in a lock can be deafening. In deep locks there is also concern for a potentially toxic carbon monoxide buildup. For these reasons, most lockmasters require that all engines (including electrical generators) be shut down after the boat is secured to the lock wall.

BOLLARDS AND LINES
The eighteenth-century method of controlling a boat inside a lock is with lines looped over

bollards atop the lock walls. Two lines are needed, one at the bow and the other at the stern. Secure one end of each line to the boat. The other end then goes around a bollard on the lock wall and back down to a deckhand on the boat. When locking down, line is paid out. Going up requires hauling in line. Lines must be at least double the length of the rise or fall of water in the lock (known as the *lift*). If the lock has a 15-foot lift, a minimum of 30 feet of line is needed, plus enough for securing to the boat.

Some locks have small-craft lines permanently attached to bollards. These eliminate the need for boats to carry and stow long lock lines. While an improvement, lock-supplied lines are universally rough and dirty. Gloves are a must when handling them. A better system consists of vertical steel cables fastened to the top and bottom of the lock walls. A loop of line around one of these cables can slide up or down as the lock water level changes. Savvy skippers carry oversize snap hooks for the purpose because metal hooks slide better on the cables. The latest improvement to locks is the floating bollard system. The floating bollards are recessed into vertical grooves in the lock walls and move up or down according to the water level. No matter which system is used, the boat end of the attachment should be attended by a deckhand at all times just in case it becomes necessary to cut loose.

LOCK CURRENTS AND EDDIES

Draining or filling a lock creates eddies and currents within the chamber. As a result, boats tend to "dance" along the lock walls as they rise and fall. The least amount of movement occurs when locking down. Considerable motion should be expected during up-bound locking, especially if the lockmaster fills the chamber rapidly. The members of your crew tending the lines will have their hands full. A third deck-

hand should be given the job of keeping fenders in place.

Leaving a Lock

Do not restart engines until instructed to do so by the lockmaster. Permission to exit the lock will come only after the gates are fully opened. Do not weave around the opening gates or pass other boats on the way out of the chamber.

When locking down-bound it is wise to remember that the lock is associated with a dam. Discharge water from the dam can cause turbulence in the river for some distance downstream.

Just as there are special signals for entering, tandem locks have sound signals for departing. One short whistle indicates that boats are free to leave the landward lock. Two short whistles tell boats to depart the riverward lock.

COMMERCIAL RIVER TRAFFIC

Most people think of towing as pulling another boat at the end of a hawser. Not so on the Western Rivers; nearly all "towing" is done by pushing. A small but powerful towboat behind a "stick" of barges pushes them to their destination. All types of cargo are moved this way, but the most popular are bulk commodities like grain, petroleum, and minerals. A stick of barges may actually be carrying as much cargo as the largest of ocean-going ships.

It is prudent to stay as far away from towboats and their barges as possible. To move all that weight takes power. Towboats are deceiving in size. They're really just floating engine rooms that can disturb a lot of water and capsize an unwary boat.

In deep water, a towboat's wake rolls out

behind in the familiar deep V shape of other vessels. The waves produced are swells that dissipate rather quickly. Things change in shallow waterways. The V shape widens as the water gets shallower. In waters less than 30 feet deep, a towboat wake usually comes off the stern almost at right angles. Worse, its leading edge is a near-vertical wall of plunging water. This sort of wake has the power to capsize small craft. These waves can also wash over the top of a boat like a waterfall, swamping it almost instantly. Pleasure boats must avoid cutting across the wake of a nearby towboat.

When giving a barge tow a wide berth, be sure to avoid the shallows near the bank. River rats say the tows "suck the bank dry." The saying is not far from the truth. The trough of a tow's wake arrives before the wave and this pulls water away from the bank. This means that boats near the bank can be set down on the muddy bottom just before the peak of the wave crashes ashore.

Much like a fog at sea, the bends and twists of the river effectively mask one barge tow from another, so warning whistle signals are used. You'll often hear a prolonged blast sounded by a towboat as it nears a sharp bend in the river to warn other vessels of its presence. The electric horns on pleasure boats are seldom powerful enough to penetrate into the pilothouse of a towboat. You may hear the warning blast of a tow around the bend, but it is unlikely the towboat operator will hear your horn. So, engaging in "whistle talk" is usually not productive. If you feel it's prudent to talk to a towboat pilot, make contact on VHF Channel 13. Most commercial vessels monitor this frequency. If that fails, try Channel 16.

Tows at Night

Pleasure boats often overtake tows on major rivers and their connected lakes. During the day

On the Western Rivers nearly all towing is done by pushing. A barge tow pushes a lot of water around when it moves; its powerful stern wake can capsize unwary small craft. (U.S. Army Corps of Engineers)

this presents no problems as the towboat and barges are visible. At night, however, towing lights are indispensable. Coming up from astern of a towboat, you will not see the usual white stern light. Instead, there will be two yellow towing lights. These show through the same arc of visibility of the white stern light that they replace. You can remember that two yellow lights in a vertical line indicate a barge tow with the phrase: "Yellow over yellow, I'm pushing a fellow."

A barge tow will display red and green sidelights both on the towboat and at the front of the stick of barges. Because the tow may be three or four barges wide, there is a large gap between these sidelights, which might fool an unwary skipper into thinking there was nothing ahead but open river. To prevent this type of accident, barge tows also display a "special flashing light" between the red and green lights on the barges. The characteristics of a special flashing light are:

- Yellow light
- Flashes 50 to 70 times per minute

Lights for Power-Driven Vessels Under Way

Deciphering Lights at Night

starboard side view   bow   stern

If you see this at night . . .

Under 164 ft. (50 m), masthead light, sidelights, and sternlight.

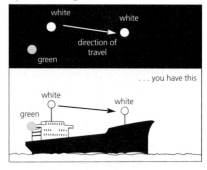

Over 164 ft. (50 m).

Lights When Towing

Under 164 ft. (50 m), two white steaming lights and towing light aft (yellow over white).

If you see this at night . . .

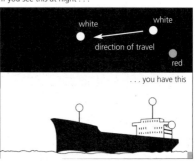

Vessel being towed shows sidelights and sternlight.

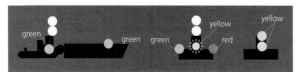

If tow is over 657 ft. (200 m), three steaming lights.

Lights When Pushing

If the two white lights are aligned . . .

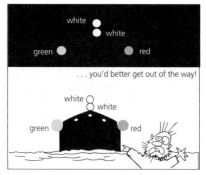

In inland waters only, the lights are as shown, with the yellow bow light flashing. In international waters, there is no yellow bow light, and the two yellow stern lights are replaced by a white stern light.

At night, the bow of a barge tow shows a special flashing yellow (amber) light between its red and green side-lights. The towboat also shows red and green lights, but not white masthead lights. Astern, the towboat shows two yellow towing lights in a vertical line instead of a white stern light. (Jim Sollers)

- Shows forward through arc of 180 to 225 degrees

For all practical purposes, a special flashing light is a hazard blinker on the bow of the barge tow. It is there to alert you that something big is coming. If you see one approaching, steer a course at a right angle to the tow's course until you can see the red or green sidelight. Only then are you outside the path of the approaching tow.

Under the Inland Rules of the Road, towboats are not required to show white masthead lights when pushing ahead. This rule acknowledges the problems associated with raising and lowering masts to go under the many bridges across the nation's river system. So when approaching a tow, do not expect to see any masthead lights.

Towboats are equipped with powerful carbon-arc spotlights. These are used to detect dangers ahead as well as to maintain distance off the river bank. It is not unusual that the loom of a spotlight will be the first indicator that a barge tow is about to come around the bend. Getting caught in the beam of an arc light can be blinding. Most towboat operators avoid shining their lights on boats for this reason (it is also against the Rules of the Road). Chances are, if you get hit by a towboat spotlight beam it is because the operator is either unsure of what you are doing, or is warning you that you are doing something he considers dangerous.

Hanging on the Bank

Towboats often drop off one or more barges along the bank of a river. Later, another tow will come along to pick up those barges and take them to their final destination. Tying a barge to the bank this way is called *hanging a barge*. Plea-sure boats often "hang" themselves on the bank in order to get a night's sleep. While this is a time-honored method of securing for the evening, you should make sure the property owner will not object. It's best to go up a slough (the mouth of a wide creek) to find a stretch of bank protected from the wakes of passing towboats.

The key to hanging along the bank is a solid tie point on shore. Sometimes, nature provides a tree in the perfect spot. Usually, however, it is necessary to create what is called a *deadman* in the ground. Some people carry steel bars, which can be driven into the ground for this purpose. If driven far enough, a steel bar works well. The problem comes in the morning, when getting the bar back out of the ground can be a chore and a half. An anchor with wide flukes can be forced into sand to create a snug anchorage. Some boats carry screw anchors similar to those used to secure mobile homes. These can be driven into the ground and later removed by turning a special crank-like handle.

Even in a protected slough it pays to keep the stern, with its valuable propellers, out in deep water. One way to achieve this is to drop a stern anchor a couple of hundred feet away from the bank as you approach it, and pay out the line as you nudge the boat up to shore. At night, haul in the stern anchor line and pay out the bow line until the boat rides a safe distance offshore. Most people sleep aboard while "hung off" the bank. If you do, be sure to place a white light where it can best be seen by passing river traffic. This light is required by the Rules of the Road. Marine stores sell all-around white anchor lights that are perfect for this purpose. The new LED lights use so little current that they can burn all night without draining the boat's starting battery.

Tent camping ashore has been traditional while cruising the rivers. These days, the threat of lawsuits has many property owners a bit nervous about permitting such activity. Look for signs showing that the land is posted against trespassing. If possible, choose public land for overnight camping. Always remember the camper's golden rule, "leave nothing behind but your footprints."

Maintenance
and Customizing

Boatownership takes work. This is as true of modern fiberglass and aluminum boats as it was of wooden craft in the days of yearly scraping, painting, and varnishing. The difference is that synthetic materials and better maintenance products have eased the burden of keeping a pontoon or deckboat in showroom condition and operating at peak performance.

Perhaps the biggest mistake most owners make is thinking of annual boat maintenance as drudgery. Sure, it's work, but it's the kind that lets the family get together on a project. Spiffing up the boat each spring is a great time to make plans for the coming summer. Kids will learn a valuable lesson when their work and planning come together in a family adventure on the water.

SIMPLE TOOL KIT

Every boat needs a basic tool kit for those unexpected minor repairs on the engine, electrical system, or plumbing. The exact choice of tools is a matter of personal taste. Instead of collecting a random assortment of tools, it's easier to

READ THE MANUAL

Before turning a wrench, read the operating manual that comes with your boat. Learn the specified intervals for changing the oil or checking trim-tab fluids. Find the specifications of lubricants and fluids. Not all oil is the same. The light mineral oil in a hydraulic steering system is far different from the 10W-40 that lubricates the engine. Some transmissions use oil from the engine crankcase, while others need special transmission fluids. Don't guess about these things. Read the instruction manual. If in doubt, see your authorized dealer for assistance. Oils and lubricants sold by engine manufacturers are a bit more expensive than generic aftermarket products. For the price comes the peace of mind of using the specified product.

purchase a ready-made tool kit in a molded plastic case. These kits can be found in hardware and boat stores at prices ranging from less than $20 to more than $200. The more expensive marine kits have stainless steel tools intended for saltwater boating. There is little need to pay extra for stainless tools for use on freshwater lakes and rivers. An occasional wipe-down with a moisture-displacing spray, like WD-40, will keep tools in serviceable condition. Corrosion is not the biggest threat to boat tools. Many are accidentally dropped overboard long before corrosion becomes an issue.

Minimum Tool Kit

Tools are expensive. If you're on a tight budget, you can get by with just these tools:

- Screwdrivers (¼-inch straight and #2 Phillips)
- 6-inch slip-joint pliers
- 8-inch adjustable wrench
- 6-inch long-nosed pliers
- Spark plug socket and ratchet wrench
- Knife
- Tape measure

Additional Tools

If money is no object, it's best to carry these tools onboard:

- Combination wrench set (SAE or metric, depending upon the engine)
- Socket set (SAE or metric)
- 10-inch arc-joint pliers
- Torx screwdriver
- Hammer
- Hacksaw
- Wire-connector crimping tool

Tool Boxes

Avoid metal tool boxes. Their sharp corners and hard sides can scratch or chip fiberglass, and steel boxes can leave rust stains where they are stored. Plastic toolboxes don't rust or chip gelcoat. Instead of an ordinary carpenter's box, however, choose one of the watertight containers sold by marine stores. A sealed box protects tools better from the moisture.

SEASONAL MAINTENANCE

Boating work follows a seasonal cycle. There is something about the first warm day of spring that draws people to work on their boats. Spring is when most of the cleaning, polishing, and painting get done. Fall's hint of frost prompts winterizing to protect the boat from winter's icy blast. Summer is when maintenance tends to be overlooked in favor of warm sun and sparkling water. Fortunately, Mother Nature provides a few rainy weekends for those necessary routine tasks.

Spring Commissioning

In nautical parlance, a boat is *commissioned* when it is made ready for use after a period of storage. In northern climates, this process has three components. One is to undo the winterization done the previous fall (see below). A second is to clean and prepare the boat for the coming season. And the third is to apply antifouling (paint) to the bottom.

ENGINE MAINTENANCE
Sterndrive Engines Most engines are laid up "wet" these days. This means that in the fall the

Sterndrive engines are fully mounted inside the hull of the boat—only the drive itself is on the outside. Most sterndrive engines are gasoline engines derived from passenger car production. These engines are "marinized" with spark-protected electrical parts, water-jacketed exhaust manifolds, and many internal changes. (Mercury Marine)

cooling system is filled with an antifreeze that is nontoxic to aquatic life. Nothing special needs to be done in the spring to remove this product other than to start the engine. An engine that is laid up "dry" had been drained of all water in the fall. In the spring it is necessary to check that all drain plugs have been replaced and are tight.

Engine fogging is the process of applying corrosion protection to the cylinder walls, pistons, and other internal parts. Fogging procedures vary depending upon the type of carburetion or fuel injection. Many mechanics remove spark plugs to spray fogging oil into the cylinders. Typically, the plugs are left loose until spring when they must be retightened. Fogging oil burns away with the first startup of the spring, and will cause a plume of white or bluish-white smoke for a few seconds.

Rubber parts like belts and hoses should be checked for signs of wear or age. In the past, the V-belts driving the engine's water pump or alternator would *take a set*—develop permanent bends that cause belt failure—over the winter. This led to many people loosening the tension on these belts in the fall. Modern belts are not plagued by set problems, but the loosening of belts continues as habit. Check each belt in spring. Unexpected looseness may be an indication that a belt is stretching and about to fail.

Engine lube oil should have been changed in the fall. If not, change it now. But either way, double-check that the level is up to the "full" mark on the dipstick.

Four-Stroke Outboard Motors Spring commissioning of a four-stroke outboard is much the same as a sterndrive engine (above). Like

---

151

CHECKLIST

After a few years of boat ownership, the tasks of spring commissioning become fairly routine. This is when memory failure can strike. Forgetting a single item can be costly. More than one engine has been destroyed by an owner who forgot to refill the oil. Outboard and I/O gearcase problems begin with failure to maintain the gearcase lubricant. Other lapses of memory are just unpleasant, like taking a swig of water from a tank that has not been properly cleared of non-toxic winter antifreeze.

Make a checklist of jobs that need doing. Write your list on a 3-by-5-inch file card, which slips easily into a shirt pocket where it stays out of the way until you need to check off a completed task or remind yourself of the next job. The spring commissioning card later serves as a guide for preparing a checklist for fall layup. Keep both of this year's cards to help prepare next year's checklists.

sterndrive engines, a four-stroke outboard should be fogged in the fall to prevent cylinder corrosion. Changing spark plugs each spring helps ensure smooth operation, but don't change the plugs until the fogging oil has burned away. Immediately after the engine starts, check the water discharge to be sure the pump is circulating cooling water. If there is no telltale stream of water, shut the engine down immediately and determine why the pump is not working. Because these motors produce so much power out of a small package, it is wise to be extra vigilant in checking lube oil level before the first start of the season. The toothed drive belt that powers the camshaft should get special consideration. Replace it when there is any sign of wear, or at the intervals recommended by the manufacturer. Internal engine damage from pistons clashing with the intake and exhaust valves is likely if the teeth on the belt slip on the toothed camshaft drive wheel.

Two-Stroke Outboard Motors An engine that was properly fogged the previous fall needs very little spring commissioning. Make sure the lube oil reservoir is full, squeeze the fuel primer bulb, and a two-stroke outboard should start and run. After startup, check the discharge to be sure the water pump is circulating cooling water. If there is no telltale stream of water, shut the engine down immediately and determine why the pump is not working. Once the fogging oil has burned away, let the powerhead cool, then change the spark plugs for a season of trouble-free operation.

I/O and Outboard Lower Units I/O drives have one or two oil reservoirs for the gear lube, depending on the make and model. Double-check that both are full. Outboard engines have lube oil only in the the gearcase of the lower unit (aka *the bullet*). Both I/O and outboard lower units have two plugs: a drain/fill plug, and an air vent. The vent is the upper plug, while the oil is both drained and filled through the lower plug. The procedure for filling is to force gear lube into the bottom plug while expelling air out the top. Lube oil should never be poured into the upper vent hole as this is sure to underfill the reservoir, causing worn gears and bearings. These days it costs about $1,500 to say, "I thought you filled the lower unit."

STEERING GEAR

Proper steering is vital to safe operation. Each spring the entire system should be checked for loose bolts or other signs of trouble. Observe the operation to make sure nothing is binding or preventing full movement of the outboard motor or I/O lower unit. Apply grease as needed to pivot points or cable attachments.

Two types of steering can be found on pontoons and deckboats. The most common system uses a mechanical push/pull cable. Hydraulic steering is less common. Mechanical systems consist of a helm (i.e., steering wheel assembly), the push/pull cable (or cables), and the engine connection. The helm converts the turning of the steering wheel into a push or pull on the cable. Little or no annual maintenance is required. Over time, however, the cable can become worn or corroded, making steering difficult. Replacement of a bad cable is the best repair. To prevent this problem, Davis Instru-

ments sells an aftermarket kit designed to lubricate steering cables. Called a *Cable Buddy*, it mounts at the outboard motor end of the cable. A fitting in the stainless steel nut allows you to add lubricant to the cable as needed.

Hydraulic steering consists of a helm, two lines of plastic or copper tubing, and the steering "ram" or cylinder. These systems lose tiny amounts of fluid over time, which must be replaced. Remove the reservoir cap on the helm and turn the wheel. Turning the wheel one direction will reduce the fluid in the reservoir, while turning the other will cause the level to rise. Add fluid only after turning the wheel so that the level is as high as possible. This ensures there will be "head space" in the reservoir after topping off with new oil.

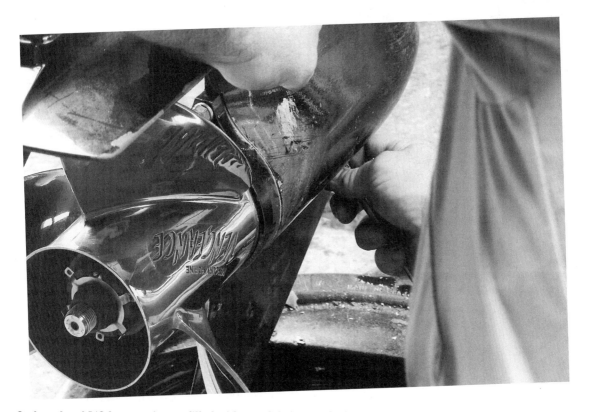

Outboard and I/O lower units are filled with gear lubricant, which should be replaced at least once a season.

POTABLE WATER SYSTEMS

When you drain the water tanks during fall layup, you can never get all of the water out. That remaining water could freeze, expand, and break water tanks, pumps, or plastic plumbing. To protect your plumbing, use propylene glycol antifreeze. This kind of antifreeze, or *pink pop* as it's often called, may be nontoxic, but it tastes horrible. Even slight traces of antifreeze absolutely ruin potable water for drinking or coffee. The best way to remove all traces of antifreeze is to pump the water system dry in spring before filling the tank. Then add a gallon or two of water to the tank and pump the system dry again. Do this several times before filling the tank with drinking water for the season. After you've filled the tank, add a couple of drops of ordinary household bleach to prevent slime and algae growth on the tank walls.

FIBERGLASS WAXING AND BUFFING

The gelcoat that gives a fiberglass deckboat its bright appearance is tough, but not impregnable. It oxidizes and fades in harsh UV light unless protected by a coat of wax or polish. The choice of waxes and polishes is bewildering. They range from old-fashioned carnauba wax to modern products based on silicone and Teflon. Before applying any of them, the boat should be washed squeaky clean with mild soap and water. Soak the surface with water to loosen any grit and dirt. Then wash with a soft cloth and plenty of soapy water. The idea is to use the soap and water as a lubricant to prevent dirt particles on your sponge or rag from scratching the fiberglass gelcoat.

In the case of stubborn dirt, beware of household cleaners that have grit in them. A onetime use won't do much damage, but using them regularly will cause rapid dulling of the gelcoat. Instead, choose chemical gel gelcoat cleaners that do their work without scratching the surface.

Dry the hull before applying polish or wax. Modern silicone and PTFE (i.e., Teflon) products do a far superior job with a lot less elbow grease than old-fashioned wax. The new products really do last a whole season. And most are resistant to gasoline. Apply these products according to the directions using clean—I repeat,

A full second deck is possible on a pontoon boat that is wide and long enough. This 31-foot Boundary Waters model from Premier has a 10-foot beam, plenty to support an upper deck as large as many smaller pontoon boats. The water slide off the stern is a favorite with kids.

clean—soft cloths. Dirty rags can scratch the surface or cause incomplete application of the polish.

Fiberglass color-restoring products and rubbing compounds are not needed on new boats, and their use is discouraged until years down the road. Eventually, however, exposure to the sunlight and oxidation will cause microscopic pitting in the gelcoat. These pits give the surface a whitish, hazy appearance. Color restorers work by removing a small amount of the surface oxidation to expose the original color beneath. Some also fill those pits with petrochemicals. An application of a sealer coat is usually necessary to make the color restoration permanent. Read the instructions and use a sealant in the same family of products as the color restorer.

Rubbing compounds aggressively remove oxidation from fiberglass that has been sadly neglected. Power buffing is needed for the best results, which can rival the original factory gloss. In inexperienced hands, however, a power buffer can quickly burn through the gelcoat. Unless you have experience in power buffing, stick to the color-restoring products.

Walking surfaces on decks should not be treated with ordinary polishes or waxes because they become slippery, especially when wet. Nonskid surfaces should be washed with a biodegradable soap and rinsed with clear water. For protection, look for products that provide protection without reducing the non-skid protection.

ALUMINUM CARE

Left on its own, unpainted aluminum forms a self-protecting oxidation. Unfortunately, while this oxidation protects the metal from further weathering, it is dull and not as attractive as the polished-metal appearance of a new boat. Aluminum maintenance chemicals have been available in the aircraft industry for years, but only recently have marine stores begun carrying products suitable for pontoon boats. Marine grade aluminum cleaners, aluminum polishes, and applicator tools are available. Painted aluminum surfaces can be cleaned and polished with any of the products available for automotive or marine use.

ANTIFOULING PAINT

Not every boat needs antifouling paint. A deckboat or pontoon boat kept on a trailer and only used for day trips does not need bottom paint. Power washing with a high-pressure sprayer should be sufficient to keep the bottom spotless (visit a do-it-yourself carwash if you don't own a machine). The only boats that need antifouling bottom paint are those kept in the water throughout the entire boating season.

Antifouling coatings consist of a biocide and a binder. The binder gives the product its color, and more importantly, it binds the biocide to the hull. Copper has traditionally been used to retard marine growth. As a biocide, copper works best in salt water. In fresh water it slows but does not stop the slime buildup, which eventually forms a barrier between the biocide and marine growth. Ciba Irgarol inhibits slime growth and is now a component in most top-end antifouling paints. International Paint uses Biolux, a similar anti-slime compound. Recently, there has been an environmentally friendly move away from copper compounds toward biodegradable biocides.

Bottom paint should never be "stretched" by adding thinner. This practice just dilutes the biocide so that the finished coating is less effective at reducing marine growth. Antifouling paint should be thinned only as needed for flow control as it is applied to the hull. Application is easiest using a standard paint roller attached to a broomstick or other long handle. Most roller frames have a threaded socket for a long handle. Cut in at the waterline and touch up around cradle parts or the launching straps with a disposable brush.

Aluminum and Copper Don't Mix Never use conventional copper-bearing antifouling paint on an aluminum hull, aluminum pontoons, or aluminum lower units of outboard motors or I/O drives. Aluminum is subject to rapid galvanic corrosion when immersed in water in the presence of copper. International Paint's Trilux 33 or Tri-Lux II can be used over a buildup of four coats of Interprotect 2000E/20001E. New Petit Paint is Alumicoat SR antifouling coating, which uses zinc pyrithione as a biocide instead of copper or cuprous oxide. Alumicoat SR can be used on boats in fresh, salt, or brackish water.

Summer Maintenance

Summer is for boating fun. Maintenance is hardly the top item on the list of things to do on a sunny Saturday afternoon. Even so, routine maintenance cannot be overlooked. Before every trip, take these steps:

- Check engine fluid levels.
- Make sure there is enough fuel for the trip.
- Check fire extinguishers, anchor and line, and other safety equipment.
- Place PFDs where they are accessible.

Once a month you should perform these steps:

- Check dock lines for chafe (if the boat is stored in water).
- Close and open all sea valves to make sure they work properly.
- Check water level in batteries.

- Inspect engine belts and hoses.
- Check automatic operation of bilge pump.

The following sections include maintenance tasks that can be performed less frequently.

HULA SKIRT

Boats kept in the water eventually build marine growth around the waterline. This "hula skirt" robs the boat of speed and causes the engine to burn more fuel. Attack marine growth with routine bottom cleanings. A variety of curved-handled brushes and scrubbing belts have been developed for do-it-yourself scrubbing of conventional boats. Most of these devices are difficult to use on pontoons. Make scrubbing the 'toons more like fun by finding a beach where you can anchor in waist-deep water. Wade around the boat wielding a stiff-bristled brush.

OIL CHANGES

Four-Stroke Outboards Engine manufacturers report that one of the biggest causes of four-stroke outboard failure is neglecting to change lube oil or maintain the oil level. Outboard engines have small oil sumps, so any carbon or corrosive chemicals that collect are more concentrated than in the larger sumps of automotive engines. Also, outboards usually operate under load, so they wear out their oil faster from pressure and heat. This all means that four-stroke outboard engine oil must be changed at regular intervals.

Most manufacturers say to change oil after the first 20 hours of break-in operation. From then on, the maximum interval between changes should not exceed 100 hours of normal operation. Engine oil of a pontoon or deckboat that is operated at idle or slow speeds most of the time should be changed at intervals of 50 hours or less. The spin-on oil filter also should be changed with every oil change.

Changing four-stroke outboard oil is easiest when the boat is ashore on its trailer. Working on land avoids any possibility of a spill on the water, which brings the threat of large oil pollution fines. Even so, neatness counts ashore. Spills on the internal surfaces of the lower shrouding unit can create an unintended oil slick after the boat is relaunched. Use a short length of hose attached to the drain plug to guide the drain oil into a container for disposal. Place an absorbent rag beneath the old oil filter to catch the inevitable drips when you spin it off.

I/Os and Outboard Lower Units Engine manufacturers recommend changing the lube oil in the outboard lower unit at the same 100-hour interval. Pressure created by spinning gear teeth inside the gearcase, or bullet, actually breaks apart the lubricant. As a result, friction increases and heat builds up. This leads to premature wear on the gears and failure of the clutch mechanism. One sign of oil breakdown is harder shifting, especially into reverse.

Place a pan beneath the lower unit before removing the lower oil plug. Oil will immediately come out in small gulps. Real draining won't begin until the top plug is also removed. The lower oil plug is usually equipped with a small magnet. Look for metal shavings on the magnet. A few are normal, but suspect gear problems if the magnet looks like a metallic porcupine. A heavy dose of metal shavings indicates the lower unit should be opened up and the internal parts inspected for damage or premature wear.

Inspect old lubricant as it drains out of the lower unit. Most of its original color should remain. A black color or strong odor indicates that heat buildup has damaged the lubricant. Coffee-colored or iridescent green oil indicates that water has entered the bullet and emulsified

Pay particular attention to oil drained from the lower unit. A milky "creamed coffee" or iridescent green appearance results from water mixed in the oil, indicating a bad shaft seal. Foul-smelling oil may indicate overheating, or that the oil should have been changed months ago.

the lubricant. Water in the oil results in rapid destruction of the gears. Replace the oil seals on the drive or propeller shaft prior to relaunching the boat.

VINYL UPHOLSTERY

Although modern vinyl is pretty tough stuff, nothing stands up to sunlight without help. A variety of products are available to keep vinyl seats and sun pads from drying and cracking. Remove dirt and stains with a cleaner designed for vinyl and rubber. Then treat the clean material with a vinyl protectant that contains UV protection to reduce sun damage.

Fall Layup

Bittersweet is the only word that describes the end of another boating season. Putting the boat "to bed" for the winter always brings back memories of the good times in the summer just past.

Laying up a big cruiser has grown so complicated these days that it is easier and safer to store those boats in heated buildings. Fortunately, pontoons and deckboats do not require such elaborate and expensive winter storage. After proper winterizing, both types of boats can be covered and stored outdoors in your back yard.

GAS TANKS

There has always been a debate over whether to store a boat with full or empty gas tanks. Most of the time, the choice is forced by the amount of fuel aboard after the last cruise of the season. It is typical for boats to go into winter storage with tanks half full. Moisture in the air above the tank can condense on the tank walls as the temperature rises and falls over the winter. This

condensation eventually finds its way into the gasoline. Storing tanks about three-quarters full (leaving room for expansion in warm spring weather) reduces condensation.

Over the winter, gasoline can go "stale" if not treated with a fuel stabilizer. This helps to prevent gum and varnish from forming during winter storage, which will cause problems in the spring. Put fuel stabilizer in the tank before you take the boat out of the water for the last time. Mercury recommends running its four-stroke outboard motors for at least ten minutes on treated gasoline before the final shutdown. This makes sure the treated fuel reaches the carburetor or all parts of the fuel injection system.

FILTERS

Some engines are equipped with a small carburetor fuel filter. Boat builders often add a larger primary filter in the fuel line between the tank and engine to trap water or particulate matter before it can get to the engine. Good practice calls for replacing fuel filters at the middle of each season and again at fall layup. The old filters contain raw gasoline, so never smoke during this job. Be sure to have plenty of ventilation in the boat to dissipate any gas fumes, and shut off any electrical equipment that might produce a spark.

OUTBOARD FUEL HOSES

The rubber fuel lines and primer bulb serving outboard engines are exposed to the sun's ultraviolet rays and weathering all summer. Over time, these parts begin to lose their flexibility and crack. Survey the hose and bulb for weathering damage once a year. Replacement parts are available from engine dealers or through aftermarket suppliers. The lowest-cost replacements are less than $15, but they are the most expensive in the long run. You will have to replace the bargain bulb and hose several times for every one made from high-quality materials. The total cost of the cheap sets is more than the price of a single good bulb and hose.

COOLING SYSTEM

Outboard engines are designed to drain away any cooling water after use. There is no need to run antifreeze through the engine. Store an outboard upright so that water will run out of the drain holes in the gear housing.

Inboard engines have more complex cooling systems that can trap cooling water, which will expand as it freezes in winter. The force of expanding water is great enough to crack the cast iron engine block. To get rid of water during winter layup, marine engines are equipped with drain plugs in their blocks and exhaust manifolds. Draining down an engine usually works fine, but there are occasions when all of the water does not get out, and a crack results.

The proven way to prevent freezing damage is to leave the block filled with antifreeze just like a car. *Hot*, or *wet*, layup circulates a non-toxic antifreeze solution through the engine at operating temperature. Kits are available to do this yourself, although the cost of a professional job is probably worth the peace of mind. Done correctly, a wet layup does more than just protect the engine against frost damage. The non-toxic antifreeze used in boat engines also helps to prevent internal corrosion of the cooling system, as well as drying and cracking of its rubber hoses.

LUBE OIL

For both sterndrive engines and four-stroke outboards, engine lube oil must be changed in the fall before winter storage. Used engine oil con-

SAVE ON SUPPLIES

It is an open secret that all the good discounts and sales on boating supplies come in the fall. Stores often liquidate a large percentage of their summer stock to generate the cash needed over the lean winter months. So, save a bundle on next year's supplies by buying them this fall when prices drop. This is when those file-card checklists come in handy to make sure you don't forget anything during your fall off-price buying spree.

tains dissolved chemicals from the combustion process which are not good for the moving parts. Removing the old oil gets rid of these potentially corrosive agents and prepares the engine for next summer with fresh lubricant. Change the oil while the engine is warm to make sure the harmful chemicals remain dissolved in the oil and that as much oil drains out as possible. New oil filters are cheap insurance against trouble. Replace the filter with every oil change. Use a felt-tipped marker to write the date of the oil change on the filter. That way you'll have a record of when it was done.

FOGGING THE ENGINE

Daily temperature changes during winter storage can cause moisture to condense inside an engine just as in a fuel tank. This can result in corrosion of internal parts, particularly the piston rings and cylinder walls. Fogging coats the internal moving parts with a protective layer of oil to fight corrosion during storage. True fogging oil has vapor corrosion inhibitors. In effect, the oil gives off anticorrosive fumes that renew the fogging protection all winter. Fogging procedures vary depending upon the type of engine and the products chosen. Follow the engine manufacturer's recommendations.

LOWER UNIT

Gear oil in an outdrive or outboard lower unit wears out over a season of use. As discussed earlier, the old oil that comes out of the bullet tells a lot about the internal condition of the seals and gears. Metal does not heal itself. The lower unit will have to be disassembled and repaired if there are any signs of trouble. If this is the case, have the work done over the winter months to avoid lost boating days next season.

Follow these steps to drain the gear oil:

1. Place lower unit in an upright position with a drain pan directly beneath it.
2. Remove the lower drain/fill plug from the bullet near the propeller.
3. Remove the upper vent plug and allow old lubricant to drain into the pan. Allow at least a half hour for all of the old oil to come out.

If there are no signs of trouble, refill the lower unit prior to winter storage. Follow these steps:

1. Cut the end of the tip off a tube of lubricant. Insert the tapered end into the lower drain/fill hole of the bullet.
2. Roll the tube of lubricant to force oil upwards into the gearcase. Air will be expelled out the upper vent hole.
3. If more than one tube is needed, seal the upper hole with your finger while changing to a new container. Sealing the upper hole prevents air from entering and keeps the new lubricant inside the bullet.
4. Continue filling the gearcase until oil surges out the upper vent hole. Keep the tube in the lower drain/fill hole while

replacing the vent plug. Then replace the drain/fill plug.
5. Dispose of old oil properly.

Both the upper and lower plugs have sealing washers, which are necessary to prevent water from getting into the gearcase. These cost only pennies and are available from authorized engine dealers. Replace both the upper and lower sealing washers with every oil change. Never attempt to run without them.

WATER PUMP IMPELLER

In years past it was common practice to remove rubber impellers from raw-water pumps on inboard engines during winter storage. This was done to prevent the blades of the pump from "taking a set," or becoming permanently bent to the shape of the pump housing. Newer rubber compounds are much less susceptible to this problem and it has become commonplace to leave impellers alone during winter storage. Still, impellers will wear out and should be inspected annually and replaced as needed. It is good insurance against overheating to change raw-water impellers on inboard engines every third or fourth year.

Outboards also have impeller water pumps located in a pump housing set just above the gearcase. Like inboard impellers, those in outboard engines should be routinely replaced every few seasons even if they appear to be in good condition. An older pump impeller can fail without warning. Repairing the water pump on an outboard requires removal of the lower unit and driveshaft. The old parts slide up and off the driveshaft. New parts slide down the shaft in the reverse manner. You can replace just the impeller, or, for a few dollars more, you can replace the entire pump assembly as a hedge against trouble during the season. The big cost in a water-pump job is tearing down and replacing

ARE ETHANOL-BLEND FUELS BAD FOR YOUR BOAT?

Contrary to popular belief, ethanol-blended fuels aren't a threat to boats. Due to environmental restrictions, boats in the Chicago area have been required to use "gasohol" since 1984 and the only drawbacks have been a slight reduction in mileage and some reports of stalling on acceleration after a prolonged period of idling.

Fear of ethanol as a marine fuel originated back in the 1980s, when engine manufacturers recommended against using blended fuels because the long-term effects of grain alcohol on engine operation were not yet known. Today, the evidence favors 10 percent ethanol-blended gasoline. All outboard and inboard engine manufacturers endorse its use.

Water has always been a problem in boat fuel tanks, and this is especially so with ethanol-blended fuels. Ethanol absorbs water in much the same way automotive "dry gas" does. On shore, this absorbed water passes through the engine without problems. Boats are a different story, however, because they sit idle for long periods of time. During idle periods, something called *phase separation* can occur.

When a tank sits idle for several weeks, the ethanol absorbs water until it can take no more. At that point the water-laden ethanol separates and accumulates at the bottom of the tank.

Fuel lines pick up gas from the bottom of fuel tanks. After phase separation takes place, the next time the engine starts, it gets a slug of water instead of fuel. Water isn't good for any engine, but that's not the only problem. The layer of gasoline above the water/ethanol mixture is now lower octane than when it came from the fuel dock. Low-octane fuel may cause a four-stroke inboard engine to hiccup, and might even damage a two-stroke outboard motor.

To prevent this, use a fuel system additive that contains a nonalcohol drying agent. Also add lubricants two or three times a season.

Aside from the separation issue, ethanol-blended gas presents no storage problems; it's more stable over time than gasoline.

---

the lower unit, so buying a few additional pump parts won't break the bank.

POTABLE WATER SYSTEM

Many pontoons and deckboats have a potable water system consisting of a tank, electric pump, plumbing, and faucet at a sink. If provision has been made for draining the tank, this is often sufficient to winterize a simple system. Check the owner's manual. It is not feasible to drain many modern potable water systems because of their complexity. In this case, protect the system with nontoxic antifreeze. Pour only enough antifreeze into the tank to fill the pump and hoses. Run the pump until undiluted antifreeze comes out of the faucet. Use as little nontoxic antifreeze as possible to get the job done. The more you use, the harder it will be to get rid of the "pink pop" taste in the spring.

MARINE TOILET

Portable toilets should be emptied of both waste and flush water. Rinse and dump the waste-holding tank several times. Heads are supposed to drain down by themselves. Operating the flush pump several times to remove as much water as possible from its workings. The pile of cracked toilet bases and china pots at most marinas is testimony to the fact that toilets do not always drain dry. Instead of worrying, run nontoxic marine antifreeze through the flush ring, pump, and hoses. The toilet's own flush pump can be used to draw "pink pop" out of a gallon jug.

ELECTRONICS

Expensive depth sounders, radios, and GPS receivers should be removed from the boat and stored in a locked building for safekeeping. They do not need to be in heated storage, just safe from sticky fingers. If repairs are needed, take the units directly to an electronics shop. That way, they will be fixed by spring commissioning. This avoids the backlog of work that electronic shops experience at the start of every boating season.

CUSTOMIZING

Once a boat casts off, it becomes a mini-world of its own. Even on a tiny lake a boat seems divorced from the realities of the evening news. Perhaps this is the reason owners are so dedicated to customizing and modifying their boats. Great satisfaction comes from having a private space that fits your lifestyle the way an old shoe fits your foot. Customizing boats can require long hours and usually costs more than anticipated. In the end, however, nothing is more valuable than the satisfaction of saying, "Yup, that's my boat."

Anyone with ordinary mechanical skills can add new equipment or modify an existing furniture layout. The key to success is to start simple. Avoid those projects that require custom-made parts or major modifications to the boat. Choose projects that center around kits that provide all the needed parts and have well-written instructions.

Vinyl Graphics

One of the easiest ways to customize any boat is with vinyl graphics. Straight-line striping materials are available at any boat or auto supply store. But for a really creative look, visit a shop that specializes in custom cutting self-stick vinyl letters. The machine that cuts the vinyl is controlled by a computer that can be programmed to reproduce just about any shape you can imagine. It's even possible to create designs on your own home computer and have them translated into cut vinyl.

Remove any old tape stripes or graphics with a plastic scraper aided by a hair dryer. A plastic putty knife is not likely to scratch fiberglass gelcoat or painted aluminum and warming the old vinyl with the hair dryer weakens the glue and softens the materials to make scraping easier. Remove the residual glue by wiping it down with mineral spirits or a specialized adhesive remover available from car parts stores.

Installing new stripes and graphics is best done with the boat out of the water so it won't move around as you apply pressure rubbing down the vinyl. A straight line on a curved surface is actually a curved line. Learning how to handle this bit of 3-D geometry is difficult. A laser level simplifies the problem by projecting a straight line onto the curved surface of the hull. Snips of masking tape can be used as removable guide marks for where the vinyl should go.

Peel the backing from just the end of the stripe and pull the tape only taut enough to get a straight line. Do not pull so hard that the vinyl stretches. Work with sections about an arm's spread in length. Attach the stripe lightly every four to six feet. Attach the taut section to the hull with the pressure of a fingertip. Light pressure in small areas is enough to keep the tape in position, while allowing the tape to be repositioned without damage. Step back to make sure the line looks good to the eye before rubbing down the entire stripe. If you don't like what you see, reposition the stripe until it looks right.

Vinyl graphics made by a sign shop are a bit more difficult to install. They come attached to a translucent backing sheet. Temporarily position the graphic with its backing sheet on the hull using masking tape. Step back to make certain it is in the correct position. Peel a bit of the graphic away from the backing sheet, bend the paper out of the way, and rub the artwork down onto the boat. Continue peeling and rubbing until the whole graphic is in position. Work slowly to avoid wrinkles and bubbles in the vinyl.

These days, easily applied vinyl graphics have replaced the tedious job of decorating pontoon or deckboats with painted stripes. Factory graphics have plenty of sizzle, but even wilder designs are available from marine suppliers and signmakers.

VECTRA

Here's proof you can have it all. This deckboat from Vectra has the speed and handling of a conventional V-hull combined with the open, flat deck of a pontoon boat. Performance comes from up to a 200 horsepower outboard. Although only a 20-footer, this boat can handle up to 12 people.

Entertainment Systems

Marine stereo components are less susceptible to corrosion from damp air than less-expensive automotive units. This is most important when boating in salt water. Using ordinary automotive equipment on freshwater rivers and lakes usually won't cause any difficulties.

Marinized or not, a stereo system should be protected in a waterproof housing or splash cover. The simplest installation uses a waterproof stereo housing that has two built-in speakers. The only wiring necessary is the 12-volt power to the unit. Another option is a universal gimbal mount—a plastic box with a watertight cover. The unit mounts in the box, which can be mounted on any flat surface. A stereo can also be mounted in a cutout in the helm console and protected by a splash-proof cover.

All boat speakers must be of a waterproof design intended for outdoor service.

ELECTRONICS

Aside from stereo systems, a boat should also be equipped with a number of other electronic devices. VHF marine radios are standard equipment on seafaring vessels. Radar units are now available in sizes suitable for trailerable boats. And with GPS, nobody should ever get lost again.

PREMIER ESCAPADE

Docks and marinas are not always necessary. Thanks to their shallow draft and aluminum construction, pontoon boats can be run ashore for a beach picnic, as this 24-foot Premier Escapade illustrates.

GPS Receivers

A decade or so ago only military ships routinely used electronic charting. Today, it's possible to hold a detailed map of the United States in your hand. Global Positioning System (GPS) receivers now track you across the country with enough accuracy to tell you in advance when to turn left on the highway. Nautical charting systems are even more sophisticated than those used for highway navigation. Unfortunately, the lakes and backwaters favored by pontoons and dockboats are not generally included in marine chart packs. For practical purposes, a GPS mapping system intended for land navigation may be better at providing critical detail for skippers on inland waters. Plus, these land units can be switched from boat to car to guide you from home to the launching ramp.

A dashboard cradle is often included with a handheld GPS receiver. You might consider buying a separate cradle so you can mount the GPS receiver in both car and boat. Choose a unit that connects to the car or boat's 12-volt system for an unending supply of power. Internal GPS batteries have a way of dying just when you need navigational information most. Boat helm stations usually come equipped with the same cigarette-lighter 12-volt outlet found in cars. If not, one can be added with only a few minutes of work. Be sure to follow the manufacturer's instructions and not reverse the polarity of the 12-volt power to the GPS receiver.

VHF Marine Radio

Although a simple process, installing a marine two-way radio must be done with care. Mistakes can reduce the output power so that if you ever do need to call for help, your radio will only whisper instead of shout. The radio should be located where it can be seen and operated by the

Global Positioning System (GPS) receivers with built-in mapping can help keep track of your boat even on inland waters. (ICOM America)

VHF marine radio. (ICOM America)

boat driver. If there is a compass on the helm station, keep the radio as far from it as possible. The radio contains a speaker with a magnet that can throw your compass off kilter.

Proper voltage is critical to radio transmitter operation. Even a small drop in voltage causes a major decrease in power output from the antenna (see Wiring Tips below). The red wire from the radio usually has an in-line fuse holder so it can be connected directly to the positive main of the boat. If no fuse holder is supplied, the radio must be connected to an existing fused circuit. The black wire from the radio goes to the negative main.

VHF Radio Antenna

The maximum legal power output of a marine VHF radio is limited to 25 watts. Additional power would not increase transmitting range significantly because the signal is limited to "line of sight." This means the efficiency and height of the antenna become critical factors. The higher the antenna, the greater the range over which you can communicate. However, there are practical limits to antenna height. Choosing a mounting location becomes a compromise between practicality and range. Special mounts are available to clamp an antenna to a pontoon boat railing. Base mounts can be bolted to the deck, the side of the helm console, or some other convenient location.

Every antenna has a decibel (dB) gain rating. This is a measurement of its effective output. Lower dB gain antennas transmit in a pattern that can be imagined as a round bubble growing ever larger with distance. Higher dB gain antennas focus their radiation into a flatter, donut-shaped field horizontal to the water. Every 3 dB of gain doubles the effective output. Boat antennas are commonly available in 3, 6, and 9 dB gain. While the larger gain is obviously preferable, height can be a problem. A 3 dB antenna is about 5 feet high, while a 9 dB antenna can be up to 24 feet tall and require special support.

Coaxial cable, or coax, connects the antenna to the transmitter. Radio frequency (RF) energy travels on the center conductor. A braided outer shield keeps the RF from leaking away before it reaches the radiating element inside the antenna. The coax attached to a new antenna comes without the special PL-259 connector needed to attach it to the radio. This allows the coax to be pulled through small openings and snaked to the helm station. Once the coax is in place, a connector must be installed. Unless you are familiar with soldering electronic cable, choose a push-on center-pin connector.

Engine Instruments

A sad truth of boating is that engine instruments have a high rate of failure. Fortunately, a variety of aftermarket instruments are available from any marine parts store. Most are less expensive than replacement parts from the original manufacturer.

No matter what the function of a particular instrument, replacement is virtually identical. All are held in position by a U-shaped metal bracket installed from underneath the panel. This bracket is secured by two nuts on studs protruding from the back of the meter case. Remove the nuts and slide the bracket off the studs. Sometimes, a ground wire is attached to one of the studs. Mark this wire as you remove it. The instrument can now be pulled out from the face of the panel.

Remove the wires to the old instrument one at a time. Note the code letter marked on the case next to the stud where each wire is

APPROXIMATE COMMUNICATIONS RANGE BASED ON VHF ANTENNA HEIGHTS

	HEIGHT OF TRANSMITTING ANTENNA		
HEIGHT OF RECEIVING ANTENNA	5 feet	10 feet	25 feet
10 feet	7 miles	10 miles	12 miles
25 feet	9 miles	11 miles	13 miles
50 feet	10 miles	14 miles	15 miles

GRILLING ABOARD

A golden sunset, a quiet anchorage, and a char-broiled steak can all come together thanks to the advent of marine-grade stainless steel barbecue grills. These come in a variety of sizes and can be either deck- or rail-mounted. Just like on the patio at home, the chef has a choice of propane or charcoal for fuel.

Don't confuse a true marine barbecue grill with one designed for patio use. Home units do not have sealed bottoms, so it is possible for burning material (even a piece of steak) to fall on deck. Nothing is worse than a fire on a boat, and grease on deck is sure to lead to a tumble. Marine grills have inner shells to protect against grease leaks and keep the fire where it belongs. On a pontoon boat, the grill should be mounted on the bow where it is as far as possible from the gasoline fuel tanks. This is also where the boat offers the most open space for the chef to swing a fork or spatula.

The choice between charcoal and propane as a cooking fuel is a matter of personal preference. Most people seem to prefer the convenience of propane afloat. Not only does the grill light instantly, but the cook has better control over temperature. Most grills can be hooked to a standard nonrefillable propane canister or a larger propane tank. The popularity of propane means that chefs who demand the "real" taste of charcoal have a much smaller range of marine grill choices.

Marine grill manufacturers offer a variety of deck and rail mounts for their units. These must be purchased separately because no single mounting system will handle every situation. Pontoon boat owners will need a square rail-mounting system. Deckboat skippers may prefer to go with a flush deck-mount pedestal or an angle mount that fits into a standard rod holder.

---

attached. Label the wire with that code letter so it can be attached to the same stud of the new instrument. On most boats these wires will also be color coded for identification.

If you have a digital camera, take a picture to document how the old instrument was wired. Install the new wires, double-checking that they are going to the correct studs on the new instrument.

Tachometers often become erratic before they totally fail. The pointer may bounce from one reading to another with no corresponding change in engine revolutions. Or the meter may stop reading for a while and then come unexpectedly back to life. The replacement instrument must be compatible with your engine.

Generally, four-stroke inboard and outboard engines can use the same tachometers, but two-stroke outboards require special instruments. Some aftermarket instruments have selector switches that allow them to be mated with any inboard or outboard engine.

Outboard engine water pressure gauges are also notorious for early failure. At nearly a hundred dollars, replacement is pricey for a new instrument likely to fail in a season or two. Better to train yourself to keep a regular watch on the tell-tale stream that shows the outboard water pump is working. On some pontoon boats, however, it is almost impossible to see this stream from on board, so replacing the pressure meter is necessary.

Powerboat speedometers use the pressure of water against a pitot tube mounted on the transom. The pitot extends about two inches downward into undisturbed water beneath the boat. As speed increases it creates pressure in a plastic tube that connects to the speedometer dial. This pressure causes the pointer to move. Adding a speedometer on a deckboat requires attaching the pitot to the transom with self-tapping stainless steel screws. Follow the manufacturer's instructions for placement. Plastic tubing is available in 25-foot lengths or by the foot from marine parts stores. A hole must be cut in the instrument panel to accommodate the instrument case.

Attaching a pitot to a pontoon boat is a challenge in creativity. One thing not to do is drill holes in the pontoon for mounting hardware. This compromises watertight integrity. A metal bracket can be made that attaches to the deck and extends downward at the back of the pontoon. The pitot attaches to this bracket so it extends the correct distance beneath the 'toon bottom. Some people have found success gluing a wooden block to the back end of a pontoon with epoxy. The pitot can be screwed to the wood without drilling into the airtight metal chamber.

Wiring Tips

None of your electronic equipment will work without a steady supply of power. This means that choosing the right wire is critical. Today's boats use the same 12-volt wiring system that is used for automobiles. There is a tendency to dismiss low-voltage boat wiring as being harmless; however, a boat's battery is capable of producing over 100 amps—enough to fry the electrical system and create enough heat to set fiberglass resin on fire.

WIRE CHOICE

Water is the enemy of electricity. Even freshwater corrosion will eventually lead to failure. In addition, the vibration of a moving boat can cause solid copper wire to fatigue and break. For these reasons, it is important to use only stranded copper marine wire. Never use solid wire in a boat. Each individual strand of the marine wire is tinned before it is twisted with other strands and coated with high-temperature insulation.

WIRE GAUGE

Wire sizes in the United States are measured by the American Wire Gauge (AWG) system. Under this system, the larger the number, the smaller the diameter of the wire. Although wire of any gauge carries current, there is more voltage loss in small-diameter wires than in big ones. This is why it is always better to go oversize on wiring. Up to 10 percent voltage drop is acceptable in noncritical applications such as convenience lighting. For electronic equipment or anchor windlasses, voltage drop should not exceed 3 percent.

CRIMP-ON TERMINALS

These handy devices come sized to match standard wire gauges. Crimp-on terminals are easily attached, although crimping is a learned art. Expect to toss away a few terminals until you get the hang of it. Strip back the wire using the crimping tool. Use the wire-stripper opening that matches the gauge of wire. The amount of insulation to strip back depends on the wire gauge and the brand of connector. Once stripped, insert the bare wire into the connector and then place the connector in the jaws of the crimping tool. Note that the jaws are color-coded to match the color of the terminal's collar. Crimp down hard! One crimp is enough for small-gauge applications. Two or more crimps are used on larger-diameter wire.

PREMIER

Few boats are better for creeping up on the big lunkers than a pontoon. These anglers have come almost into the weeds in search of their quarry. By careful maneuvering, the propeller of the outboard is well out of danger.

WIRING SIZE CHART FOR NONCRITICAL APPLICATIONS
SUGGESTED WIRE GAUGE FOR 10 PERCENT VOLTAGE DROP

AMPS ON CIRCUIT	LENGTH OF WIRE				
	10 feet	15 feet	20 feet	25 feet	30 feet
5	18	18	18	18	18
10	18	18	16	16	14
15	18	16	14	14	12
20	16	14	14	12	12
25	16	14	12	12	10

WIRING SIZE CHART FOR CRITICAL APPLICATIONS
SUGGESTED WIRE GAUGE FOR 3 PERCENT VOLTAGE DROP

AMPS ON CIRCUIT	LENGTH OF WIRE				
	10 feet	15 feet	20 feet	25 feet	30 feet
5	18	16	14	12	12
10	14	12	10	10	10
15	12	10	10	8	8
20	10	10	8	8	8
25	10	8	6	6	6

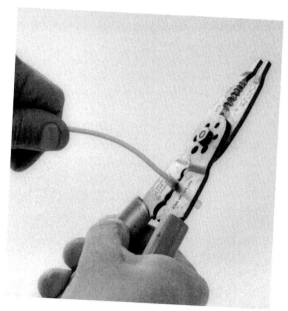

Crimping tool.

ROUTING

Wires must be routed so they do not come into contact with water. They should not go through the bilge of a deckboat where water might collect. On pontoon boats, wires should not run beneath the deck unless they are contained in a watertight conduit. Where possible, bundle wires together and support them every foot or so with cable ties, clamps, or similar devices. Due to vibration, captive-eye terminals are preferred on boat wiring in place of the U-shaped lugs used ashore. If the screw holding the terminal loosens, the wire does not disconnect.

U.S. manufacturers have adopted color coding for boat wiring. It pays to continue using this color code when you install additional equipment. Color coding makes it easy to troubleshoot problems later.

PREMIER

Premier's line of Sportdeck boats blurs the line between deckboats and pontoon boats. The fiberglass tri-hull is similar to a conventional boat. It is topped with a large, flat deck the same as a pontoon vessel. Premier says the combination gives the handing of a ski boat and the fun of a pontoon boat, but it requires less horsepower.

BOAT WIRING COLOR CODE

Wire Color	Circuit Description	Typical Uses of Circuit
Black	Negative mains	Return wire to battery
Red	Positive mains	Main power, unfused from the battery
Dark Gray	Navigation lights	From fuse or switch to lights
Purple	Ignition	Switch to coil and instruments
Purple	Instruments	Distribution panel to instruments
Dark Blue	Lights	Distribution panel to interior lights
Green	Bonding	Noncurrent boat bonding system
Brown	Generator	Armature to regulator
Brown	Pumps	Fuse or switch to bilge pumps
Tan	Water temperature	Engine water temp sender to gauge
Yellow	Alternator	Field to regulator
Yellow	Bilge blower	Fuse or switch to blower motor
Yellow w/Red Stripe	Starter	Switch to solenoid
Orange	Accessories	Ammeter to alternator and accessory fuses to switches
Pink	Fuel gauge	Fuel tank sender to gauge
White	Negative mains	Return wire to battery

Appendix
LEGAL MATTERS

OWNERSHIP AND TITLING

MSO

New boats are shipped from the factory with a paper known as the Manufacturer's Statement of Origin, or MSO. This document gives all of the particulars about the boat, ranging from its size and model year to the dimensions and style of accommodations. The most important piece of information on the MSO is the Hull Identification Number, or HIN. Since 1972 all boats built in the United States have carried

HINs. These numbers must be permanently attached to the transom on the starboard side. The first letters of the HIN identify the manufacturer and the last numbers indicate the model year. In addition to the transom, the HIN must be permanently attached to a second, unexposed portion of the hull. As a theft deterrent, many manufacturers also attach a third HIN in a secret location.

When a dealer sells a new boat, the MSO is converted to either a state or federal title. Each of the fifty states has its own titling process. Issuance of a state title allows you to register your boat and obtain a bow number.

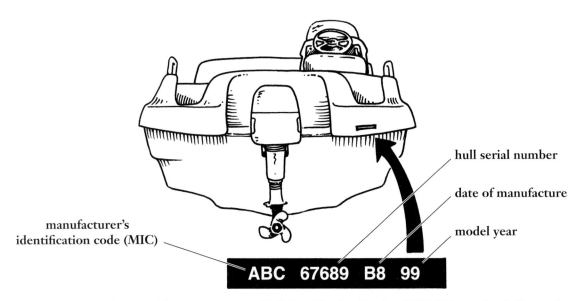

manufacturer's
identification code (MIC)

hull serial number

date of manufacture

model year

ABC 67689 B8 99

Every boat sold in the United States must carry a Hull Identification Number (HIN). This number indicates the boat's manufacturer, model year, length, and the boat's individual serial number. (In this case, the date of manufacture is February 1998.) (Christopher Hoyt)

State Titles

Requirements for titling boats vary slightly, but most states require all powerboats to carry titles. The rules for nonpowered craft and sailboats vary widely. Dealers know the titling requirements and guide buyers through the process. In fact, most boat dealers handle all of the paperwork, much like the service provided by car dealers. The MSO is surrendered and a state title is issued in its place. At the same time, your bank or lending institution will place a lien on the new title if you borrow money to purchase the boat. Again, this works the same as in a car purchase. It is necessary to obtain a title before the boat can be registered and issued bow numbers. Separate titles are required for outboard motors in most states. Proof of payment of state sales and use taxes is required to obtain a title.

State Registration

Titles refer to ownership, while registration involves paying annual fees and attaching numbers to the bow of the boat. Under guidelines set up by the U.S. Coast Guard, all fifty states now require registration of powerboats. Sailboats and muscle-powered rowboats may be exempt from registration if they are under a certain length—often 14 feet. Registration fees are charged on a graduated scale that increases with the size of the boat. State registrations are valid for one to three years. To prove payment of the required fee, states issue validation stickers.

Boats are registered in their state of primary use. This can create confusion for owners who live in one state, but operate on waters in a different state. Casual trips to other states are permitted under reciprocity provisions that vary from state to state. Some states allow up to 90 days of visitation privileges, but most are 60 days and a few are as short as 30 days. It is up to the boatowner to determine the local registration requirements.

Most states issue a wallet-size registration card. Others give a larger paper registration. Either way, the original proof of registration must be carried at all times when the boat is in operation.

BOW NUMBERS Metal license plates are not used on boats. Instead, each boat is issued a certificate of number. As the name implies, this certificate provides the boat with a unique identification number that must be displayed on both sides of the bow. The first two letters of the number indicate the issuing state. Then come four numbers, followed by two more letters. State numbers must be displayed on the forward half of the vessel. Most people use self-stick vinyl letters and numbers, which provide years of service. The size and type of numbers are controlled by federal regulation as well as state law:

- The letters and numbers must read from left to right (conventional display).
- Letters and numbers must be in bold block letters a minimum of 3 inches in height.
- They must be of contrasting color to the boat hull or background.
- Letters must be separated from numbers by either a space or a hyphen.

Correct	Incorrect
MO 1234 ZZ	MO1234ZZ
MO-1234-ZZ	(no spaces or hyphens)
	ZZ 1234 MO
	(wrong order)
	MO-1234-ZZ
	(not block letters)

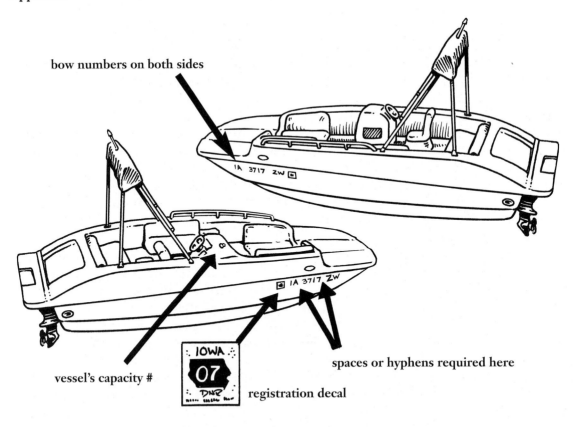

bow numbers on both sides

vessel's capacity #

IOWA
07
DNR

registration decal

spaces or hyphens required here

Bow numbers must be displayed by all state-registered boats. The size and placement of the numbers is dictated by law. A sticker placed behind the numbers shows the boat has a valid registration. (Christopher Hoyt)

Law-enforcement officials are fairly lenient about where on the boat the registration numbers are displayed as long as they are plainly visible. However, federal regulations specify they must be placed as high above the waterline as is practical. Most pontoon-boat owners apply self-stick numbers to the aluminum filler panels of the deck fences. Avoid the temptation to install registration numbers on pontoons. Wave action will soon wash them away. Deckboat owners can usually find space on the hull just below the deck joint.

Some owners object to spoiling the "look" of their new boats with numbers. Admittedly, they are not pretty. One way to make them less objectionable is to purchase vinyl letters in a hue that complements the boat's color scheme. Boat stores usually sell only black or white letters. Check with a local sign maker for a better choice of colors. The law does not specify the color of registration numbers, except that they must contrast with the background color. Avoid getting too creative with the style of lettering. Federal regulations specify block letters.

VALIDATION STICKERS Each boat gets two stickers, one for the port bow and the other for the starboard bow. They are displayed immediately aft of the identification numbers. Be careful when handling validation stickers. They are printed on special 2-ply vinyl that separates if the sticker is removed from the boat. Once the plies separate, the sticker is no longer valid. This prevents theft of the stickers. However, it also prevents you from repositioning a sticker once its adhesive touches the hull. Check with your state's division of watercraft for a replacement validation sticker should you damage one.

Insurance

While we all hope we will never need it, insurance for your boat is a good idea. As with all commodities, the price of comparable coverage varies. It pays to get quotes from several companies or agents. Most homeowner policies cover smaller boats, but the cost, complexity, and horsepower of modern deckboats and pontoon craft put them outside the homeowner policy restrictions, making it necessary to buy specific coverage just for the boat. Among the things that should be included in any boat policy are:

- **Liability** — This coverage protects you in case someone else is injured or their property is damaged as a result of your actions or negligence. The amount of liability coverage is usually based upon your net worth.
- **Hull and Machinery** — Accidents happen. You might go aground, or the boat may catch fire or sink. Some policies base payments for this type of claim on the depreciated value of the boat. Others, usually more expensive, allow you

to recover an agreed fixed value for your boat.
- **Pollution** — Insurance cannot pay fines imposed for negligence. However, it can cover the substantial cost of containing an oil spill and cleaning it up.
- **Salvage** — In most cases, a sunken boat cannot be left where it lies, but must be removed. This is always true if the hull blocks a navigable channel or is leaking oil or gasoline. Few services are more expensive than the salvage of a sunken boat.
- **Jones Act** — Occasionally, on federally navigable waters you may be responsible for federal worker's compensation for injuries to someone you employ to work upon your boat. The law that governs this is called the "Jones Act."

The U.S. Coast Guard is not obligated to tow disabled boats back to port except under life-threatening conditions. As a result, should you break down it will be your responsibility to hire a marine-assistance towing company to do the job. Towing on the water is expensive, so it pays to have some sort of protection against this cost. If your marine policy does not cover towing, consider becoming a "member" of a local towing service. In most cases the cost of membership is less than one-fifth the cost of a single tow home.

ANTI-POLLUTION REGULATIONS

Although the environmental protection movement is new, laws against throwing refuse into federal waters go back to 1899. The Refuse Act of that year still prohibits throwing, discharging, or depositing any refuse matter of any kind into the waters of the United States. "Refuse" under the law includes trash, garbage, oil, and other liquid pollutants. Myriad new federal laws have been enacted since that original statute. States, too, have passed anti-pollution legislation, which is often more stringent than federal laws.

Oil Pollution

The discharge of oil or oily waste into federal navigable waters is prohibited. Violators are subject to substantial civil and criminal sanctions. The various states have similar laws against oil pollution of non-navigable waters. Laws covering reservoirs used for drinking water are particularly restrictive.

All vessels operating on federal waters with an internal motor must have the capacity to retain oily mixtures on board until they can be discharged to a reception facility. Big ships have expensive oily-waste recovery units. On small craft such as deckboats, an oil-absorbent pad in the bilge and a bucket are sufficient to meet the requirement.

Fines for discharging oily bilge water are harsh. Instead of risking a hefty fine, it makes sense to spend a few bucks on an oil-absorbent sponge and secure it in the bilge. Oil floats and most bilge pumps cannot get the last drop of water out of the boat. The absorbent material soaks up oil on the surface of bilge water, while the pump draws clean water from underneath the sponge. Change absorbent material at least once a season. If it becomes completely oil-soaked in less than a season, the engine has an oil leak that must be repaired.

All vessels over 26 feet in length must display an anti-oil-pollution placard in a conspic-

uous place in the machinery spaces or at the bilge pump controls. This placard must be at least 5 by 8 inches in size and made of durable material. Self-stick vinyl placards are available for free from many boating supply stores and marinas. More durable plastic placards cost a few dollars. Federal law requires the following wording:

DISCHARGE OF OIL PROHIBITED

The Federal Water Pollution Control Act prohibits the discharge of oil or oily waste upon or into any navigable waters of the U.S. The prohibition includes any discharge which causes a film or discoloration of the surface of the water or causes a sludge or emulsion beneath the surface of the water. Violators are subject to substantial civil and/or criminal sanctions including fines and imprisonment.

Garbage

International treaties now govern the discharge of garbage and other wastes from ships at sea. Because the United States signed these treaties, the prohibitions now extend inland to cover all federal waters and the Great Lakes. Like oil pollution regulations, the states have also enacted laws against dumping garbage on non-federal lakes and streams. As with oil pollution, all vessels 26 feet and over must display a garbage placard when operating on federal waters. The federal regulation specifies wording that has little relevance to rivers and lakes, because most of the rules specify what may be discharged within a certain number of miles offshore. Even a large pontoon boat will never visit waters covered by the language on the placard. However, the impact of the regulations does affect all federal waters by prohibiting the discharge of plastics, floating dunnage (packing materials), food waste, paper, rags, crockery, and even ground-up food waste. Whatever trash you create on the water should come ashore in a garbage bag for disposal ashore.

Marine Toilets

The simple "toilet" has undergone a bureaucratic transformation into a "marine sanitation device," or MSD for short. Federal regulations specify three types of MSDs: Type I, Type II, and Type III. The first two types allow flow-through discharge (untreated in Type I, treated in Type II). The third type of MSD is a holding-tank system to be pumped out ashore. Federal regulations allowed the states to declare "no discharge" zones and most have done so. Some states, like Michigan, have declared every puddle big enough to float a boat as a "no discharge" area. This means that from a practical standpoint, the holding-tank toilet is the only legal MSD on pleasure boats. This is why a portable toilet that can be taken ashore for dumping into a sanitary disposal station has become standard equipment on most small boats.

LAW ENFORCEMENT

Although there is more freedom on the water than anywhere else, boats are not beyond the long arm of the law.

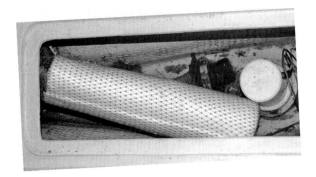

Deckboats with inboard engines run the risk of oily bilge water being pumped overboard. One easy way to prevent a fine for water pollution is to install oil-absorbent material in the bilge to trap and hold any spills. (Don Lindberg)

Safety Boardings

When hailed by a federal, state, or local law-enforcement officer, a vessel is required to heave-to, or maneuver in a manner such that a boarding officer can come aboard. If the boarding is related to a safety check, you may request permission to move to safer conditions if you do not feel comfortable attempting such a maneuver in open water.

During a safety boarding you will be asked to show your boat registration card and one approved personal flotation device of the correct size for each person on board. In addition, the officer may ask to inspect your fire extinguisher, distress signals, anchor, and any other required equipment. Safety inspections usually take about fifteen minutes.

An inspection by one enforcement authority does not exempt your boat from inspection by any other police agency. It is not unusual to be stopped several times within a single day on waters patrolled by the Coast Guard, state watercraft agencies, and local police departments. One way to reduce the chances of being stopped is to have your PFDs visible to officers as they cruise past. Perhaps the best deterrent to overzealous inspections is to participate in the Vessel Safety Check program sponsored by the U.S. Coast Guard, U.S. Power Squadrons, and the U.S. Coast Guard Auxiliary. By passing this voluntary inspection, your vessel receives a bright decal indicating it meets all safety requirements.

Surprisingly, one-fourth of all vessels voluntarily inspected under the safety check program fail to pass. Nearly 12 percent of the boats fail to carry the required distress signals. The second most common reason for failure is noncompliance with state regulations that are not on the Coast Guard list (e.g., anchor requirements or other equipment). Nonfunctional navigation lights round out the big three reasons for failure. The lights on nearly one boat in ten do not work properly.

Homeland Security

Following the 9/11 attacks, the Coast Guard has become the lead federal agency for on-water homeland security. Except in major deepwater ports and some sections of the Western Rivers, the new security measures generally do not affect pleasure boats. The one exception is when operating in the vicinity of U.S. Naval vessels. Strict rules apply as to how close any boat may approach a Navy ship and at what speed. These rules resulted from the attack on the U.S.S. *Cole*, which was accomplished in a small inflatable boat.

All boats are prohibited from approaching within 100 yards of any U.S. Navy vessel. If for safety you must pass with 100 yards, you must first contact either the Navy ship directly or the U.S. Coast Guard escort vessel on Channel 16 of the marine radio. Outside the 100-yard "no approach zone" there is a mandatory speed zone. Boats from 100 to 500 yards distant from Navy ships must operate at minimum safe speed and be prepared to respond to instructions from either the ship or its official patrol vessels. Violating these requirements is a felony, punishable by up to six years in prison and up to $250,000 in fines.

No-Wake and Speed Zones

Federal Rules of the Road require boats to operate at a "safe speed" at all times. This means a speed at which the vessel can be maneuvered to avoid collision with another boat under the prevailing conditions of weather and darkness. In addition, local and state regulations can set tighter restrictions on boat speed. Some harbors have speed limits, while most are posted as *no-wake* zones. Other waters may be marked as a *minimum-wake* zones.

Channels in harbors and other areas crowded with boats are often marked *no wake* for safety. In addition, many states limit boats to no-wake speed within 100 feet of the shore, docks, and anchored or drifting boats. When operating in a no-wake zone the boat must operate at idle speed, or the slowest speed at which it can be safely maneuvered. Most no-wake zones are marked by buoys on the water or signs on shore.

Negligent Operation

When carelessness rises to the point of endangering lives and property, it becomes either *negligent operation* or *gross negligent operation*. The Coast Guard may impose a fine for negligent operation, or a fine and imprisonment for gross negligence. Some examples of actions that may be either negligent or grossly negligent include:

◆ Operating a boat in a swimming area, particularly if swimmers are present

- Operating a boat while under the influence of alcohol or drugs
- Excessive speed in the vicinity of boats or in dangerous waters
- Hazardous towed water activities such as waterskiing, wakeboarding, or tubing
- Bow-riding or riding on seatbacks, gunwales, or transom

Under Title 46 of the United States Code (§2302) operating a vessel in a negligent manner that endangers the life, limb, or property of a person is punishable by a fine of up to $1,000. Gross negligence can be punished by a $5,000 fine, one year in jail, or both. The terms *negligent* and *grossly negligent* are used in federal regulations. State laws may use different wording, such as *reckless* or *careless* operation. State penalties vary, but are similar to the federal punishments.

No-wake zones are created either for public safety or to protect nearby docked boats from damage. Many states limit boats to no-wake speed within 100 feet of the shore, whether speed limits are posted or not.

Accidents and Reports

Just like on shore, certain accidents must be reported. Under Coast Guard regulations, an accident must be reported when:

- There is loss of life
- Personal injuries require medical treatment beyond simple first aid
- Damage to the boat or other property exceeds $2,000
- There is complete loss of the boat

Various states have stricter requirements for reporting accidents than the Coast Guard. Some require reporting of all accidents. If in doubt, make a report.

In general, accidents should be reported first to the nearest law-enforcement division having jurisdiction over the waters involved. This is usually a local sheriff's office or police department. Additional reports may be required by the state watercraft division and the Coast Guard. Under federal regulations, only a death or disappearance of someone from the boat must be reported immediately. Otherwise, boat operators have up to 48 hours to prepare the federal report. State reporting time requirements vary.

RENDERING ASSISTANCE

You are required to provide assistance to anyone else who is in danger on the water. However, in doing so you are not required to put yourself, your vessel, or your passengers into danger. If you are one of the boats involved in a collision, you are also required to exchange your name and address with all of the parties involved. Failure to provide assistance or to exchange information can result in a federal fine of up to $1,000 and two years in jail.

GOOD SAMARITAN

Federal law protects you from lawsuits if you render assistance at the scene of a marine accident without the objection of the person you help. This "good Samaritan" provision covers rendering assistance, arranging salvage, towage, medical treatment, or other assistance, provided that you "act as an ordinary, reasonable, and prudent individual would have acted under the circumstances."

Under the Influence

Boats and good times go together, especially pontoon boats and deckboats. These craft are perfect for rafting together on a lazy Saturday afternoon. Pretty soon, the music is playing and everyone is having fun. Adult beverages are often part of the activities. Putting all the legalities aside, there are solid fun-related reasons for moderation. Most people are not used to drinking during the day under a hot sun. All too often, the drinker falls into a deep sleep as a result of mixing alcohol with sun and the gentle motion of a boat. You can't have a lot of fun when you're asleep. Worse, you can get a blistering sunburn.

Alcohol causes people to lose their inhibitions. Unexpected falls overboard are not uncommon. After all, we don't use the term *tipsy* without good reason. Like all mammals, people have a reflex called the *mammalian diving response*. In whales and dolphins this response is highly refined so they can dive for extended periods of time without breathing. The heartbeat slows and other bodily functions are altered while underwater. In people, alcohol mixes up the diving response. An unexpected fall into cold water can literally stop the heart of someone who has consumed even a modest amount of alcohol. The result is a so-called dry drowning in which no water gets into the victim's lungs.

It is as illegal to drive a boat under the influence of alcohol as it is to drive a car. The big difference is that boat operators become impaired far more quickly than motorists on the highway. The reason is the boating environment with its sounds, vibration, and bright sunlight. Coast Guard records show that one-third of all boating accidents are alcohol-related. Federal and state laws carry heavy penalties for operating a vessel while impaired. These penalties include large fines, suspension or revocation of boat operator privileges, and jail terms. In general, the same laws apply to boating while "buzzed" on illegal drugs.

Impaired is now universally defined for adults as having a blood alcohol content of more than 0.08 percent. Many states consider anyone under 21 years of age as impaired at a much lower 0.02 percent blood alcohol content. Coast Guard and state officials cooperate when it comes to arresting drunk operators. Federal officials will apprehend and hold an operator if requested to do so by local law-enforcement officers. Generally, the voyage is terminated and offenders go to jail. Breath-alcohol testers are in common use on the water. Refusal to "blow" can result in loss of state boating privileges. The federal penalty for operating under the influence of drugs or alcohol is a fine of up to $1,000 for first-time offenses and up to $5,000 for subsequent convictions.

Without exception, a "sober skipper" should be designated for every trip on which adult beverages are consumed. One of the crew agrees to consume nothing intoxicating. That person should be the only one to handle the boat at any time after the caps come off the bottles.

INDEX